A Syntactic Grammar of Hindi

A Syntactic Grammar of Hindi

Prof. Suraj Bhan Singh

DIVE IN THE OCEAN OF KNOWLEDGE
Ocean Books
Ocean Books Pvt. Ltd.
ISO 9001:2015 Publishers

Published by
Ocean Books (P) Ltd.
4/19 Asaf Ali Road,
New Delhi-110 002 (INDIA)
e-mail: info@oceanbooks.in

ISBN 978-81-84300-83-3
A SYNTATIC GRAMMAR OF HINDI
by Prof. Suraj Bhan Singh
Edition
2026

Price
₹ 600.00 (Rupees Six Hundred only)

Printed at
R-Tech Offset Printers, Delhi

INTRODUCTON

Hindi is today being learnt and taught in many Indian and foreign universities and institutions at different levels – initial, intermediate and advanced. Though initial level grammar and self-taught books are adequately available for Hindi learners, the intermediate and advanced levels of Hindi grammars written through the medium of English are still rare. Still rarer are the pedagogically conceived Hindi grammar books based on sound linguistic principles which may be used by learners, teachers, linguists and computer scientists working in the allied fields of Natural Language Processing (NLP) and machine aided English-Hindi translation which in fact need finer rules of grammar.

The book also provides an updated material on Hindi syntax for the students and teachers of Linguistics who will not only find the latest material on Hindi syntax through the medium of English, but also the finally evolved 45 sentence patterns of Hindi for the non-Hindi speaking learners of Hindi which have been pedagogically and linguistically arranged with ample examples and explanatory comments.

The book thus meets the long-felt needs of the intermediate to advanced Hindi learners, students, teachers, linguists, computer scientists, NLP workers as well as foreign nationals working on some aspects of Hindi through the medium of English.

The book is divided into two parts: *theory* and *application*. The first part (theory) examines and evaluates the various grammatical notions such as phrase, complex verbs, compound verbs, conjunct verbs, causatives, voice, aspect, mood and tense etc. It depicts the latest developments in the related fields and provides critical assessment and comparisons on each topic in comprehensible language.

The second part of the book (Application) deals with the discourse part of the language. It displays the actual language *in use* and in interaction. It displays how the words and phrases in actual discourse acquire a different meaning at the discourse level. It highlights the difference between the language and the *language in use*. The book contains a valuable database of 45 kernel (or basic) Hindi sentence patterns/sub-patterns at discourse level. It illustrates the structural, semantic and pragmatic features of the sentences and marks them in their respective sentence frames, called sub-patterns. The sub-patterns thus marked with these features have the capacity to generate innumerable Hindi sentences by using the three broad rules of expansion, substitution and transformation.

The grammar in this book is basically descriptive and is not based on any particular model or theory, but it does assimilate almost all the new significant and relevant findings which are available in structural grammars, tagmemics, transformational-generative grammar, case grammar, systemic grammar and relational grammar etc. The overall approach of this book has been to clarify the grammatical and technical concepts through examples and comparisons rather than technical jargons. The objective has been to ensure that the book meets the requirement of the general language learners, advanced language learners, language teachers, linguists and computer professionals working in the fields of NLP, computer-aided English-Hindi translation, in particular those who have the required knowledge of English but are not able to follow the advanced Hindi grammars written in Hindi.

Therefore, for the facility of those who are not adequately acquainted with certain grammatical or linguistic terminology used in the book, there is a large word index in the appendix of the book, which mentions the page numbers where the technical words or phrases are shown as occurring in the real context. The meaning and usage of these words is also given and thus becomes self-explanatory.

2. The changing concept of sentence

The ultimate objective of the sentence in real life is the communication of the message, but in fact what is communicated in the interaction is not just the linguistic message consisting of some sounds, grammatical constructs and semantic inputs. It is important to remember that a sentence often hides as much as it reveals. Often there is a social grammar hidden in the sentence. For instance, it tells us as to which sentence, sentence-form or expression is appropriate for use in a certain context or environment and which not. Besides, there is sometimes the speaker's own attitude, his opinion or his own viewpoint, which remains hidden in the sentence. It is in this total environment that the sentence becomes communicable to us in real life. This is the reason why Austin calls the sentence a *speech act* and not just a speech. The sentence, as it were, is as good as an action or an activity because it involves a complete environment. For instance, take the two Hindi sentences:

आप कहाँ के नवाब आए।

अब तो तुम्हारा दोस्त आने से रहा।

These sentences hide much more than they reveal. For instance, if we analyze, the hidden elements in these sentences it may come out to be something like this: आप नवाब नहीं हैं and अब तुम्हारा दोस्त नहीं आएगा + satire etc.

These are called the verbal extensions of the sentence. They surround the language unit and help to determine their interpretation. This is what Austin calls a *discourse*. The discourse is an extended verbal expression in speech or writing. The discourse represents the full intent of the speaker. It may consist of a single word (e.g. जाओ) which is a full sentence (e.g. वह किताब लाओ) or more than a sentence (e.g. मेज पर एक किताब है. उसे यहाँ लेकर आओ). Till now the sentence was considered to be the basic unit of the language but now discourse, and not the sentence, is considered to be the basic unit of the language. Sentence, however, still remains the largest physical unit of the grammatical structure.

The present book is as much concerned with the language syntax as with the discourse of the living language. It's focus on the current grammatical operations of Hindi syntax and at the same time its practical link-up with the actual sentence patterns is likely to make the book more useful and illustrative. Thus combined with the updated Hindi syntax and its finer rules of discourse, the book is likely to have far-reaching implications not only in language studies and linguistics but also in many natural language processing (NLP) applications and computational linguistics where syntax and semantics play a larger role in machine-assisted translation activities.

Functionally, the book has two objectives: (i) to examine, asses and update the various grammatical notions emerged during the last couple of decades in Hindi and (ii) to identify the kernel or basic Hindi sentence patterns, which should be able to generate innumerable sentences of the language through some known rules of expansion, substitution and transformation and marked for certain structural, semantic and pragmatic features.

The grammar used in this book is basically descriptive and is not based on any particular model or theory. In other words, it does not rigidly follow any particular linguistic school or model. It assimilates and absorbs almost all the new significant findings, which were available in structural grammars, tagmemics, transformational-generative grammar, case grammar, systemic grammar and relational grammar etc.

In the analysis of Hindi sentence patterns the method used is that of feature analysis or componential analysis placed within a physical sentence frame with explanatory comments on each sub-pattern.

3. The sentence and sentence patterns

A sentence is a concrete and definite construction made of various phrases. A sentence pattern is an abstract frame made up of the slots of these phrases from which we can generate innumerable sentences by inserting appropriate words in appropriate slots. The sentence has a concrete and definite entity. The sentence frame, on the other hand, is an abstract and symbolic frame. The number of words used in a sentence is limited, but the number of words that can be used in the sentence pattern is unlimited. It is concrete because the words (or phrases) in the sentence appear before us in the form of an audible or visible string which we can hear or see. For instance, 'लड़का चिट्ठी लिख रहा है' is a definite construction which we call sentence. Every phrase occurring in the sentence has a definite place of its use from where it performs its allotted function in the sentence. For instance, in the above sentence लड़का is performing the function of a subject, the चिट्ठी is performing the function of an object and लिख रहा है is performing the function of a verb. The places where these phrases occur in the sentences are called slots or functional slots. Thus we can have more than one slot in the sentence like a subject slot, an object slot, a verb slot, a complement slot or an adverb slot etc. If we choose to represent the various phrases of the sentence through such functional slots we get a sentence pattern like S O C V (i.e. subject object complement and verb).

Subject	Object	Complement	Verb Phrase
निदेशक ने	राधिका को	अपना निजी सचिव	नियुक्त किया
मैं	आपको	अपना सबसे अच्छा दोस्त	मानता हूँ
वकील ने	लड़की के भाई को	मुज़रिम	सिद्ध कर दिया

The slots of the frame here provide simply the grammatical information about the sentence, i.e. whether the slots belong to the subject, object, complement or verb etc. They do not specify any other semantic, structural or pragmatic features like <+ animate,> < -lexical> <-physical>. In other words the unmarked slots cannot specify whether the slot should be occupied by an animate noun or inanimate noun, by an abstract noun or a concrete noun etc. This information is available in the feature-marked sentence patterns in which each slot of the frame is marked with structural, semantic and pragmatic features as we find in almost all the sentence patterns given in the part 2 of this book.

The symbol + before the word indicates the presence of the feature and the symbol - before it indicates the absence of the feature. The symbol ± indicates that the feature may be interpreted both ways - plus as well as minus feature. See, for instance, the features in sub-pattern-22 (Phrasal Object), (b) कर activisation, (c) कि-clause and (d) animate को-subject.

Sub-pattern-8 सिद्ध हो (Confirmation)

NP (subject) <+member>	NP (complement) <+class, + quality addition>	Linking verb सिद्ध हो (confirmation) <+lexical, -कि,+stative, +aspect>
(1) वह	कुशल अध्यापक	सिद्ध हुआ।
(2) हेमा	एक सफल पत्नी	सिद्ध होगी।
(3) यह नुस्खा	रामबाण	साबित हुआ।

Explanatory comments:

(a) *Proof and Quality Addition* : There is a relationship of class and member between the subject and the complement. The additional feature of the verb of this sub-pattern is *confirmation* and *reinforcement* and that of complement is *quality addition*, that is, not only a teacher but also an *efficient* teacher. In other words, only such nouns can occupy the place of the noun complement which basically represent the quality or which can be associated with some adjectives. See:

(1) a) - वह कुशल अध्यापक सिद्ध हुआ। (acceptable)
b *वह अध्यापक सिद्ध हुआ। (unacceptable)

(2) a - हेमा एक सफल पत्नी सिद्ध हुई। (acceptable)
b- *हेमा एक पत्नी सिद्ध हुई। (unacceptable).

It will be clear that it is only because of the epithets like कुशल and सफल that the phrase acquires the quality of an adjective.

The features in the slots of the sentence frames are indicated through the three symbols +, - and ±. The symbol + before the word indicates the presence of the feature and the symbol - before it indicates the absence of the feature. The symbol ± or indicates that the feature may be either present or absent.

Needless to say, a description of this sort brings some sort of mathematical precision to the description of the grammatical features and makes them distinct from each other. With the help of these symbols, these sub-patterns are supposed to be potentially capable of generating innumerable Hindi sentences using the known linguistic processes like addition, transformation and substitution etc.

All the 45 sentence sub-patterns and their distinctive features have been defined and marked so that each sentence sub-pattern is ultimately reduced to a configuration of features. A similar configuration of features must automatically generate similar types of sentences. The idea is that given a similar set of structural, semantic and pragmatic features the sub-patterns should automatically generate a draft Hindi sentence.

It must be confessed at this juncture that to capture all the meanings and nuances of a living language is a stupendous task and still more difficult is to attempt to formulate the rules for their use. In the present circumstances all we can do is to customize our description of the language for our specific purposes and remember the words of Samuel Johnson, the first lexicographer of English language who said this long back:

Language does not follow a beaten path. Grammarians do not make the rules of the language. They only follow them. It is the language speakers who make the rules.

At the conclusion of the book I will here like to express my gratitude to my friend Dr Vijay Kumar Malhotra who not only constantly inspired and goaded me to complete the book but also rendered academic and other help whenever I needed.

Prof. Suraj Bhan Singh

About the book

The first version of the author's *Hindi ka Vakyatmak Vyakaran* was published in 1980 in Hindi but there was a constant demand from many quarters to bring out the English version of the book for the benefit of the foreign or non-Hindi speaking learners, scholars, advanced language learners and specially computer professionals working on natural language processing and machine-aided translation systems because they need the finer rules of grammar. Hence the present new English version of the book is a vastly revised, enriched and updated form with a user-friendly format.

CONTENTS

PART-1 THEORY

Chapter-1 SENTENCE

Chapter-2 PHRASE

Chapter-3 SENTENCE PATTERNS

PART-2 APPLICATION

Chapter-4 COPULA SENTENCE PATTERN

PART-1

THEORY

Chapter-1

SENTENCE

1.1 Defining a Sentence

Sentence is the largest unit of the grammatical structure of the language and is also the basic unit of the language at the communication level. This is by far the most neutral interpretation of the sentence which recognizes the sentence as a part of language structure and defines its social function. Sentence infact is a heavy-duty word and its definition will depend on whether we are looking at it as a semantic unit, a structural unit, a psychological unit or a component of the context. The various views expressed by linguists and scholars to define the sentence can be broadly grouped into the following categories for convenience.

(a) Philosophical Interpretation: According to the western logicians and सत्तामीमांसा, a sentence is basically an overt form of a subject, a predicate and a copula (linking verb). For instance, in a sentence like 'Ram is a scholar', Ram is a subject, scholar is a predicate, and *is* is a copula or a linking verb. The traditional grammarians held a different view. They recognized only two entities in a sentence – *subject* (about whom something is said) and the *predicate* (whatever is said about the subject) (Barker 1938 : 4).

(b) Sanskrit Grammatical Tradition: Patanjali says in महाभाष्य that a verb together with both its forms *तिङंत* and *कृदंत* constitute a sentence (आख्यातं सविशेषणं वाक्यम्). According to Bhartrihari, a sentence is the one whose components, when analyzed, anticipate each other, but which do not anticipate words from another sentence, which is concentrated around a verb, which conveys a meaning and is at times associated with adjectives. Indian न्याय दर्शन has enumerated three attributes of a sentence योग्यता, आकांक्षा and सन्निधि. Out of these योग्यता stands for semantic compatibility, e.g. a sentence like *The chair is eating fruits* lacks semantic compatibility (congruence). आकांक्षा means anticipation of another word/phrase by a word/phrase, e.g. the word/phrase राधा ने फल automatically demands or anticipates another word or phrase, like खाया. The word सन्निधि means appropriate nearness of the various components of a sentence. An undesirable distance or time gap between the pronunciation of two words or components can mar the comprehensibility of the sentence. Hence there should be a reasonable closeness or distance between the components or words.

(c) Semantic Definition: Till around the beginning of the twentieth century the sentence continued to be defined as an 'independent meaningful expression'. Jesperson (1924 : 307) defined the sentence as a relatively complete and independent human utterance whose completeness and independence lies in the fact that it is, or it can be, used independently'. According to Gardiner (1926 : 80), a sentence is a word or a group of words which expresses a comprehensible meaning. Guru (1920 : 55) has also defined a sentence as 'a word-group that expresses a complete thought'. According to these definitions, *a sentence is the basic unit of a grammatical structure that expresses the intent or thought of a speaker*.

(4) Structural Definition: The completeness of a meaning or an idea is always relative and, therefore, no objective or neutral rules can be formed on its basis. Hence the structural linguists tried to provide the definition of a sentence on the basis of its structure. According to them, a sentence is a construction which cannot be a part or constituent of a larger construction in an utterance (Bloomfield 1926 : 156). In this definition, a sentence has been viewed merely in terms of a construction separate from its meaning. According to them, a sentence is a construction which is made up of a few constituents (words, phrases) in the same way as the word is a construction which is made up of a few sounds. Looked at this angle, a sentence is *the largest grammatical construction* of the language.

The word 'utterance' mentioned in Bloomfield's definition is itself relative and ambiguous – it is difficult to specify as to how much portion of a speech can be an utterance. Bernard Bloch, C.C. Fries and some others accepted this definition with some reservation. Skirting all these objections, some structural linguists devised a new definition of the sentence taking the spoken aspect of the language as a central point, as for instance, the *sentence is the utterance between the silence and the terminal stress* (James Sledd and Scott 1959 : 167)

(5) Language-specific Definition: Some structural linguists (Palmer 1971 : 72) provided a language-specific, rather than generic, definition of a sentence. According to them, a sentence is a structure made up of various linguistic elements arranged in a specific order. These linguistic elements occur in the sentence in the form of structural categories (noun, pronoun, adjective, verb etc.) and functional categories (subject, object, complement, verb, particle etc.) and their pattern of distribution differs from language to language. Hence the definition of language will be different for each language. On this basis, we can formulate the definition of a Hindi sentence as follows:

<Hindi sentence = (+ Subject +/- Object +/- Complement +/- adverbial# + Verb>

In this definition, the verb is a compulsory component (+) and the object and complement are obligatory in a few sentences and optional in others (+/-) and adverbial is an optional component which can occur at any place before it (+/-/#). In other words, an adverbial can occur before and after the subject or object and before the verb but not after the verb.

(6) Mentalistic View: The structural linguists had viewed the sentence as a construction which is concrete and analyzable, but

Chomsky (1965), the father of the Transformational Grammar, viewed the sentence as an abstract concept situated or residing inside the human mind whose manifest or overt form is an utterance. In its abstract (mental) form a sentence is an *ideal sentence.* The form of the sentence that is expressed in the outer surface may have one or more sentences embedded in it through some particular structural and semantic processes. For instance, the sentence 'I saw Champa passing through here' has two sentences embedded in it – 'I saw Champa' and 'Champa was passing through here'.

The analysis of the sentence in transformational grammar starts with a bilateral division –noun phrase (NP) and verb phrase (VP), which in some ways is parallel to the traditional division of *subject* and *predicate*. In transformational grammar the hierarchy and relationship existing between the different levels and components of the sentence are specified (marked) which at one stage also includes the semantic component. Contrary to this, the structural analysis is mainly linear where the semantic component is normally ruled out because it is deemed to be un-analyzable and abstract. For instance, in the sentence प्रमोद ने शीला को मुस्कुराते हुए देखा it is not clear whether the phrase मुस्कुराते हुए refers to प्रमोद or to शीला. This can be better represented through transformational hierarchy rather than the linear analysis. That is why the transformational grammarians define the sentence as a 'structured string of words' (Jacobs and Rosenbaum 1968 : 10).

(7) Sentence in Case Grammar: According to the Case Grammar, the sentence is a structure made up of a verb and one or more noun phrases where every noun remains linked to the verb under certain (case) relationships (Fillmore 1968). This case relationship is completely meaning based. The case relationship is determined mainly on the basis of the inherent features of the verbs and the nouns (e.g. animate-inanimate, active-inactive, agent-experiencer, goal, volition etc.) and not on the basis of their structural functions. Sentences which are different on the basis of their inherent case relationships are also different in their sentence structures. This difference is often proved through their structural constraints or restrictions. For instance, in the sentence, राधा नाची, राधा is an agent (or active subject) (see 3.5.3 a), but in a superficially similar sentence राधा चौंकी, राधा is an experiencer. The two sentences are not the same in case relationship. There is a restriction in Hindi on the use of volitional constructions (like –ना है, ना पड़ etc). For instance, while a sentence like राधा को नाचना है is possible, a sentence like राधा को चौंकना है or राधा को चौंकना पड़ा is not possible.

(8) Sociolinguistic Interpretation: As a result of the new developments in the field of sociolinguistics and subsequently pragmatics, the concept of a sentence underwent a drastic change. The sentence now came to be regarded as a simple unit of communication and not the basic unit of the language (as the structural linguists used to hold). From the point of view of communication, the basic unit of the language is *discourse* (Austin 2007). The discourse represents the full intent or thought of the speaker. Depending upon the necessity, the intent or message of the speaker can be communicated by a single word (आओ !), by more than a word (वह किताब ले आओ), by more than a sentence (ज़रा देखो !, वहाँ एक किताब रखी है उसे ले आओ !), by a paragraph and sometimes by a whole chapter or a book.

From the contextual point of view, sentences are of two types: *system sentences* and *text sentences*. At the communication level only text sentences are real sentences (i.e. real life sentences) because they are related to the context or real situation. On the other hand, grammatical sentences which are not related to the real context of situation are nil from the point of view of communication or message. For instance, if we read a sentence तुम्हारे पिताजी बस से गिर पड़े in a grammar book as a piece of an example, it is an artificial sentence even though it is meaningful and grammatical and will not revoke any reaction from us. But if the sentence is spoken before us in a real life situation, we will be concerned about the health of our father. Here it is a system sentence, because it has not been used for communication of message to someone in a real life situation and not just for providing an example for the expression of meaning even though the meaning of the sentence is complete in itself.

The above discussion will reveal that the concept of the sentence has long been a favourite topic of debate amongst linguists, philosophers and scholars and has been revolving around three central points—meaning, structure and communication in one form or the other.

1.2 Sentence in the Language Structure

Language structure has three dimensions - sound, grammar and meaning. *Sound* is the physical and concrete aspect of the language, which we can perceive with our senses. *Grammar* is the abstract and system-based aspect of the language.*Sound* is a substance and*grammar* is the shape of the substance. Sentences and words fall under grammar. *Meaning* is the mental aspect of the language, which basically resides in the mind of the speaker or audience.

Sounds*per se* are meaningless but they become meaningful when they acquire the form and shape of words and sentences through some grammatical system. It is in fact grammar that links the sound to the realm of meaning. Grammar is the link between the sound and meaning. The structure of the language can thus be illustrated as follows:

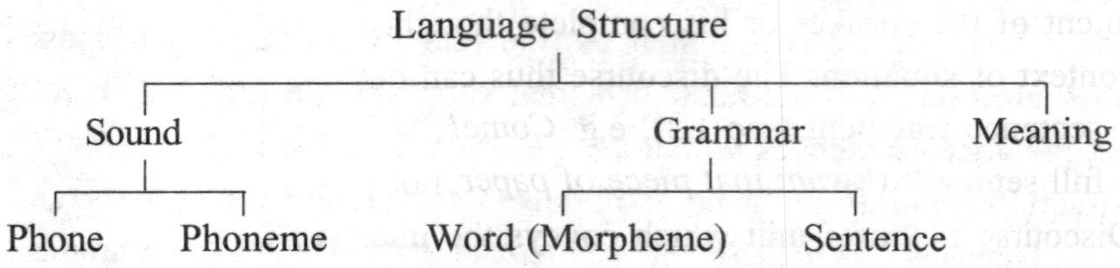

The chart displays the multi-layered and systemic structure of the language where every level has its own internal system (e.g. phonic system, phonemic system, morphological system, sentence structure or system and semantic system) and each level is connected to its higher and lower levels. This is precisely the reason why the language is called *the system of systems.*

There is yet another angle to look at the language which takes into account the context or the social dimension of the language. For instance, Halliday (1961) and Firth (1957) have conceived three levels of language – *substance, form* and *situation*. The substance represents the sound and writing which can be heard and written. The *form* includes grammar and words. Phonology is a link between the substance and the form, and context is the link between the grammar and the situation. See -

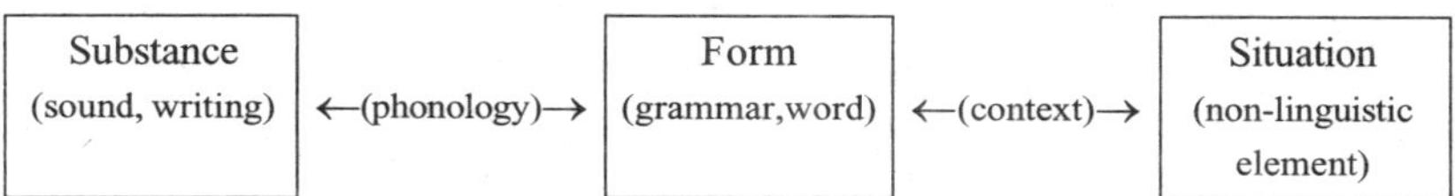

Context is a non-linguistic element and is mainly related to the function and the social domain of the language and influences the language structure and the selection of sentence options.

The structure of the language can also be viewed as a well-organized hierarchy of pure linguistic components - smaller unit, then a larger unit and then a still larger unit etc.

We had seen earlier in section 1.1 that in terms of grammatical construction the *sentence* is the largest unit of the language, but in terms of language communication, *discourse,* and not the sentence, is the largest unit of the language. *Discourse* represents the full intent of the speaker or his complete thought and is related to the context or situation. The discourse thus can be a minor sentence or a sentence fragment (see 1.3), e.g. *Come!*, हां /yes!, etc.). It can be a full sentence (*I want that piece of paper*.) or a group of sentences. Discourse is thus a unit which coveys the intended message of the speaker in its totality.

The unit smaller than the sentence is a *clause*. The sentence may consist of a single clause or more than one clause. When the sentence consists of a single clause it is called an independent clause and called a *simple sentence* (see 1.4). In such a situation there is no distinction between the sentence and the clause. For instance, यह मकान मेरा है is an independent clause as well as a simple sentence. यह मेरा

मकान है, लेकिन मैं अब इसे बेचना चाहता हूँ is also a sentence but it consists of two clauses.

The unit smaller than the clause is a **phrase.** A clause is made up of one or more phrases. A phrase is basically a functional unit and, therefore, it may consist of a single word or more than one word (see 2.1), because in a sentence the grammatical function (e.g. subject, object, complement, verb and adverbial etc.) can be performed by a single word as well as more than one word. For instance, in the sentence लड़का बीमार है 'लड़का' is a single word, but it can be replaced by 'मेरा लड़का', 'मेरा बड़ा लड़का', 'मेरा सबसे बड़ा लड़का' and all these are phrases irrespective of whether they are made up of a single word or a combination of words.

The unit smaller than the phrase is a **word.** A phrase is made up of words, e.g. मेरा + बड़ा + लड़का = 'मेरा बड़ा लड़का', but the phrase which consists of a single word acts both as a phrase as well as a word. For instance, in the sentence, लड़का आ गया, लड़का is a word as well as a phrase.

The unit smaller than the word is a **morpheme**. A sequence of sounds which is meaningful and which cannot be divided into further meaningful parts is called a morpheme. Morpheme is the minimum meaningful unit of the language. A morpheme can be in the form of a word or a unit larger than a word. For instance, सहनशीलता is a word but it contains atleast three morphemes – सहन + शील + ता, but in a word which contains only one morpheme, the word and the morpheme are identical, e.g. मकान.

The unit smaller than the morpheme is a **phoneme**. A phoneme is a group of sounds used in a language and whose members share some features but none of the members can be used in each other's place. The sequence of phonemes makes for a morpheme, for instance the five phonemes m+k+aa+n put together make a morpheme (or word). Phoneme is the smallest unit of the language though some linguists consider phonic features (such as aspiration, voice, friction etc.) as the smallest unit of the language because it is a combination of these features that makes for a phoneme.

Thus we find that the language is a multi-layered structure and its each level is linked to the other in a hierarchy , as shown in the following illustration:

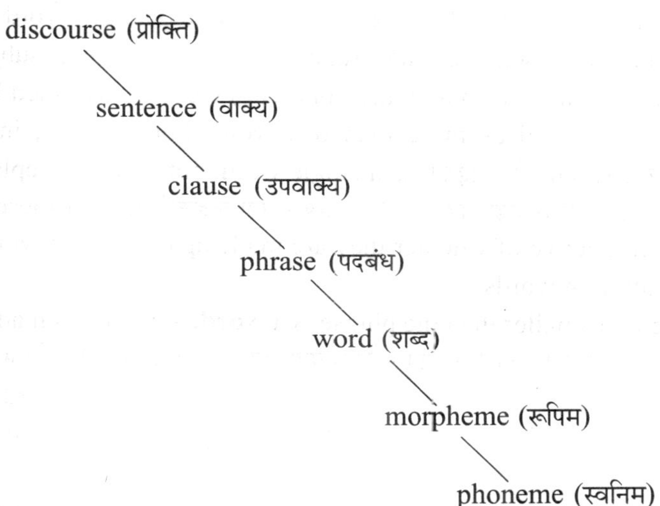

The basic unit of language at the communication level is	:	discourse
The largest unit of the grammatical structure of the language	:	sentence
The minimum unit of expression of thought	:	sentence
The smallest meaningful unit of the language	:	morpheme
The smallest structural unit of the language	:	phoneme

For the study of sentence patterns the analysis of only sentences and phrases is relevant.

1.3 Minor Sentences

Minor sentences (also called sentence fragments) are incomplete from the point of view of grammatical structure but are complete in terms of the communication of message or thought, e.g. नमस्ते !, बैरा !, कौन ? The early grammarians did not consider these expressions as sentences. According to Sweet (1891: 452), these are not brief sentences but are something in between a word and a sentence. Even though incomplete in outer structure, these minor sentences are complete in their meaning and inner structure. For instance, the minor sentence जाओ has a complete comprehensibility even though the word तुम is missing in it, because the omission of तुम here is the basic structural requirement of imperative sentences. Similarly, in reply to the question तुम कौन हो, the answer in only one word रामलाल which is understood as मैं रामलाल हूँ. Here the comprehensibility has been possible because it is linked to the context.

The minor sentences can be divided into two categories – (a) structure-dependent minor sentences and (b) context-dependent minor sentences:

(a) Structure-dependent Minor Sentence: The structure of certain types of sentences requires the omission of some part of the sentence as a structural requirement. Such sentences are usually modal (i.e mood-based) in nature and can be used as discourse starters without any pre-linguistic reference, e.g.

(1) Imperative: आइए !, उधर मत जाओ !, इधर आना !
(2) Vocative: बैरा ! हे भगवान् !, पिताजी !
(3) Exclamation: अरे !,वाह !, छि: !, शाबाश !
(4) Greetings: नमस्ते, हैलो !, शुक्रिया !

(b) Context-dependent Minor Sentence: Some sentences require omission of one of their portions because of the necessity of the context. Such sentences are often used in context with some prior linguistic reference and are, therefore, completely linked to their contexts. Outside the context they may often lose their communicability. Sometimes these minor sentences can be used in non-linguistic contexts also, e.g. the question by the clerk while registering somebody's name– आपका नाम? (meaning 'आपका नाम क्या है?') A minor sentence of this type can not be used if there is no relevant context. Some examples of such context-sensitive minor sentences are being given below (expressions in bold letters are minor sentences):

(1) Question sentence : (Hearing the knock at the door) **कौन?**
- (मैं सुंदरम् हूँ, **और आप?)**

(2) Reply sentence :
- बाहर कौन है?
- **मैं।**
- आप ही रामप्रसाद हैं?
- **जी हाँ।**

(3) Confirmatory sentence:
- मैं कल जा रहा हूँ।
- **अच्छा!**

(4) Complementary sentence:
- मैं तुमसे शादी करना चाहता हूँ। **आज, अभी।**
- मैं कल यहाँ से चला जाऊँगा। **तीन की गाड़ी से।**

Minor sentences are also used in co-ordinative sentences, e.g *माँ सो रही है और* **बच्चे भी** (see contracted sentence 1.5.4c).

1.4 Types of Sentences

The types of sentences can be determined at two levels—structure and meaning.

1.4.1 Structural Classification

Based on the structure, sentences can be classified into two types—simple and non-simple. The non-simple sentences can be further subdivided into compound and complex sentences:

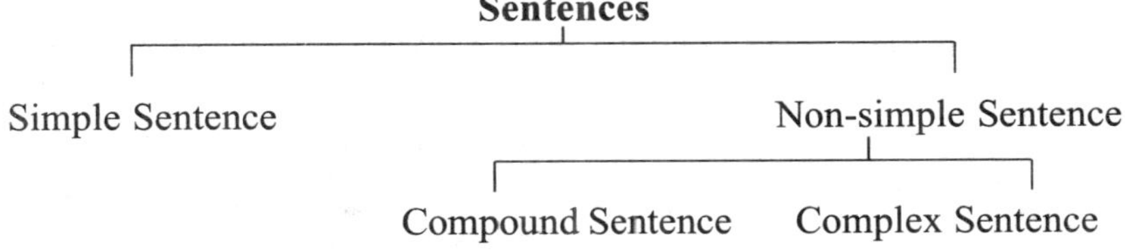

(i) Simple sentence # A #

(ii) Non-simple sentence (i) Compound sentence # A + A #
(ii) Complex sentence # A + B #

'*a*' represents an independent clause and '*b*' represents a subordinate clause. The dots '...' represents that it is limitless, i.e.

the sentence has the capacity to accept more clauses. The symbol '#' indicates the beginning and end of the sentence. Example:

(1) डॉक्टर ने मरीज को देखा। (simple sentence)

(2) डॉक्टर ने मरीज को देखा और उसे दवा दी। (compound sentence)

(3) डॉक्टर ने उस मरीज को देखा जो पंक्ति में सबसे आगे खड़ा था। (complex sentence)

It will be evident that a sentence may consist of a single clause or more than one clause. Where the clause is single, it becomes an independent clause which is called a **simple sentence** (e.g. sentence 1). If the sentence consists of two or more clauses, it is called a **non-simple** clause (e.g. sentences 2, 3). If all the clauses of a non-simple sentence are independent main clauses, it is called a **compound sentence** (see 1.5) (e.g. sentence 3). If one clause of the sentence is independent or the main clause and the rest are dependent clause(s), it is called a complex sentence (sentence 3) (e.g. see 1.6). If a sentence consists of two or more independent clauses and one or more dependent clauses, it is called a **compound-complex sentence**, e.g.

वह तुरंत खड़ा हुआ और बोला कि मैं इसका सख्त विरोध करता हूँ।

1.4.2 Semantic Classification of Sentences

Based on the meaning or semantics, sentences can be classified into three categories – referential, imperative and expressive which are related to the three familiar functions of the language – (a) referential function, (b) conative function and (c) expressive function.

(a) Referential Sentence – One of the functions of the language is to communicate information about some subject or proposition. This is called the *referential* function of the language. The sentences that are used to fulfill this function are also called indefinite (or narrative) sentences. In sentences of this type, the subject or theme has the dominance and not the speaker or hearer, e.g. यह संसार नश्वर है, दूध गिर गया।

(b) Conative or Imperative Sentence – The second main function of the language is to control or direct the activities of others which is called the *conative* function of the language. In order to perform this function the sentences used are generally imperative sentences which are directed to control the hearer's activities. Here the hearer is the dominant factor and not the speaker or the subject, e.g. बाहर जाओ, थोड़ी देर इंतज़ार कीजिए (see 2.10.3a).

(c) Expressive Sentence – The third main function of the language is to express the various emotions and feelings of the speaker which is called the *expressive* function of the language. This is materialized through emotive sentences centered on the speaker rather than the subject or the hearer. Sentences expressing doubt, wish and exclamation are speaker-oriented and subjective expressions. Therefore, all subjunctive sentences (2.10.3b) and sentences expressing wish fall in this category, e.g. शायद वह अब न लौटे, आपकी यात्रा शुभ हो!, भगवान् आपका भला करे !, काश, मैं आपकी जगह होता!,अहा कितना सुंदर दृश्य है ! छि: यह भी कोई मकान है !

Out of these, the referential sentences can have both negative and interrogative forms. Imperative sentences can have only positive and negative forms. Exclamatory sentences can not have interrogative forms. Expressive sentences have certain rules and restrictions in forming interrogative and negative forms.

Generally the forms of referential, imperative and expressive sentences in the language are more or less fixed, e.g.

a) the use of imperative verb forms (जा, जाओ, जाइए, जाना) conative sentences,
b) the use of different tense forms in referential (indefinite) sentences.
c) the use of various modal forms in expressive sentences,
d) the use of k-words (क्या, कौन, कब etc.) or special intonation in interrogative sentences, the use of न, नहीं or मत in negative sentences.

But if we analyze the actual sentences in use in real life situations, we may sometimes come across contradictions in their sentence forms and their social functions. For instance, we may find that in certain contexts the overtly indefinite sentences are performing the function of an imperative and even, interrogative sentences, e. g.

(1) मुझे बड़ी प्यास लग रही है। (i.e. = पानी पिलाइए)

(2) मुझे एक कप चाय चाहिए। (i.e = एक कप चाय दीजिए)

(3) मैं कल आपके यहाँ आना चाहता हूँ। (i.e.= क्या मैं कल आपके यहाँ आ सकता हूँ?)

It may be noted that all these sentences convey a certain meaning at the surface level as dictated by their sentence frames, but at the deeper level their intent or meaning is different as shown within brackets against each sentence called.

1.5 Compound Sentences

1.5.1 Defining a Compound Sentence

Structurally, a *compound sentence* is made up of two or more independent sentences which are related together in appositional relationship, i.e., semantically they are not dependent on each other. In *complex sentences*, on the other hand, this relationship is that of a main and dependent clause. At the surface level the clauses of compound sentences are linked together through appositional conjunctions (और, या लेकिन etc.) e.g. बाहर बारिश हो रही है और लोग इधर-उधर भाग रहे हैं।

Sometimes two or more clauses of compound sentences partially map on each other and it is difficult to recognize them as compound sentences at the surface level. For instance, the sentence सतीश और दीपक सुबह व्यायाम करते हैं is a combination of the following two independent sentences in their deep structure:

(1) सतीश सुबह व्यायाम करता है।

(2) दीपक सुबह व्यायाम करता है।

These sentences when merged into a single compound sentence are conjoined through a coordinative conjunct और.

Similarly the compound sentence आप कल आए थे या परसों contains two underlying sentences conjoined by the conjunct या:

(3) आप कल आए थे ?

(4) आप परसों आए थे ?

These are the underlying sentences which are present in the deep surface of the sentence, but while appearing at the surface structure some of their portions get deleted (see 1.5.3)

1.5.2 Semantic Classification of Compound Sentences

There is an appositional (parallel) relationship between the clauses of compound sentences, but this relationship cannot always be said to be parallel. The constituent clauses of a compound sentence are called parallel when both the constituent clauses are capable of being reversed in order without damage to the central meaning of the sentence. For instance, the relationship between the constituent clauses of the following compound sentences can be said to be parallel because even after the inversion of the two clauses, their semantic compatibility remains intact, i.e. there is merely a shift in their theme or priority. See–

(1) रात सुनसान थी *और* चारों ओर अंधेरा था।

(1a) चारों ओर अंधेरा था *और* रात सुनसान थी।

(2) लोहा पिघल जाएगा *या* अपनी जगह छोड़ देगा।

(2a) लोहा अपनी जगह छोड़ देगा *या* पिघल जाएगा।

On the contrary the constituent clauses of some compound sentences are linked to the context (e.g. cause and effect) and, therefore, do not permit inversion of clauses, e.g.

(3) चिड़िया को गोली लगी *और* वह नीचे आ गिरी।

(3a) *चिड़िया नीचे आ गिरी *और* उसे चोट लगी।

(4) वह उठा *लेकिन* लोगों ने उसे बिठा दिया।

(4a) *लोगों ने उसे बिठा दिया *लेकिन* वह उठा।

Based on the relationship existing between the various constituent clauses of a sentence, the following semantic categories can be enumerated as follows:

(a) Co-ordinative Relationship: When the constituent clauses denote a collection or conjunction of two or more events, situations or actions they are supposed to have a co-coordinative relationship. Such a relationship is indicated by placing the following conjuncts between the two clauses: और (तथा, एवं), फिर, ही नहीं, बल्कि etc. Examples –

(1) रात सुनसान थी *और* चारों ओर अंधेरा था।

(3) चिड़िया को गोली लगी *और* वह नीचे आ गिरी।

(5) वह थोड़ी देर *रुकी, फिर* चल दी।

(6) उसने रिक्शेवाले को गाली ही नहीं दी, *बल्कि* पीटा भी।

(b) Disjunctive Relationship: When the constituent clauses of a compound sentence denote either the acceptance of one event, situation or action, or rejection of both, they are supposed to have a divisive relationship. This relationship is just the opposite of coordinative relationship. Some important divisive conjuncts used are: या (अथवा), या ...या, न...न, न कि, न, नहीं तो, अन्यथा, चाहे...चाहे, न कि, (या). Examples:

(2) लोहा पिघल जाएगा *या* अपनी जगह छोड़ देगा।

(7) *या* तुम स्वयं चले जाओ या मुझे जाने दो।

(8) *न* वह मुझे जानता है न मैं उसे।

(9) जल्दी चले जाओ *नहीं तो* वह यहीं आ जाएगा।

(10) चाहे तुम यहाँ रहो *चाहे* ससुराल।

(11) मैं आपसे अपना वेतन माँग रहा हूँ *न कि* भीख।

(12) तुम पढ़ते हो *कि (या)* नहीं।

(c) Opposite Relationship: When the two constituent clauses of the sentence denote opposition or contradiction between two events, situations or actions, it is supposed to have opposite relationship. Such sentences indicate the negation or limitation of the first clause. Both the clauses of this category have mutual relationship and, therefore, it is not possible to inverse the clauses without damage to the central meaning. Important conjuncts used to denote the contradictory relationship are: लेकिन (किंतु, परंतु, मगर, पर), बल्कि, प्रत्युत् etc. Examples:

(4) वह उठा *लेकिन* लोगों ने उसे बिठा दिया।

(13) उसने मुझे पैसे नहीं लौटाए *बल्कि* मुझसे कुछ और पैसे ले लिए।

The difference between the usage of *बल्कि* in sentence (6) and (13) need to be noted.

(d) Resultative Conjunct: When the two constituent clauses of a compound sentence denote the cause and effect relationship even without being semantically or structurally dependent on each other they are supposed to have resultative relationship. Some important resultative conjuncts are : अरे, इसलिए, अत:, अतएव, सो Examples :

(14) मैं बीमार हूँ *इसलिए* कल बैठक में नहीं आ सकता।

Here it should be treated as different from the causative adverbial clause of a complex sentence (see 1.6.4d). The subordinate clause in the complex sentence denotes the reason while the main clause denotes the result. In a compound sentence both the clauses are independent clauses out of which the second clause informs about the result. In causative complex sentence the main intention of the speaker is to inform about the fact contained in the main clause and the 'reason' is presented as an auxiliary or support information which is contained in the dependent clause. On the other hand, in the case of the resultative compound sentence, the object of the speaker is to provide information of both–the fact and the reason and, therefore, both are expressed by two different independent/main clauses. This will be evident from the fact that in a resultative compound sentence the conjunct इसलिए can be replaced by और or और इसलिए while it is not possible in the case of causative complex sentences, e.g.

(14) मैं बीमार हूँ **इसलिए** कल बैठक में नहीं आ सकता।

(compound sentence)

(14a) मैं बीमार हूँ **और (इसलिए)** कल बैठक में नहीं आ सकता।

(compound sentence)

(15) मैं कल बैठक में नहीं आ सकता **क्योंकि** मैं बीमार हूँ।

(complex sentence)

(15a) *मैं कल बैठक में नहीं आ सकता ***और क्योंकि** मैं बीमार हूँ।

(unacceptable)

A comparative description of the conjuncts used in the compound and complex sentences can be seen below:

Complex sentence:

In the main clause	In the subordinate clause
ϕ (no conjunct)	क्योंकि
इसलिए	कि
इतना	कि
ϕ (no conjunct)	जिससे, ताकि

(15) मैं कल बैठक में नहीं आ सकता **क्योंकि** मैं बीमार हूँ।

(16) पीतांबर **इसलिए** दिल्ली जाना चाहता है **कि** वहाँ उसकी ससुराल है।

(17) वह इतना कंजूस है **कि** चाय में चीनी तक नहीं डालता।

(18) तुम ये पैसे भी चुकता कर दो **ताकि** बाद में कोई शिकायत न रहे।

Compound sentence:

In the first clause	In the second clause
ϕ (no conjunct)	इसलिए, अत:, अतएव, सो

(14) मैं बीमार हूँ **इसलिए** कल बैठक में नहीं आ सकता।

(19) उसे लड़की पसंद थी **सो** उसने हामी भर दी।

1.5.3 Formation of Compound Sentences

Both the traditional grammar as well as the transformational grammar agree that the two constituents of a compound sentence are related to each other in appositional or parallel relationship. The transformational grammar, however, describes the formation rules as to how the two underlying sentences get merged with each other in the surface structure. According to this, the formation of compound sentences involves as many as three transformational processes:

(a) Coordination process: An appositional coordinative conjunct is inserted between two or more constituent sentences (clauses), e.g. the insertion of the appositional conjunct *और* between the two sentences – रात सुनसान थी and चारों ओर अंधेरा था thus generating a single sentence – रात सुनसान थी और चारों ओर अंधेरा था।

(b) Deletion process: If two or more constituent sentences have similar portions (phrase or phrases) and belong to the same grammatical category and perform the same function, the identical portion of the second sentence gets deleted, e.g. the deletion of सो रही है in the second clause of the sentence – माँ सो रही है और बच्चे भी।

(c) Transformation process: The non-similar portions of the second constituent clause are shifted to the first sentence where they are attached through a coordination process. For instance, when the two constituent clauses लोहा धातु है and सोना धातु है merge into one sentence, the word सोना of the second sentence is shifted to the first sentence to make the full sentence– लोहा और सोना धातु हैं।

1.5.4 Structural Classification of Compound Sentences

Some compound sentences undergo a single transformation process; some undergo three and some four processes. Based on this, the Hindi compound sentences are classified into three categories:

(a) Full Compound Sentence: Sentences belonging to this category undergo only a single process of insertion in which a coordinate conjunct is inserted between the two sentences and there is no deletion or shifting of components. Consequently both the constituent sentences remain in their full form without any change except the insertion of a coordinative conjunct, e.g.

(1) रात सुनसान थी *और* चारों तरफ अंधेरा था।

(9) जल्दी चले जाओ *नहीं तो* वह यहीं आ जाएगा।

(4) वह उठा *लेकिन* लोगों ने उसे बिठा दिया।

(b) Partial Compound Sentence: The partial compound sentence undergoes two processes – coordination and deletion through the coordination process, a coordinative conjunct is inserted between the two sentences and under the deletion process, the identical and similar portion in the second sentence is deleted. This deleted portion is normally a verb phrase. If a conjunct belonging to the *और* -class the word *भी* may be used at the end. e.g.

(20) माँ सो रही है और बच्चे भी।

(21) मैं आपको जानता हूँ (लेकिन) आपके लड़के को नहीं (जानता)।

(22) आप कल आए थे या परसों (आए थे)?

(c) Constricted Compound Sentence: The constricted compound sentences undergo all the three processes – insertion of a coordinative conjunct between the two sentences, deletion of the identical portions from the second sentence and shifting of all the non-identical portions to the first sentence. Remember that this process is largely the same as that of the partial coordinative sentence except that in the constricted sentence no portion of the second sentence is shifted to the first sentence, e.g.

(23) *लोहा और सोना* धातु हैं। (joint subject phrase)

(24) ठेकेदार ने *सभी मकान और पेड़* तोड़ डाले। (joint object phrase)

(25) उल्लू *दिन को सोता है और रात को जागता* है। (joint predicate)

(26) दिल्ली और लंदन क्रमश: भारत *और* इंग्लैण्ड की राजधानियाँ हैं।

(parallel joint sentence)

Sentences of this type are also called *squeezed* sentences because here two or more sentences are squeezed into one. Similarly the phrases squeezed into one are called squeezed phrases, as for instance लोहा और सोना, सभी मकान और पेड़ etc.

Sentence (25) should be considered a squeezed compound sentence and not a partial compound sentence, because here there is the deletion of the subject phrase and not the verb phrase and secondly, the expression दिन को सोता है और रात को जागता है constitutes a joint predicate whereas no portion of a partial compound sentence has the capacity to form a compound phrase.

Now see the following sentences:

(27) आपका मकान *सुंदर और हवादार* है। (joint complement phrase)

(28) चोर ने *समझ कर और बड़ी सफाई से* काम किया।

(joint adverbial phrase)

(29) *मेरा और आपका* पैसा आ गया है। (attributive phrase)

Theoretically, the joint complement phrases, joint adverbial phrases and joint attributive phrases are also compound sentences because they contain two or more underlying sentences even though at the surface level they merge together. For practical reasons, however, many grammarians do not subscribe to this view and find it unnecessary to include them under compound sentences. According to Kamata Prasad Guru (1920) "Only that sentence should be taken as a constricted (संकुचित) sentence where many predicates have one subject or where many subjects have many predicates."

1.5.5 Restrictions on Compound Sentences

A compound sentence cannot be formed by simply conjoining

any two sentences of any type. Similarly, a constricted phrase cannot be constituted by simply conjoining two compound phrases of any type by additive conjuncts like *और*. In other words, they do not necessarily contain two underlying sentences in their deep structure. There are certain structural and semantic constraints for the formation of Hindi compound sentences which are described below:

(a) Co-agent Constraints: Some bi-directional or bilateral verbs (see sub-pattern-33) inherently require the existence of two parties for the same action to take place – the agent and the co-agent. In such sentences both the agent and the co-agent together accomplish the action and are joined by the conjunct *और*. In sentences of this type, there is no existence of two underlying sentences in their deep structure simply because they are not derived from any underlying sentences, e.g.

Group - *A*

(30) राम *और* अशोक रास्ते में मिले।

(31) रमेश *और* राधा ने शादी की।

(32) उसका बाप *और* वह एक जैसे हैं।

Group - *B*

(33) मोहन *और* सोहन मित्र हैं।

(34) दो *और* दो चार होते हैं।

We cannot look for underlying sentences in these strings, e.g. *राम रास्ते में मिला। *अशोक रास्ते में मिला or *मोहन मित्र है और *सोहन मित्र है etc., because the verb per se demands or anticipates a co- participant, i.e. co-agent.

Sentences under group *A* are different for another reason also. According to the transformation grammar, they are supposed to have been derived from the adverb since they are basically expressed by adverbial phrases, e.g.

(30a) राम *अशोक से* रास्ते में मिला।

(31a) रमेश ने *राधा से* शादी की।

(32a) वह *अपने बाप के जैसा* है।

(b) Semantic Field Constraints: The constituents or portion of the compound sentences which form a combination or a group, must belong to the same semantic fields otherwise a meaningful combination is not possible, e.g.

(35) मुझे रास्ते में [सतीश और राकेश] मिले।
[*सतीश और तीस रुपए]

(36) उसे [भूख और प्यास] लगी।
[*भूख और चोट]

(37) उन्होंने [जलेबी और लड्डू] खाए।
[*जलेबी और चाँटे]

(c) Functional and Structural Constraints: The two constituents combined in the compound sentences must belong to the same functional and structural categories , e.g.

(38) मैं [एक किताब और पेंसिल] चाहता हूँ।
[*एक किताबऔर लेटना]

(39) रामलाल [समझदार और होशियार] है।
[*समझदार और मेरा बड़ा भाई] है।

(40) वह [आने से पहले और जाने के बाद] खाँसता है।
[*आने से पहले और धीरे से]

(d) Contextual Constraints: The contextual category (e.g. statement, order, question, and request) of both the constituent clauses of the compound sentences should be similar. Similarly the mood, aspect and tense of both the constituent clauses should be uniform or compatible, e.g.

(41) *वह रोज़ सात बजे उठता है और आप कहाँ जा रहे हैं।

(42) *जल्दी से एक गिलास पानी लाओ और तुम होशियार हो।

In certain special contexts where two sentences are related to the same theme or reference, the conjunction of two sentences with different functional categories and different aspects, tenses and moods may become possible, though such combinations are limited. Basically such a mixed combination falls within the domain of *stylistics* rather than grammar. Similarly in certain contexts, conjuncts *और* and *या* also perform some additional stylistic functions other than their normal function of co-ordination. For instance, note such stylistic functions (shown within brackets) in the following examples:

(43) मैं तुमसे उम्र में बड़ा हूँ *और* तुम मुझे सिखा रहे हो! (लेकिन फिर भी)

(44) मैं चुपचाप अपना काम कर रहा था *और* वह अचानक आ धमका। (तभी)

(45) आप तो सारा दिन बाहर रहते हैं *और* हम एक घंटे को भी बाहर नहीं जा सकते (यह कहाँ का न्याय है कि है ...!)

(46) तुम आ रहे हो *या* मैं जाऊँ! (नहीं तो)

□

Chapter-2

PHRASE

2.1 Defining A Phrase

A phrase is the next smaller unit after the sentence. A sentence is made up of phrases. Phrases are the units which perform grammatical functions in a sentence and whose existence is relevant only within a sentence and not outside it.

Every sentence has a defined place or slot for the object, complement, adverb and verb in its string where nouns, adjectives, adverbs and verbs etc. occur and perform certain specific roles in the sentence and accomplish certain functions. The places where they occur are called slots and the word or group of words that are used in these slots are called phrases. A phrase may consist of a single word or more than one word. For instance see the following sentences:

(1) लड़की	शाम को	लौटेगी.
(2) मेरी लड़की	कल शाम को	लौटेगी.
(3) मेरी सबसे बड़ी लड़की	कल या परसों शाम को	लौट रही है.

Sentence (1) contains three phrases – 'लड़की', 'शाम को' and 'लौटेगी', which occur in the slots of the subject, the adverb and the verb respectivley. Sentence (2) shows some expansion of the same slots (मेरी लड़की x कल शाम को x लौटेगी), but by virtue of their being used in the same respective slots, they are also called*phrases* , that is, phrase wise, there is no difference between the three constituents 'daughter', 'my daughter' and 'my eldest daughter' because all the three are phrases and occur in the same slot of the subject. Similarly all the three word groups 'शाम को', 'कल शाम को' and 'कल या परसों शाम को' are phrases because they all occur in the same slot of an adverb. Similarly, both लौटेगी and लौट रही है are verb phrases because they occupy the same slot of the sentence string where a verb occurs. In other words, a phrase whatever its size in the sentence can be expanded by adding modifiers or some other compatible constituents which will become a part of the phrase.

A word needs to be distinguished from a phrase. A *word* in isolation is a lexical entry that exists in dictionaries and conveys only its lexical meaning. The same word when used in a sentence acquires a context and becomes a phrase. Sometimes a distinction is made between the Hindi words पद and पदबंध by some scholars. According to them, if a phrase consists of a single word in a sentence, it is a पद and if it consists of two or more words it is a पदबंध, but this definition is no more accepted in the modern syntactic analysis in linguistics. As of now, the Hindi word पदबंध is used both for a single word phrase or a multi-word phrase.

In terms of grammatical structure, Hindi phrases can be grouped into four structural classes: (i) noun phrase, (ii) pronoun phrase (iii) adjective phrase (iv) adverb phrase and (v) verb phrase. (See below 2.2)

In terms of the functions Hindi phrases perform in a sentence, they can be grouped into five functional categories – (i) subject phrase, (ii) object phrase, (iii) complement phrase, (iv) adverb phrase and (v) verb phrase. (See below 2.3)

Some constituents of a phrase are semantically more closely related to each other than others. Such constituents are called*immediate constituents* and are supposed to share the relationship of immediate constituents among themselves. For instance in sentence (2) above, मेरी and लड़की are the immediate constituents, but *लड़की* and *कल* are not immediate constituents even though they also occur close to each other. Hence the constituents *मेरी लड़की* form a phrase, while the constituents **लड़की कल* do not.

The construction of a phrase is defined in terms of the relationship that holds between the various constituents of the phrase i.e. whether they are obligatory or optional constituents in the formation of the phrase, whether any of their constituents can singly perform the function of the whole phrase or whether there is any hierarchical relationship amongst its constituents. Based on these features, the construction of a phrase is divided into two types – endocentric construction and exocentric construction (see below 2.2.1 and 2.2.2). The endocentric construction has three sub-classes – Attributive, Coordinative and Appositional. The exocentric construction has further two sub-classes – axis-relator construction and close-knit construction.

Some constituents of a phrase are semantically more closely related to each other than others. Such constituents called *immediate constituents* and are supposed to share the relationship of immediate constituents among themselves. For instance in sentence (2) above, *मेरी and लड़की are the immediate constituents, but *लड़की* and *कल* are not immediate constituents even though they also occur close to each other. Hence the constituents मेरी लड़की form a phrase, while the constituents *लड़की कल do not.

2.2 Structrual Classification of Phrases

Based on the internal structure, the Hindi phrases can be divided into the following classes:

Construction of Hindi Phrases

Endocentric | Exocentric

Attributive	*Coordinative*	*Appositional*	*Axis-Relator*	*Close-knit*
गरम चाय	चाय और कॉफी	(मेरा) नौकर रामू	कमरे में	आ रहा है
(adj+head)	(head+head)	(head : head)	(axis+relator)	(close-knit)

2.2.1 Endocentric Construction

A phrase is called *endocentric* if atleast one of its constituents is capable of performing the function of the whole phrase. For instance, the sentence, नौकर चाय ला रहा है, contains three phrases – 'नौकर', 'गरम चाय' and 'ला रहा है' of which the phrase 'गरम चाय' has an endocentric construction because the function of गरम चाय can also be performed by only one constituent. In other words, if we replace the phrase *गरम चाय* with a single constituent चाय, the structure of the sentence will remain intact (e.g. नौकर गरम चाय ला रहा है). Here one single constituent (*चाय*) possesses the capacity to replace the whole phrase without damaging the basic structure of the sentence but the second constituent (*गरम*) does not have this capacity (*नौकर गरम ला रहा है). An endocentric construction of this type is called an *attributive construction* because the relationship between the two constituents is that of a modifier/ attribute + head. In yet another sentence having endocentric construction नौकर चाय और समोसा ला रहा है, the phrase *चाय और समोसा* can be successfully replaced by any one of the two single constituents *चाय* or *समोसा*, (e.g *नौकर चाय ला रहा है। नौकर समोसा ला रहा है*). The difference here is that both the constituents of the phrase (चाय और समोसा) are heads and share the mutual relationship of head + head and not modifier +head.

The constituent of the phrase which qualifies the head is called a *modifier*. For instance, the word चाय in the phrase गरम चाय is the head and the word गरम is the modifier (adjective). The modifier in this construction, however, does not have the capacity to perform the complete function of the whole phrase singly (e.g.*नौकर गरम ला रहा है). The head is the obligatory constituent of the phrase and the modifier is the optional constituent. Hence the head can occur even without a modifier without affecting the structure of the sentence, but the modifier cannot occur singly.

An endocentric construction must have atleast one constituent as the head and the rest may be either modifier(s) or yet another head. Based on the structural status of the heads in the phrase, the endocentric construction is divided into three categories: (a) attributive phrase, (b) coordinative phrase and (c) appositional phrase.

(a) Attributive Phrase: Attributive phrase has one head and one or more modifiers, e.g. गरम चाय. Here चाय is a head and an essential constituent of the phrase. गरम is a modifier and an optional constituent of the phrase. More than one modifier can be used along with one head, e.g. बहुत गरम चाय, बहुत ही गरम चाय, लिपटन की बिना दूध की गरम चाय. Some phrases may have more than one modifier for the same head. In such phrases, some modifiers may directly qualify the head while some others may qualify the modifier itself, as for instance, in the above example, the three modifiers 'गरम', 'लिपटन की' and 'बिना दूध की' qualify the same head (चाय), but the modifier बहुत qualifies yet another modifier (गरम) and ही qualifies the modifier बहुत. It needs to be noted that there is normally a certain order or stratification in the sequencing of these modifiers in the phrase. However, in the present discussion on syntax, their stratification or order in the phrase is not relevant because it falls in the domain of morphology.

(b) Co-ordinative Phrase: A co-ordinative phrase has two or more heads which may be combined by some coordinative conjuncts like और, तथा, या etc. e.g. 'चाय और कॉफ़ी', 'दिन और रात', 'दूध, चाय या कॉफ़ी'. In such phrases no single head can perform the function of the whole phrase, because each head represents an underlying sentence, e.g. नौकर चाय और कॉफी ला रहा है = नौकर चाय ला रहा है + नौकर कॉफी ला रहा है। (compare squeezed sentence 1.5).

(c) Appositional Phrase: Appositional phrase also contains two or more heads but they are linked together in appositional (or equivalent) relationship, e.g. समिति के अध्यक्ष श्री वर्मा, भारत की राजधानी दिल्ली. The appositional relationship can be defined by markers or symbols like 'i.e' or 'that is' as, for instance, 'समिति के अध्यक्ष, that is, श्री वर्मा', 'भारत की राजधानी, i.e दिल्ली'. In appositional phrases any single head out of the two or more can structurally perform the function of the whole phrase without damaging the structure of the basic sentence, e.g. समिति के अध्यक्ष श्री वर्मा अब भाषण देंगे = श्री वर्मा अब भाषण देंगे = समिति के अध्यक्ष अब भाषण देंगे।

It may be noted that, like a noun phrase, an appositional phrase can also accept adjective phrases as attributes wherever required, e.g. गरम चाय और बिना चीनी का दूध/ समिति के अध्यक्ष श्री वर्मा।

2.2.2 Exocentric Construction

Any construction which is not endocentric is an exocentric construction. In other words, a construction is called exocentric if none of its constituents are capable of singly performing the function of the whole phrase. This is as much as to say that all the constituents of an exocentric construction are obligatory. None of the constituents can be removed without damaging the structure of the main sentence. For example, in the sentence कमरे में कौन है, the phrase कमरे में, is an exocentric construction because neither of the two constituents 'कमरे' or 'में' is capable of performing the function of the whole phrase. In other words, if we remove either of these constituents, the sentence will collapse, e.g. *कमरे कौन है, *में कौन है। Generally Hindi phrases that end in a postposition are exocentric in construction, e.g. कमरे में, सड़क पर, लड़की के लिए, घर में, सोहन को, etc.

We may often find the existence of an attributive phrase within a larger adverbial phrase e.g. ऊपर वाले मकान में, where 'ऊपर वाला' is a modifier of the noun 'मकान' and the phrase 'मकान में' is an adverbial phrase which forms an exocentric construction. Thus the whole phrase 'ऊपर वाले मकान में', taken as a whole becomes an adverbial phrase and a part of an exocentric construction.

Exocentric constructions have neither a head nor a modifier, but based on the inter-relationship between their constituents, they are divided into two types – (a) axis-relator phrase and, (b) close-knit phrase.

(a) Axis-relator phrase: Though there is no head in the exocentric construction, but from the point of view of internal structure, one constituent of the phrase, which is normally a noun, acts as an *axis* and the second constituent, which is normally a postposition or adverbial, acts as a *relator*, i.e., it denotes the mode of relationship with the axis, and thus manifests its linkage with other constituents of the sentence. For instance, in the phrase कमरे में, the constituent कमरा is an axis and में is a relator (denoting the relationship of location) and in the phrase लड़की के लिए, the constituent लड़की is an axis and के लिए is a relator (denoting the relationship of with beneficiary).

It may be noted that the postposition का in an endocentric construction is a modifier at the phrase level (e.g. राम का मकान), but at the sentence level when used at the end of the adjective phrase it constitutes an exocentric construction. For instance, in the sentences वह मकान राम का है and ये सभी चिट्ठियाँ पैसा माँगने वालों की हैं, the phrases राम का and पैसा माँगने वालों की are exocentric constructions.

(b) Close-knit Phrase: Constituents of some exocentric phrases are so closely knit together that they neither show the interrelationship of head-modifier nor that of axis-relator. Such phrases are called closely-knit phrases, meaning that they are so closely knit that they cannot be segmented as separate categories neither structurally nor semantically and thus form one single unit, e.g verb phrases like ला रहा है, लिखा जा रहा होगा, चाहिए था, उड़नछू हो गया। In fact all Hindi verb phrases belong to the category of close-knit phrases.

2.3 Structural and Functional Classification of Phrases

Phrases are normally classified in terms of their structure and function. The five structural categories of phrases are: (i) noun phrase, (ii) pronoun phrase, (iii) adjective phrase, (iv) adverb phrase and (v) verb phrase. In terms of functions, these phrases are classified into five functional categories: (i) subject phrase, (ii) object phrase, (iii) complement phrase, (iv) adverbial phrase and (v) verb phrase.

2.3.1 Noun Phrase

A phrase which has a noun as its head is called a *noun phrase*. It consists of a noun as an obligatory constituent and modifiers as optional constituents. For instance, in the sentence 'मेरा नया ड्राइवर बीमार है', the phrase 'मेरा नया ड्राइवर' is a noun phrase and the *ड्राइवर* is the head of the phrase while मेरा and नया are its modifiers. It is an endocentric construction (see 2.2.1) which has a noun as its head.

The modifier in Hindi generally precedes the noun, e.g. सुंदर लड़की, पीली वाली साड़ी, राम का लड़का. However, in some very limited cases and certain types of expressions, the adjective may be placed after the noun for some special effect or emphasis, e.g. उसने लड़की *सुंदर* छाँटी है, राधा ने साड़ी *नीली वाली* पहन ली।

Modifiers of nouns in Hindi may belong to one of the following seven structural classes:

Qualitative:	बड़ा, अच्छा, सुंदर (घर); सबसे लंबा, लाल-सा (कपड़ा)
Participle/-वाला:	बहता (पानी), टूटी कुर्सी, तीन बजे छूटने वाली (गाड़ी)
Pronominal:	कोई (काम), कुछ (बहाना), कौन-कौन (लोग), यह (लड़का)
Numeral/quantity:	चार, चारों, दुगुना, पहला, कुछ (लोग), थोड़ा (आराम)
का-adjective:	राम का (लड़का), मेरा (जूता)
Apposition:	मेरा भाई रमेश, हिमालय पर्वत
Honorific title:	*श्री* रामलाल, डॉ. बोस, वर्मा *जी*, निदेशक *महोदय*

Though most of these modifiers are used before the noun, the epithets जी and महोदय are placed after the noun, e.g. मंत्री महोदय, मंत्री जी. In certain idiomatic expressions, some unusual construction of noun phrases can also be seen, e.g. *शहर का शहर* उजड़ गया, *परेशानी में परेशानी* सामने आ रही है।

Where a noun phrase has more than one modifier, the normal order of modifiers is like this:

का-modifier + demonstrative pronoun + numeral + qualitative modifier + noun, e.g. आपकी ये तीनों नीली साड़ियाँ। An inversion of words is, however, possible in certain contexts between the modifiers ये and आपकी, e.g. आपकी ये तीनों नीली साड़ियाँ > ये आपकी तीनों नीली साड़ियाँ।

Noun phrases in Hindi can occupy all those slots in a sentence where a normal noun word is used, i.e. subject, object and complement. When used as a subject or an object in a sentence, the noun phrases take the usual case signs: ने, को, से, etc. wherever required, e.g.

(1) अंग्रेजी के प्रोफेसर *ने*/ सभी लड़कों *को*/ बुलाया। (subject/object)

(2) बाहर बैठे हुए यात्रियों *से* नहीं चला जाता। (subject)

2.3.2 Pronoun Phrase

The pronoun phrase has a pronoun as its head and one or more modifiers, e.g. *वह बेचारा* and *तुम लोग* in the sentence 'वह बेचारा कर ही क्या सकता था? and *तुम लोग कहाँ जाना चाहते हो*? Here वह and तुम are heads of the phrases and बेचारा and लोग are modifiers. Having a head-modifier relationship, the pronoun phrase is also an endocentric construction like a noun phrase. Unlike the adjective phrase, however, the modifier of the pronoun is used after the adjective and not before it.

Pronoun phrases are very limited in number in all the languages and, therefore, at the level of sentence analysis they are included under noun phrases, because both noun and pronoun perform the same grammatical function in the sentence.

2.3.3 Adjective Phrase

An adjective phrase has an adjective as its head and one or more modifiers, for instance in the sentence मकान बहुत सुंदर है, the constituent बहुत सुंदर is an adjective phrase in which सुंदर is the head and बहुत is its modifier. Having a head-modifier relationship, the adjective phrase is also an endocentric construction which has an adjective सुंदर as a head and modifiers (बहुत, ही, ज़्यादा) as its optional constituents. The modifiers attached to the adjective may be more than one, e.g. बहुत सुंदर, बहुत ज़्यादा सुंदर, बहुत ही ज़्यादा सुंदर. In these examples, बहुत does not necessarily qualify सुंदर; it first qualifies its immediate constituent ज़्यादा. Similarly in the construction बहुत ही ज़्यादा सुंदर, ही also qualifies its immediate constituent ज़्यादा.

An important characteristic of an adjective phrase is that it can be used both as a modifier of a noun as well as a predicate of a sentence where it is called a predicate adjective. Compare these sentences-

(3) उसका काम *बहुत सुंदर* है। (predicative adjective)

(4) उसने बहुत सुंदर काम किया है. (modifier)

In sentence (3) the adjective phrase (*बहुत सुंदर*) has been used as a separate phrase occupying the place of a complement whereas in sentence (4) the same adjective phrase (बहुत सुंदर) has been used merely as a modifier of the noun काम. In sentential analysis, however, only adjective phrases which occupy the position of a predicate in a sentence are taken into consideration, such as sentence (3).

Though a majority of adjective phrases can be used both as modifier as well as predicative adjective, there are certain constraints on the use of certain adjectives in the attributive position, i.e. before a noun. For instance, while the sentence लड़का तैयार है is acceptable, the expression 'तैयार लड़का' is not acceptable. Similarly, while the use of adjective निहाल in a predicative position is acceptable, as in 'बच्चों को गोद में लेकर माँ निहाल हो गई, its use in the attributive phrase as *'निहाल माँ' is unacceptable.

Semantically, the modifiers of the noun generally provide information about the quality, quantity, size, intensity, comparability, approximation and various other attributes related to the noun, and at times even adjectives, e.g. अत्यंत (विशाल), बहुत (अच्छा); तुमसे बड़ा, सबसे छोटा (comparative), आप जैसा शरीफ (simili); लगभग, कोई (तीन सौ) (approximation) etc.

Chafe (1970) holds that all adjectives provide information about the state of the noun. The state of the noun denoted by the modifier (adjective) may be of two types - *relative* state and ***absolute*** state. Compare the two adjectives बीमार and जिंदा in these two sentences:

(a) मोहन *बीमार* है। (relative state)

(b) मरीज *जिन्दा* है। (absolute state)

In sentence (a) the adjective बीमार can be quantified or graded by modifiers like बहुत, बहुत ज्यादा, थोड़ा etc. because it denotes a relative *state* which is flexible and comparable. On the other hand, in sentence (b) the adjective जिन्दा cannot be quantified, graded or compared because it denotes an *absolute state*. Hence a phrase like *बहुत जिंदा, or *ज़रा-सा जिंदा is not possible. The difference between the two can be explained in these examples.

(a) Adjective denoting relative state: Adjectives like छोटा, बड़ा, चौड़ा, लंबा, संकरा, पुराना, ऊँचा, गरीब, हलका, भारी, दुखी etc. normally denote a relative state of the noun which can be quantified or graded, e.g. बहुत छोटा, सबसे छोटा, जरा-सा छोटा etc. It is so because when we refer to a thing as small what we mean is that the form or shape of the thing is smaller than the prescribed norm. This norm does not rest in that particular thing but in the other members of that class which are larger than it. For instance, यह मकान छोटा है means that this house is smaller as compared to other houses. Adjectives of this category have the capacity to be expressed in relative terms by using various quantitive or comparative attributes like बहुत, की अपेक्षा etc. e.g. *बहुत* छोटा, *बिल्कुल* छोटा, *मेरे मकान से* छोटा, etc.

If the state of a thing we refer to has been expressed in terms of its class and not member, the norm will be shifted from the member to its larger class (called norm-shifting). For instance, in the sentences हाथी बड़ा होता है and सुई छोटी होती है the bigness of the elephant and the smallness of the needle are their generic characteristics and not specific. These sentences do not give the meaning that the sizes of the elephant and the needle are larger or smaller than other elephants or needles. They give the meaning that the whole of the elephant-class is larger in size compared to that of the other members of the animal class (like dog-class, goat-class or lion-class) and, similarly, the needle is smaller as compared to the other members of this instrument.

(b) Adjective denoting absolute state: Adjectives like जिंदा, खुला, बंद, सच, झूठ, बेहोश, मृत, विभक्त, गिरा हुआ, सोया हुआ, लटका हुआ etc. normally denote an absolute state. The absolute state of the noun cannot be quantified, graded or divided into parts. It either exists or does not exist. For instance, the norm of being जिंदा lies in its state itself and not in any other thing or class of things. Hence relative, comparative or quantifying modifiers like बहुत, की अपेक्षा etc. are not possible in this category of adjectives. (*मरीज जरा-सा जिंदा है, *मैं उसकी अपेक्षा सोया हुआ था).

Certain basically stative adjectives can, however, be transformed into non-stative or active forms by using the verbalizers होना and करना, e.g. छोटा > छोटा करना, बड़ा > बड़ा होना। Similarly many basically active or process verbs can be transformed into resultative state verbs or participles, e.g. टूटना > टूटा हुआ, गिरना > गिरा हुआ, etc.

(c) Neutral vs. Perception-based Adjectives: Some adjectives denote the value or features inherent in the noun in a neutral way where there is little or no scope for projection of speakers' personal viewpoint or his value judgment, e.g. काला, टेढ़ा, छोटा, खट्टा, रंगीन, कीमती, पथभ्रष्ट etc. The properties or characteristics of the thing or object lie in the object itself and are not subject to speaker's interpretation or perception and are, therefore, referred to as *neutral adjectives*.

Some adjectives, may, however, have certain scope for the speaker's own perception or interpretation of the meaning and may partly influence his value judgment about the adjective. Such adjectives are called *perception-based adjectives*, e.g. अच्छा, बेकार, सही, सफल, कारगर, उपयोगी etc. There is, however, a constraint on the use of the perception-based adjectives in certain types of sentences. For instance, while we can say यह दवा उपयोगी सिद्ध हुई, we cannot say यह दवा खट्टी सिद्ध हुई (sub-pattern-15). Similarly, while we can say फिल्म अच्छी रही, we cannot say फिल्म रंगीन रही (sub-pattern-17). It may be noted that sometimes some neutral adjectives may be used in the place of perception-based adjectives, but in such cases, the subjective perception of the speaker becomes too evident, e.g. पार्टी कुछ छोटी रही.

2.3.4 Adverb Phrase

An adverb phrase in Hindi can be formed in many ways. Normally it is formed by combining a noun with a postposition/adverbial, e.g. कमरे में, घर के बाहर, आराम से, जनवरी से मार्च तक, दिन-भर etc. A verbal noun or gerund can also take the place of a noun, e.g. उठने से पहले, जाने के लिए etc. In certain cases the postposition is also omitted in the adverbial phrase, e.g. हम घर गए, मैं कल रात नहीं सो सका. For the deletion of postposition in घर गया, see sub-pattern 32 (c). The deletion of the postposition को in the phrase कल रात is due to the use of the modifier कल (compare: मैं रात *को* नहीं सो सका. There is normally (but not always) a tendency to drop को after the noun if there is a modifier (adjective) before it (e.g. वह कल रात आया). The postposition को is also deleted if the place or time referred to is not specific.

A single or a pair of adverbial words in a sentence can also form an adverb phrase, e.g. यहाँ, रोज, ऐसी की तैसी, कभी-कभी etc. Participles can also form an adverbial phrase, e.g. हँसकर, पढ़ते हुए, चलते-चलते etc. Sometimes the reduplication of certain nouns also forms an adjective phrase, e.g. जगह-जगह, घर-घर (वह घर-घर वोट माँगने जाएगा).

Adverb phrases made up of two or more constituents are exocentric in construction and not endocentric, i.e., they have the relationship of axis and relator and not modifier and head (e.g. कमरे में, जाने के लिए). Within the phrase neither the noun (axis) can be optionally removed nor the postposition (relator).

Adverb phrases occur as optional constituents in most sentences, e.g. वह (कमरे में) पढ़ रहा है. However, in certain categories of sentences adverb phrases are used as obligatory constituents, e.g. वह कमरे में है (sub-pattern 18-20, 31, 38). As optional constituents, the adverb phrase provides some additional or new information and helps in the extension of the sentence.

The adverb phrases mainly provide the following types of information with the help of certain postpositions, adverbials or suffixes:

1. Locative: ऊपर, यहाँ, चारों ओर, आसपास, में, पर etc.
2. Temporal: आज, रोज, कभी-कभी, के बाद (सोमवार) को, से/तक etc.
3. Manner: (आराम) से, कई तरह, ऐसे, (हँस) कर, (ध्यान) पूर्वक, के अनुसार etc.
4. Causal: के कारण, के मारे, (प्यास) से, पढ़ते-पढ़ते etc.
5. Purposive: के लिए/वास्ते, (खाने) को, अर्थ (सहायतार्थ) etc.
6. Instrumental: (चाकू) से, (आँखों) से etc.
7. Associative: के साथ, से, सहित, साथ-साथ etc.
8. Presence-absence (भाव-अभाव) : के बिना, के बावजूद, के होते हुए भी etc.

2.3.5 Non-declinables/Adverbials

There are certain phrases or words in a sentence which by definition cannot be included under adverbs but which have a sentential significance, e.g. affirmative and negative particles (हाँ, नहीं, जी नहीं, जरा, etc.), conjuncts (लेकिन, फिर, फिर भी, तथापि, मानो etc.) and words of exclamation (वाह, हाय etc.). They are also optional constituents like adverbs. For the purpose of broad classification, these as well as the adverbs are often loosely grouped under the adverbials or indeclinables (अव्यय in Hindi). Thus all such phrases which are not noun phrases, pronoun phrases, adjective phrases or verb phrases have been grouped under adverbials which also include normal adverbials. For the purpose of the analysis of Hindi sentence patterns, the broader term *'adverbials'*, instead of 'adverb phrase', has been used.

2.3.6 Verb Phrase

In Hindi the *verb phrase* consist of a main verb and an auxiliary verb and is normally used at the end of the sentence, e.g. पढ़ सकता है, लिखा जा चुका है, चला गया, दिखाई दे रहा था etc. Hindi verb phrase is an endocentric as well as exocentric construction (see 2.2.b), hence all its constituents are obligatory and not optional. Hindi verb phrase consists of the following constituents:

(a) Main Verb: The portion of the verb that carries the lexical meaning is called the *main verb,* e.g. पढ़-, चल-, माना कर-, भूल जा-etc. The following constituents form the main verb in Hindi:

(i) Simple root which includes the intransitive, transitive and causative forms of the root (see 2.7), e.g. कट, काट, कटवा, सो, सुलवा etc.

(ii) *Compound root*, which are formed by combining two roots which are semantically related to each other, e.g. पढ़-लिख, खा-पी, चल-फिर etc. Verbs of this type are very limited in number.

(iii) *Complex Verb* (see 2.4) which is formed by combining – कर or हो with a noun or a verb, e.g. इंतजार कर-, सिद्ध हो-, मालूम कर-, सुनाई पड़- etc.

(iv) *Conjunct Verb* (see 2.6) which is formed by a combination of two roots but have an inherent existence of कर in between the two, e.g. ले जा (ले कर जा), ढूँढ निकाल- (ढूँढ कर निकाल) etc.)

(v) *Compound Verb* (2.5) which is formed by a combination of root and the intensifier, e.g. कर दे-, भूल जा, रो पड़- etc. The intensifiers intensify or influence only the lexical meaning of the first constituent and, therefore, they are included under the main verb.

(b) Auxiliary Verb: The portion of the verb phrase that carries the grammatical information of the sentence is called an auxiliary verb, e.g. -ता है, था, -एगा, -या, जा- etc. Auxiliary verbs in Hindi include the suffixes or markers denoting voice (see 2.8), aspect (see 2.9), mood (see 2.10), and tense (see 2.11). All these are called grammatical categories at sentence level.

A consolidated diagram of the verb phrase in Hindi is being given below:

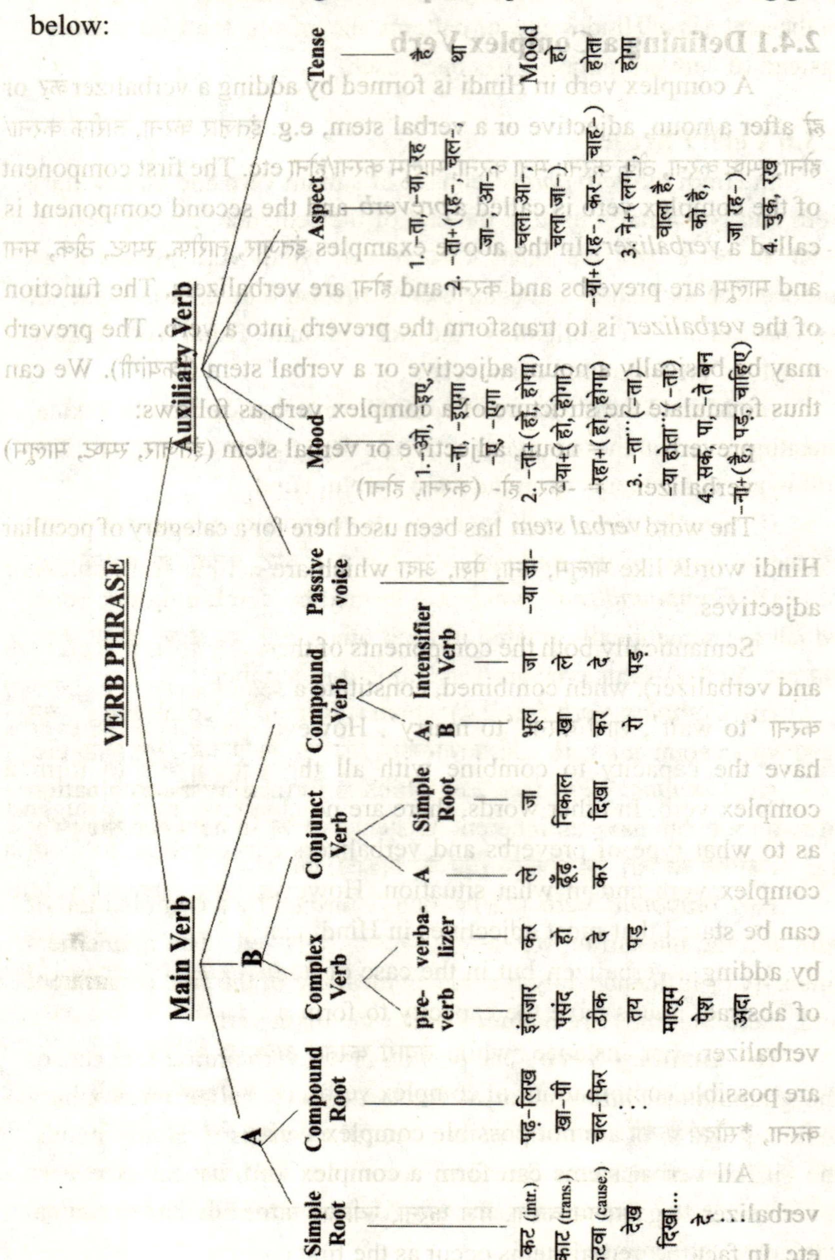

2.4 Complex Verbs

2.4.1 Defining a Complex Verb

A complex verb in Hindi is formed by adding a verbalizer *कर* or *हो* after a noun, adjective or a verbal stem, e.g. इंतज़ार करना, तारीफ़ करना/होना; स्पष्ट करना, ठीक करना; मना करना, मालूम करना/होना etc. The first component of the complex verb is called a *preverb* and the second component is called a *verbalizer*. In the above examples इंतज़ार, तारीफ़, स्पष्ट, ठीक, मना and मालूम are preverbs and करना and होना are verbalizers. The function of the *verbalizer* is to transform the preverb into a verb. The preverb may be basically a noun, adjective or a verbal stem (क्रियांगी). We can thus formulate the structure of a complex verb as follows:

preverb = noun, adjective or verbal stem (इंतज़ार, स्पष्ट, मालूम)
verbalizer = -कर, हो- (करना, होना)

The word *verbal stem* has been used here for a category of peculiar Hindi words like मालूम, मना, पेश, अदा which are neither full nouns nor adjectives.

Semantically both the components of the complex verb (preverb and verbalizer), when combined, constitute a semantic unit, e.g. इंतज़ार करना 'to wait', शादी करना 'to marry'. However, not all the preverbs have the capacity to combine with all the verbalizers to form a complex verb. In other words, there are no clear-cut rules to suggest as to what type of preverbs and verbalizers can combine to form a complex verb and in what situation. However, as a general rule it can be stated that most adjectives in Hindi can form a complex verb by adding a verbalizer, but in the case of nouns only a limited class of abstract nouns have the capacity to form a complex verb through verbalizer. For instance, while तैयारी करना, अय्याशी करना, बेवकूफ़ी करना are possible combinations of complex verbs, combinations like *सच्चाई करना, *सौंदर्य करना are not possible complex verbs.

All verbal stems can form a complex verb with the help of a verbalizer, e.g. मालूम करना, पेश करना, स्वीकार करना, अदा करना, खत्म करना etc. In fact the verbal stems occur as the first constituent of a complex verb. They are not used as independent words like nouns and adjectives. That is why they are treated as different from normal adjectives or nouns. Some lexicographers and linguists, however, place them in the category of adjectives on the ground that in intransitive usages these words are used in the position of predicative adjectives, e.g. आपको मालूम/ज्ञात होगा, यहाँ सिगरेट पीना मना/निषिद्ध है, उन्हें आपकी शर्तें स्वीकार हैं/स्वीकार्य हैं, but they cannot be used as modifiers of nouns, e. g. *अदा पैसा, *खत्म बात, *पेश काग़ज़, *मालूम बात, *मना सिगरेट, and *स्वीकार शर्त.

The second component of the complex verb is generally either करना or होना (respectively transitive and intransitive), e.g. मालूम करना - मालूम होना, प्रयोग करना - प्रयोग होना. Both the verbalizers करना and होना are lexically empty. Their only function is to provide the form and meaning of a verb to the preverb (i.e. the noun, the adjective and the verbal stem).

A limited number of complex verbs in Hindi, however, have some unusual or idiomatised verbalizers, like खाना, मारना, बाँधना, बजाना, कसना, चलना, होना, पढ़ना, आना etc, e.g. घूस खाना, धोखा खाना, डींग मारना, थप्पड़ मारना/कसना, ढाढस बँधाना, आदाब बजाना, सलाम ठोकना, भाग लेना, चकमा देना, सज़ा देना, दिखाई पड़ना/देना. It is not just a coincidence that most of these verbalizers also occur in the list of the intensifiers of compound verbs which give some intensive colour to the meaning (see 2.5.1, 2.5.4). These verbalizers can be grouped into two categories on the basis of their actual function in the phrase:

(i) *Verbalizers* which regularly or primarily accompany the preverbs of the complex verbs and do not directly influence their verbal meanings, e.g. दिखाई देना, बदला लेना, भाग लेना, मुक्का मारना, ढाढस बंधाना etc. It may be noted that normal verbalizers (करना or होना) are not normally used in these positions, rather they are a sort of substitutes for them in these complex verbs. For instance, a combination like *दिखाई होना or *दिखाई करना is not possible.

(ii) *Verbalizers* which actually influence or alter the meaning of the complex verb, e.g. सलाम करना - सलाम *ठोकना* - आदाब अर्ज़ करना -

आदाब बजाना - लात मारना - लात कसना; पता होना - पता चलना; मालूम होना - पता चलना; मालूम होना : मालूम पड़ना; याद करना - याद आना etc. It may be noted that the verbalizers ठोकना, बजाना, कसना, चलना, पढ़ना, आना etc. used in these complex verbs give additional information about the speakers' attitude or motive (2.5.4)

2.4.2 The Semantic and Syntactic Value of the Preverb

The first component (i.e. the preverb) of the complex verb is important from many points of view. Semantically it is this component that carries the lexical meaning and determines the semantic categories of the subject and the object in the sentence. For instance, the preverb मालूम in the complex verb मालूम करना demands an animate subject and an inanimate object and the preverb शादी in the complex verb शादी करना demands an animate subject as well as an animate object.

At the syntactic level also it is the first component i.e. the verbalizer that determines the choice and use of the postposition. For instance, if the verbalizer belongs to the category of an adjective or a verbal stem, it will not require a postposition before it, e.g. मिस्त्री ने मेरी कार ठीक की, मुझे सारी बातें मालूम हैं. If, however, the verbalizer is a noun, it will generally require the use of a postposition का/की and sometimes even से, में, पर, को की etc. before it, e.g.

(1) रमेश ने सीता **का** इंतज़ार किया। (का)

(2) लोगों ने **आपकी** तारीफ़ की। (की)

(3) मैंने पशुपतिनाथ **के** दर्शन किए। (के)

(4) छात्राएँ अध्यापक **से** बात कर रही हैं। (से)

(5) सभी यात्रियों ने झटपट डिब्बे **में** प्रवेश किया। (में)

(6) श्रीकांत ने सारी जायदाद **पर** अधिकार कर लिया। (पर)

(7) क्या तुम सीता **को** प्यार करते हो? (को)

(8) उन्होंने पहली लड़की **की ओर** इशारा किया। (की ओर)

(9) कल तुम **किसके** साथ गुफ्तगू कर रहे थे? (के साथ)

(10) सरकार **आपके बारे में** छानबीन कर रही है। (के बारे में)

Out of these postpositions का can be used only before the complex verbs and not before the simple verbs, e.g. मैंने इन तथ्यों की खोज की is a possible sentence, but a sentence like *मैंने इन तथ्यों की खोज़ी की is not grammatical. On the contrary, all other postpositions can be used both before and after the simple and complex verbs, e.g. से लड़ना – से लड़ाई करना, को डाँटना – को डाँट लगाना, में घुसना – में प्रवेश करना etc. See -

(11) वह अपने पड़ोसी *से* लड़ा।

(12) उसने अपने पड़ोसी *से* लड़ाई की।

It may be noted that wherever देना occurs as a verbalizer in a complex verb, it is the verbalizer and not the preverb that determines the choice of the postposition and the semantic category of the object, because the verb देना in its basic lexical meaning demands an animate subject and an animate dative, e.g. (को) सजा देना, (को) धोखा देना, (को) चकमा देना, (को) गाली देना, (को) वचन देना, (को) ताने देना etc. See -

(13) मैनेजर ने हम सबको नोटिस दिया है। (को + simple verb)

(14) मैनेजर ने हम सबको धोखा दिया है। (को + complex verb)

Functional and Non-functional Complex Verbs

The complex verbs can be divided into two classes depending upon the roles they play in the agreement pattern of the sentence - functional and non-functional. *Functional complex verbs* are the ones which accomplish a function or a role by affecting the verb agreement pattern of the sentence. Such complex verbs are called *functional complex verbs*. For instance, in the sentence रमेश ने सीता का इंतज़ार किया, the agreement of the verb किया is with the first component (i.e. preverb इंतज़ार) and not with the object सीता. Here the first component of the complex verb possesses the capacity to affect the verb agreement pattern of the sentence. Complex verbs which do not have the capacity to affect the verb agreement of the sentence are called *non-functional* complex verbs. For instance, in the sentence मिस्त्री ने मेरी कार ठीक की, the verbalizer की has an agreement with the object कार.

2.4.3 Functional Complex Verbs

The first component (i.e the preverb) of the functional complex verbs has the capacity to control the number-gender agreement of the second component (verbalizer) in the ने-environment (i.e. where the sentence has a ने-construction). The first component of the functional complex verb is always a noun and never an adjective or any other word. Complex verbs in Hindi are used in three types of structural roles or situations:

(a) Postpositional Situation: A situation where a postposition precedes the complex verb, as in *का* इंतज़ार करना, *से* बात करना, *को* प्यार करना, *की ओर* इशारा करना, *के बारे में* छानबीन करना etc. In other words, the complex verbs belonging to this class always demand a marked object, a marked co-agent and a marked co-adverbial (*marked* here stands for *marked by a postposition*) (see 3.5.3 a-c). For examples see sentences 1 to 10 above (रमेश ने सीता का इंतज़ार किया etc.) (Also see sub-pattern 41 a and 37 b).

(b) Object-oriented Situation: A situation where the complex verbs, even while being basically *ने*-transitive, do not demand a separate object. The noun preverb of the complex verb here performs a dual role of the object as well as the preverb, as in the case of the following noun preverbs: हड़ताल, आत्महत्या, and भोजन -

(15) मज़दूरों ने *हड़ताल* की। (object as well as the verb)

(16) रामू ने *आत्महत्या* कर ली है। (object as well as the verb)

(17) मेहमानों ने *भोजन* कर लिया है। (object as well as the verb)

(c) Subject-oriented Situation: A situation where the basically intransitive verbs do not even require a subject in the sentence and take over the dual role of a subject as well as a verb, e.g. अकाल पड़ना, बर्फ़ पड़ना, बारिश होना, गर्मी होना/पड़ना, सर्दी होना/पड़ना, e.g.

(18) *बारिश* हो रही है। (subject as well as a verb)

(19) *बर्फ़* पड़ रही है। (subject as well as a verb)

In these sentences, the words बारिश and बर्फ़ are, on the one hand, the noun components or preverbs of the complex verb and, on the other hand, the grammatical subject of the sentence, too. Such complex verbs normally denote the occurrence of some natural phenomenon, not controlled by men (see sub-pattern 30). These phenomena take place because of natural factors and not because of some human effort or will. They are, therefore, basically intransitive in nature and cannot be normally transformed into transitive constructions, e.g. *बारिश करना, *बर्फ़ पड़ाना, etc. On the contrary, many other complex verbs which are transitive and superficially similar can have transitive forms, e.g हड़ताल हो रही है and >लोग हड़ताल कर रहे हैं (see sub-pattern 37)

Some complex verbs have the capacity to be used with more than one postposition, e.g. मैंने अपनी लड़की की शादी की, शेखर ने राधा से शादी की : मैं तुमसे प्यार करता हूँ : मैं तुमको प्यार करता हूँ. Some complex verbs can be used both with and without a postposition, e.g. मैंने एक गलती की : मैंने उसे बुलाने की गलती की.

Though the noun components (preverbs) of the complex verbs are generally in singular number, but some noun components can be used both in singular as well as plural, e.g. बात करना : बातें करना; (कई) जुर्म करना, (कई वादे करना), कई प्रश्न करना, गलती करना : गलतियाँ करना. In the complex verb दर्शन करना, दर्शन is usually used in plural, e.g. मैंने पशुपति नाथ के दर्शन किए.

2.4.4 Non-functional Complex Verbs

As against the functional complex verbs, the non-functional complex verbs do not play any monitoring role in the agreement system of the sentence. In other words, the preverbs of the non-functional complex verbs do not affect or control the gender and number agreement of the sentence.

There are three major classes of complex verbs in Hindi from the point of view of कर-construction:

(a) *adjective + कर* construction: e.g. ठीक करना, स्पष्ट करना, इकट्ठा करना, सिद्ध करना, बंद करना etc.:

(20) मिस्त्री ने मेरी कार ठीक की। (object-verb agreement)

(21) मिस्त्री ने मेरा रेडियो ठीक किया।   -do-

(b) *Verbal stem + कर* construction ,e.g., मालूम करना, खत्म करना, मना करना, स्वीकार करना, पेश करना etc.

(22) मैंने सभी बातें मालूम कर ली हैं।   (object-verb agreement)

(23) मेरे सारे पैसे खत्म हो गए।   -do-

(c) *Noun + कर* construction which are comparatively fewer in number, e.g. याद करना. पसंद करना, खर्च करना, शुरू करना, etc.

(24) महेश ने यह गाना याद किया।   (object-verb agreement)

(25) लड़कियों ने नया खेल शुरू किया है।   -do-

Normally complex verbs made of noun + कर are supposed to be functional complex verbs, but in sentences (24-25), they appear as non-functional complex verbs and are not in a position to influence the number-gender agreement of the sentence despite the presence of the noun components (याद, शुरू) in the complex verbs. Hence modern linguists differ on this issue whether they should be treated as a noun or a verbal stem in the complex verb system. Some linguists (Olphen 1978:174) treat this category of nouns as different from normal nouns and recognize their double role. Accordingly, words like शुरू, याद, क्षमा are supposed to have two structural categories (i) as an independent noun (e.g. आपकी याद में मैं घुला जा रहा हूँ) and (ii) as an inseparable component or verbal stem of the complex verb, e.g. sentences (24 – 25).

Table of Functional and Non-functional Complex Verbs

Functional **(noun-verb agreement)**	**Non-functional** **(object-verb agreement)**
1. संज्ञा + verbalizer <+post-position>का/की + इंतज़ार करना, सेवा करना, शादी करना-1, प्रयोग करना, तारीफ़ करना, स्मरण करना, मरम्मत करना, मदद करना, पालन, बेवकूफ़ी करना, इरादा करना, वादा करना, दान करना-1, (के) दर्शन करना से + बात करना, शादी करना-2, लड़ाई करना, प्यार करना-1, नफ़रत करना, में + प्रवेश करना, हस्तक्षेप करना, भाग लेना/रुचि रखना/लेना पर + अधिकार करना, गुस्सा करना, विश्वास करना, शक करना को + (1) माफ़ करना, प्यार करना-2, खबर करना (2) सज़ा देना, धोखा देना, चकमा देना, गाली देना, ताने देना, वचन देना, इजाज़त देना, (की ओर) इशारा करना, (के साथ) गुफ़्तगू करना, (के बारे में) छानबीन करना	**1. adjective + कर** ठीक करना, स्पष्ट करना, इकट्ठा करना, संतुष्ट करना, बंद करना, तय करना, तैयार करना, ज़ाहिर करना, जमा करना, सिद्ध करना, प्रयुक्त करना, सूचित करना **2. preverb + कर** मालूम करना, पता करना, पेश करना, अदा करना, मना करना, ख़त्म करना, देर करना, स्वीकार करना, वहन करना **रूढ़ प्रयोग :** दिखाई देना, सुनाई देना/पड़ना, जान पड़ना, पता लगना/चलना, मालूम पड़ना, बख़्श देना **3. noun + कर** याद करना, पसंद करना, ख़र्च करना, दान करना-2, प्रदान करना, धारण करना, शुद्ध करना, सहन करना, इनकार करना
2. noun + कर <postposition> (1) हड़ताल करना, भोजन करना, सफ़र करना, ऐय्याशी करना, गलती करना, आत्महत्या करना (2) बारिश होना, बर्फ पड़ना, गर्मी होना/पड़ना, सर्दी होना/पड़ना, अकाल पड़ना	***Special Usage*** **:** डींग मारना/हाँकना, घूस खाना, धोखा खाना, परेशानी उठाना (को) आदाब बजाना, सलाम ठोकना, थप्पड़ मारना/कसना, लात मारना/कसना, ताने मारना, डाँट लगाना, चोट पहुँचाना (पर) सवार होना, (की) बलि चढ़ाना, (की) खबर लेना, (की) याद आना, (का) पता लगाना

2.4.5 The Grammatical value of the Noun Component Object

From the point of view of grammatical agreement the noun component of the complex verb has the same value as the unmarked object of the transitive verb, because both of them govern the number-gender agreement of the verb in a sentence which has a subject + ने construction, i.e. Past tense transitive. Since in the sentences (1-3) the subject is marked by का, the responsibility of the verb agreement falls on the unmarked nouns of the complex verbs, i.e. इंतज़ार, तारीफ़, दर्शन. It is so because the verb in a Hindi sentence always agrees with the unmarked object of the sentence, i.e an object which is not followed by any postposition. See sentences (1-3)

(1) रमेश ने सीता का इंतज़ार किया।

(2) लोगों ने आपकी तारीफ़ की।

One of the rules of the universal grammar is that no component of a phrase can influence or alter the agreement pattern of another constituent of the same phrase at the sentence level. If it does, they are supposed to be the members of another phrase. The position of the functional complex verb in Hindi is, therefore, a little peculiar. While on the one hand both the components of the functional complex verbs form a single unit, structurally they form two different phrases, because it is how the rationale of their agreement with the noun component can be explained. Even while recognizing the two components of the complex verbs as separate phrases, these noun components cannot be given the status of objects, because they do not share all the features of a normal object. For instance, they cannot accept the common object marker को in possible situations, e.g. *मिस्त्री ने कार की मरम्मत को किया in the analogy of शेखर अपनी पत्नी को पीटता है. (*cf* sub-pattern 34 b).

Hence the analysis of this class of compound verbs will have to be shown on the basis of two parameters – structural and semantic:

(i) Structural analysis :

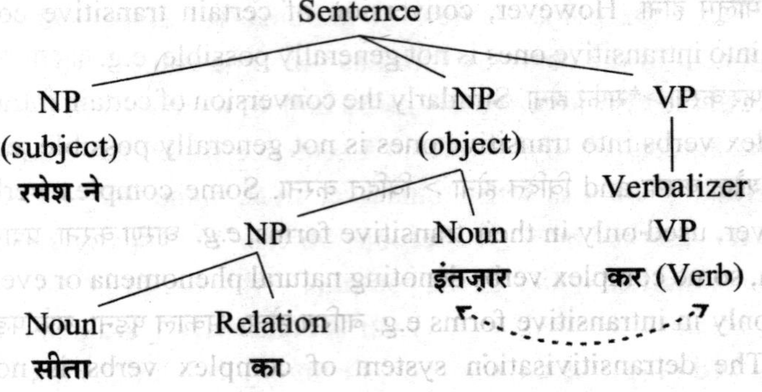

रमेश ने/ सीता का / इंतज़ार/ किया

(ii) Semantic Analysis

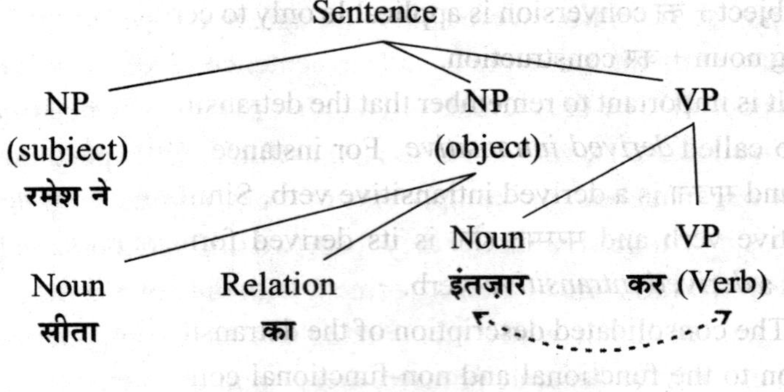

रमेश ने/ सीता का / इंतज़ार/ किया।

2.4.6 Detransitivisation of Complex Verbs

It is possible to detransitivise most of the transitive complex verbs constructed by the verbalizer कर by converting it into हो, *e.g.* शादी करना >शादी होना, ठीक करना>ठीक होना, मालूम करना>मालूम होना. Though both the transitive and intransitive forms of these complex verbs are in use, yet certain complex verbs have a stronger tendency to be used in the transitive forms and others in the intransitive forms. For instance, both the transitive and intransitive forms of these complex verbs are equally frequent in use, e.g. शादी करना >शादी होना, ठीक करना >ठीक होना, मालूम करना>मालूम होना. However, conversion of certain transitive complex verbs into intransitive ones is not generally possible, e.g. दान करना >*दान होना, सफ़र करना >*सफ़र होना. Similarly the conversion of certain intransitive complex verbs into transitive ones is not generally possible, e.g. शौक होना>*शौक करना and विदित होना > विदित करना. Some complex verbs are, however, used only in their transitive forms, *e.g.* धारण करना, प्रदान करना. Again, some complex verbs denoting natural phenomena or events are used only in intransitive forms e.g. बारिश होना, अकाल पड़ना, बर्फ पड़ना etc.

The detransitivisation system of complex verbs is not, not however, limited to verb form conversion from कर to हो, but this also includes some syntactic processes. The process of detransitivisation includes three syntactic processes – (i) the deletion of the subject, (ii) subject + को conversion and (iii) subject + का conversion. Out of these, the subject + का conversion is applicable only to certain complex verbs having noun + कर construction.

It is important to remember that the detransitivised verb in Hindi is also called *derived intransitive*. For instance, सुखाना is a transitive verb and सूखना is a derived intransitive verb. Similarly मरम्मत करना is a transitive verb and मरम्मत होना is its derived form and is, therefore, called a *derived intransitive* verb.

The consolidated description of the detransitivisation process in relation to the functional and non-functional complex verbs is being illustrated below where derived intransitives are shown as Derived intransitive. In the chart below the derived intransitive complex verbs are stative as they show the state of the verb and not the process.

(a) Detransivisation of Functional Complex Verbs

Deletion of subject:

(1) मिस्त्री ने कार की मरम्मत *की*। (transitive)

> कार की मरम्मत *हुई*। (derived intransitive)

Subject + को:

(2) सतीश ने अपनी *पत्नी पर विश्वास* किया। (transitive)

> सतीश को अपनी पत्नी पर *विश्वास हुआ*। (derived intransitive)

> सतीश को अपनी पत्नी पर विश्वास है। (stative)

Subject + का :

(3) छात्राएँ अध्यापक से बातें *कर* रही हैं। (transitive)

> छात्रों की अध्यापक से बातें *हो* रही हैं। (derived intransitive)

(4) उसने भाषा पर अधिकार *किया*। (transitive)

> उसका भाषा पर अधिकार *हुआ*। (derived intransitive)

> उसका भाषा पर अधिकार है। (stative)

(5) उसने *जाने* का इरादा किया। (transitive)

> उसका जाने का इरादा *हुआ*। (derived intransitive)

> उसका जाने का इरादा *है*। (stative)

(b) Detransivisation of non-functioal Complex Verbs

Deletion of subect :

(6) मिस्त्री ने कार ठीक *कर* दी। (transitive)

> कार ठीक *हो गई*। (derived intransitive)

(7) उसने सभी पैसे अदा *कर दिए*। (transitive)

> सभी पैसे अदा *हो गए*। (derived intransitive)

Subject + को :

(8) मैंने सभी बातें मालूम *कर* लीं। (transitive)

> *मुझे* सारी बातें मालूम *हो गईं*। (derived intransitive)

> *मुझे* सारी बातें मालूम हैं। (stative)

(9) महेश ने वह गाना याद किया। (transitive)

> महेश *को* वह गाना याद हो गया। (derived intransitive)

> महेश *को* यह गाना याद है। (stative)

The detransivisation of other complex verbs which are formed by verbalizers other than कर or हो is generally achieved by a transformation process or lexical words, e.g. दाँत लगाना > दाँत लगना/खाना/पढ़ना, चोट पहुँचाना, गाली देना > गाली खाना, लात मारना > लात खाना, धोखा देना > धोखा खाना, सज़ा देना > सज़ा भुगतना, e.g.

(10) साहब ने रामू को *डाँट लगाई*। (transitive)

> रामू ने डाँट खाई। (patient, non-active)

> रामू को डाँट *लगी/पड़ी*। (को-sentence, non-active)

2.4.7 Cognate Complex Verbs

Complex verbs related to common lexical words or common semantic fields are called cognate complex verbs. For instance, the following complex verbs are cognate complex verbs because they share the same lexical words despite the fact that they belong to two different structural categories or may be each other's derivatives:

तैयार करना – तैयारी करना　　　　प्रयोग करना – प्रयुक्त करना

याद रहना – याद रखना　　　　सहायता करना – मदद करना

No two cognate complex verbs are perfect synonyms of each other in their meaning, distribution and context. There is always some difference between them, even though very slight, in connotation or usage, e.g.

(10) इस साबुन का *प्रयोग कीजिए* (*प्रयुक्त)।

(11) मैंने सफ़र की *तैयारी कर ली है*।

*मैंने सफ़र तैयार *कर लिया है*।

(13) मुझे अचानक आपकी *याद आई*।

*मैंने अचानक आपको याद रखा।

(14) मैं आपकी मदद (सहायता) करना अपना *फ़र्ज़* समझता हूँ।

(stylistic variation)

The cognate complex verbs can be grouped into three major categories where semantic, distributional and contextual differences can be identified. Some semantic distinctions related to the noun + कर complex verbs can be seen in Bahal (1974).

(a) Structural/distributional Difference:

तैयार करना – (की) तैयारी करना; मना करना – की मनाही करना; शुरू करना – की शुरुआत करना; प्रयुक्त करना – (का) प्रयोग करना; तलाश करना – की तलाशी करना; निर्धारित करना – (का निर्धारण करना)

(b) Stylistic Difference:

(की) सहायता करना – (की) मदद करना; (का) इंतज़ाम करना – (की) व्यवस्था करना; का प्रयोग करना – का इस्तेमाल करना

(c) Verbalizer-based Difference:

भाषण देना – भाषण करना; याद आना, याद रखना; वापस करना – वापस देना; रुचि रखना – रुचि लेना : सुनाई देना –सुनाई पड़ना.

2.5 Compound Verbs

2.5.1 Defining a Compound Verb

A *compound verb* in Hindi is formed by combining two verbs together, of which the first one is in the form of a verb root and the second verb takes on the suffixes of aspect, mood and tense, e.g. कर लेना, भाग जाना, फेंक देना, रो पड़ना, उतर आना etc. The first verb denotes the dictionary meaning and is called the lexical verb. The second verb does not represent any independent lexical meaning, but only developes, limits or intensifies the meaning of the first verb, i.e. the lexical verb. The verbs लेना, जाना, देना, पड़ना, आना used in these examples may have separate lexical meanings elsewhere but when used as an intensifier in a compound verb they shed their lexical meanings and become lexically empty, called lexical *emptiness* (Hook 1974) or *dramatization* (Porizka 1954).

The formation of the compound verb can be illustrated as follows:

Hindi Compound Verbs

Verb -1	Verb-2
+ root form	+ inflection
+ lexical verb	+ intensifier
+ lexical meaning	–no lexical meaning

(1) सभी चोर *भाग गए* ।

(2) मैं कल तक *आ जाऊँगा* ।

(3) सभी मेहमानों ने खाना *खा लिया* ।

The number of intensifiers in Hindi is, however, limited, though grammarians are divided on their numbers. (Kamtaprasad Guru recognizes 11 intensifiers, Aryendra Sharma 18, Macgregor 13, Bajpeyi 12 and Olphen 17). The eight major intensifiers generally recognized by most grammarians are – 1. भाग जाना, 2. लेना (कर लेना), 3. देना (फेंक देना), 4. आना (उतर आना), 5. पड़ना (रो पड़ना), 6. उठना (काँप उठना), 7. बैठना (कर बैठना), 8. डालना (कर डालना) । The intensifier चला जाना is an exception in that the first constituent चला is not in the root form. There are certain other less frequently used intensifiers also, of which the more prominent ones are: 9) निकलना (बढ़ निकलना), 10. मारना (छान मारना), (11) मरना (जा मरना), 12. छोड़ना (बना छोड़ना)।

There is yet another category of compound verbs called *irregular compound verbs*. These compound verbs do not conform to the normal structure of the compound verbs and in general infuse an additional intensity to the meaning of the compound verb. They can also be classified into three types: (a) Fast mode Irregular compound verbs, (b) continuous compound verbs and (c) Inverted compound Verbs.

(i) *Fast mode Irregular Compound Verbs*: Sometimes a perfective suffix -या is added to the first constituent of the verb in its ए-ending form (किए देता हूँ) to denote an immediate or quick action on the part of the subject (sentence 1-2). The first constituent of the compound verb in such cases may agree with the number and gender of the subject if the verb is intransitive (sentence 3-4). The intensifiers of such compound verbs require either a habitual (-ता), or a continuous (-रहा) aspect accompanied by a present tense marker (है, था). See:

(1) मैं अभी फोन किए देता हूँ/*किया देता हूँ। (transitive)

(2) मैं खुद *देखे* लेता हूँ/*देखा लेता हूँ। (transitive)

(3) उसका दिल *बैठा* जाता है/*बैठे* जाता है। (intransitive)

(4) दुश्मन *चढ़ा* आ रहा है। (intrastitive)

(ii) *Continuous Compound Verbs*: Normally compound verbs in Hindi do not take continuous aspect marker रहा because it may result into a duplication of two verb stems in sequence - one of the compound verb and the other of the continuous aspect marker. Thus, there is a restriction on the occurrence of double stems in a sequence, e.g. *फेंक दे रहा है. Hence only simple non-compound verbs are used in such situations, e.g.

(5) वह सभी सामान *फेंक रहा है*। (**फेंक दे रहा है*).

However, if there is a need for using a compound verb, an aspect marker -या is placed after the first verb constituent. In such a situation it becomes ए-ending if the verb is transitive and if the verb is intransitive, it may change according to the gender and number of the subject, e.g.

(6) वह सब सामान *फेंके* दे रहा है। (transitive)

(7) लड़की पानी *पिए* जा रही है। (transitive)

(8) बच्ची भूख से *मरी* जा रही है/*मरे* जा रही है। (intransitive)

(9) उसका दिल *बैठा* जा रहा है/*बैठे* जा रहा है। (intransitive)

(iii) *Inverted Compound Verbs*: If there is a need to express the sense of anger or speed with verbs denoting physical action, the two constituents of the compound verbs can be at times inverted in Hindi, e.g.

पटक देना > दे पटकना; उड़ चलना > चल उड़ना;
मार देना > दे मारना; खींच देना> दे खींचना;

2.5.2 Distinctive Features of Compound Verbs

(a) Lexical Emptiness of Intensifiers: Only the first verb component of a compound verb carries the lexical meaning while the second verb component (i.e. the intensifier) loses its lexical meaning, e.g. in the compound verbs आ जाना and रो पड़ना, the independent lexical meanings of आना 'to come' and पड़ना 'to lie' are lost.

The lexical emptiness of the intensifiers, however, does not prevent them from being meaningful and significant at a functional level (see below). Secondly, some intensifiers even though bereft of their original lexical meanings often retain some trace of their original meaning. For instance, the intensifier लेना covers in it the sense of the speaker being a beneficiary while the intensifier देना covers the sense of some other character being a beneficiary. Similarly, the intensifier आना hints at the sense of moving towards the centre (i.e. nearness), the intensifier जाना, on the other hand, covers the sense of moving away from the centre (i.e. distance). Hence the so called lexical emptiness of the intensifiers is rather a relative feature and not an absolute one.

Despite the fact that the intensifiers lend some value to the meaning of the verb, the functional value of the intensifiers is always subordinate to the lexical value of the main verb. For instance, in compound verbs like आ जाना both the constituents (आना, and जाना) denote a single meaning *to come* Similarly, in the compound verb ले आना, both the constituents लेना and आना denote a single meaning *to bring.* Such constructions are often called unipolar construction, that is, having two poles but having a single meaning. Different from this are conjunct verbs (for which see 2.6)

(b) Co-occurrence of Intensifiers and Lexical Verbs: Not all the intensifiers can occur with all the lexical verbs. There exists a relationship of collocation and constrains between them. Some lexical verbs have the capacity to occur with a larger number of intensifiers whereas some others are used with only one or two. For instance, the verb खाना has the capacity to occur in the company of a larger number of intensifiers, e.g. जाना, देना, लेना and डालना (खा जाना, खा लेना, खा देना, खा डालना) while the verb टूटना can occur only in the company of one intensifier जाना (टूट जाना). The combination *टूट लेना or *टूट देना) is not feasible.

Some compound verbs show an extremely stronger tendency of collocation than others and, therefore, their lexical verbs occur only in the company of their specific intensifiers, e.g. भूल जाना, खो जाना, गुम हो जाना, गायब हो जाना, मुकर जाना, ऊब जाना, उकता जाना, गोल कर जाना, भाग जाना (in the sense of running *away*) and हो जाना (in the sense of *becoming,* i.e. change of state). See below:

मैं आपकी बात *भूला (भूल गया)।

ऐन वक्त पर वह *मुकरा (गया)।

It is, however, possible to use these verbs without intensifiers only in complete negative environments (see 2.10.4 a), e.g.

मैं आपकी बात नहीं भूला।

मैं कब मुकरा, बताओ?

There are, however, no clear-cut rules to predict as to which intensifiers can legitimately accompany which lexical verbs. This practice is ultimately determined by usage and not by cut and dried grammatical rules. That is why there has been a practice of presenting such lexical verbs in a *list* form along with their likely intensifiers instead of formulating grammatical or usage rules.

(i) Restrictions of Grammatical Categories: Transitive intensifiers (e.g. देना, लेना, डालना, छोड़ना, मारना) normally occur in the company of transitive verbs and intransitive intensifiers (e.g. जाना, आना, पड़ना, उठाना, बैठना, निकालना, मारना) occur in the company of intransitive verbs. In certain contexts, however, some of these verbs can occur with both the types of lexical verbs – transitive as well as intransitive. See:

जाना –	आ जाना (intr + intr)	देना --	फेंक देना (tr. + tr)
	पी जाना (tr + intr)		चल देना (intr + tr)
बैठना –	उठ बैठना (intr + intr)	लेना –	ले लेना (tr + tr)
	कर बैठना (tr + intr)		सो लेना (intr + tr)

(ii) Restrictions of Semantic Categories: The intensifiers लेना, देना, बैठना, डालना and छोड़ना are normally used with *controllable verbs* (see 3.5.3 a) and not with verbs which represent uncontrollable actions (*वह मार दिया, *बच्ची गिर ली). Even amongst verbs denoting controllable actions the intensifier लेना is most naturally used where the beneficiary of the action is necessarily or by reference the subject, e.g. खा लेना, पहन लेना, पी लेना, पी लेना (necessarily): पढ़ देना, रख देना, लिख देना (by reference). The use of the intensifier देना is also natural along with causative verbs, e.g. पिटवा देना, पहुँचा देना, लौटा देना, बिकवा देना, पिलवा देना etc. though depending upon the nature of the context, combinations (or collocations like करवा देना, रखवा लेना etc. are possible.

Similarly, the use of the intensifier डालना is more natural in the company of verbs denoting violence e.g. मार डालना, फाड़ डालना. In the same way, the use of the intensifier निकलना is more natural in the company of verbs denoting motion, e.g. चल निकलना, बढ़ निकलना, just as the use of the intensifier पड़ना is natural in the company of immediate or uncontrollable actions, e.g. चल निकलना, बढ़ निकलना (see ahead the table 2.5.4).

(iii) *Restrictions on Negativity*: Compound verbs in Hindi cannot be used in normal negative sentences (10-11) or sentences where the successful accomplishment of the action is in doubt (12-16. See –

(10) मैंने काम *कर लिया* (*नहीं कर लिया)।

(11) वह किताब लाना *भूल जाएगा* (*नहीं भूल जाएगा)।

(12) मैंने बटुआ ढूँढा *(* ढूँढ लिया)* लेकिन नहीं मिल पाया।

(13) उन्होंने खाना खाया *(*खा लिया)* लेकिन वे पूरा नहीं खा सके।

(14) मैंने उन्हें पैसे *लौटाए* (*लौटा दिए) लेकिन उन्होंने नहीं लिए।

(15) मैंने बड़ी मुश्किल से यह किताब *पढ़ी* (*पढ़ ली)।

(16) जब तक पुलिस *पहुँची* (*पहुँच गई) तब तक चोर भाग चुके थे।

There are, however, two exceptions where the intensifiers can be used in a negative environment:

(i) where the sentence is in the indirect imperative form i.e. –ना and –इएगा form, i.e. देना, जाना : In such sentences the negative particle मत or न is placed between the two components of the compound verb or before it, e.g.

किताब *खो मत देना।*

बीच में *न चले आना।*

हमें *भूल न जाइएगा।*

(ii) where the sentence involves the use of कहीं, जब तक न .., क्यों नहीं, अगर न लिया and double negation, e.g.

कहीं वे हमें *देख न लें।*

तुम *क्यों नहीं* सो जाते।

जब तक पुलिस *न* आ जाए, तब तक हम यहाँ से नहीं हटेंगे।

अगर तुम्हें *पकड़ न* लिया तो मेरा नाम जग्गू नहीं।

कोई कारण नहीं कि तुम पकड़े *न जाओ।*

Absence of negation is a genetic feature of compound verbs. On the contrary, the conjunct verbs (see 2.6.2c) do not show this characteristic where negative sentences can be freely used, e.g.

वे अपनी किताब नहीं *ले गए।*

अभी तक उन्होंने कुछ नहीं *लिख भेजा* है।

2.5.3 Compound Verbs and the use of ने

The following intransitive and transitive situations are possible for the use of ने after the subject:

Group 1	vi. + vi.	- ने	वह भाग गया/रो पड़ा/काँप उठा/उतर आया/चल निकला/जा मरा।
Group 2	vt. + vt.	+ ने	उसने कागज फेंक दिया/ले लिया/छान मारा; उसने क्या कर डाला/बना छोड़ा?
Group 3	vi. + vt.	- ने	वह चल दिया/हँस दिया/रो दिया, मुस्करा दिया/सो लिया/हो लिया।
Group 4	vt.+ vi.	- ने	वह दूध पी गया; यह तुम क्या कर बैठे?

It will be clear from this chart that the use of ने after the subject is possible only when both the components of the compound verb are transitive. As an exception some native speakers optionally use ने after the subject in sentences having transitive and intransitive components of the compound verbs, e.g. उसने हँस दिया.

2.5.4 Functional, Aspectual and Attituditional Value of Intensifiers

Despite the fact that the intensifiers of the compound verbs are mostly deprived of their lexical meanings, they nevertheless provide some important **functional, aspectual** and **attituditional** information about the sentence. At the **functional level**, the intensifiers intensify, develop and limit the lexical meaning of the first component (i.e. verb). For instance, it highlights the functional difference between the verbs रखना, रख लेना and रख देना as in sentences:

नौकर ने पैसे रख *लिये*। (self beneficiary)
नौकर ने पैसे रख *दिए*। (other beneficiary)
(see page 78-79)

Based on the **functional value**, the intensifiers can be divided into two categories : (i) where the intensifiers really influence the meanings of the concerned lexical verb, e.g. रख देना, रख लेना, हँस पड़ना, रो

उठना, etc., and (ii) where the intensifiers are used as a part of collocation (i.e used regularly or routinely) at a structural level in admissible environments and do not directly affect the meanings of the lexical verb, e.g. भूल जाना, टाल देना, ऊब जाना, मुकर जाना, फेंक देना.

There are also some intensifiers, though small in number, which bring about a qualitative change in the lexical meaning of the compound verbs, e.g.

1. मारना = पीटना 'to beat'
   मार डालना = जान से मारना 'to kill'
2. मानना = समझना (वह मुझे अपना भाई मानता है)
   मान जाना = सहमत होना (वह मेरी बात मान जाएगा)
3. होना = घटित होना 'to be'
   हो जाना = बन जाना 'to become'
4. चलना = पैदल चलना 'to walk'
   चला जाना = बाहर जाना 'to go away'

Under the **aspective role** some intensifiers denote the successful accomplishment of an action (see the table below). Some grammarians (Hacker 1958), Porizka (1967-69) consider the aspective role of the intensifiers more significant than others. Normally the intensifiers जाना and लेना denote the completion of an action, but the sense of completion denoted by the perfective aspect marker -या is different from it in the sense that the sense of completion denoted by the aspect marker -या has an additional sense of the successful completion of the action. Therefore, no condition or restriction can be imposed in the linguistic environment. See sentences (12-16) above and the following:

(17) मैंने किताब पढ़ी > मैंने मुश्किल से किताब *पढ़ी*।
> * मैंने मुश्किल से किताब *पढ़ ली*।

(18) मैंने बटुआ ढूँढा, लेकिन नहीं मिला।
*मैंने बटुआ ढूँढ लिया, लेकिन नहीं मिला।

The accomplishment of the action denoted by the intensifires is not limited to only the perfective aspect but it also extends to other tenses and moods as well, e.g. बैठ जाएगी, कल आपको पैसे मिल जाएँगे, तीन बजे तक मैं खाना खा लेता हूँ.

At the *attituditional* level, many intensifiers provide some additional information about the specific attitude or viewpoint of the speaker towards the action. For instance in the sentence बिल्ली सारा दूध पी गई, the intensifier गई does not only indicate the completion of the action of drinking, but it also gives a hidden indication of disapproval suggesting that the action was undesirable. Similarly the sentence वह मुस्करा दिया indicates that there was no other option, the sentence उसने सारा कमरा छान मारा indicates an attitude of hurriedness. Thus it will appear that the attitude of the speaker is determined by various factors like the nature of the action, the *speech act*, the participants and their mutual relationship. This is the reason many linguists (Kachru 1979) hold that a complete meaning of the compound verbs in Hindi would require not only the lexical and sentential meaning but also the analysis of the speaker's attitude. It may, however, be noted that not all the compound verbs display the element of speaker's attitude.

A broad classification of the functional, aspective and attitudional values of Hindi intensifiers is presented in the following table:

Functional, Aspective and Attitudional Values of Hindi Intensifiers

Intens-ifiers	Usage	Values		
		Functional	Aspective	Attituditional
जाना	वह चला *गया* । (भाग-, निकल-) लोग *आ गए* । (पहुँच-, बैठ-)	distance	accomplish-ment	
	बिल्ली सारा दूध *पी गई* । (खा-, निगल-, कह-, उगल-) वह किताब भूल *गया* । (ऊब-, मुकर-, *गायब हो*-)	quickness	accomplish-ment	disapproval
आना	बादल घिर *आए* । उसकी आँखों में आँसू भर *आए* । (छलक-, याद हो-)	nearness	coming	emotion

लेना	उन्होंने खाना खा *लिया*। (पी-, सुन-, पहन-) नौकर ने पैसे रख *लिए*। (कर-, पढ़-) मैं थोड़ी-सी पी *लेता हूँ*। (सो-, टहल-) वह उर्दू पढ़ *लेता* है। (लिख-, बोल-, गा-, बजा-) मैं आपके भी कपड़े धो *लूँगा*।	intake self-beneficiary limited quantity incomplete competence	accomplishment accomplishment self	
देना	रमेश ने मकान बेच *दिया*। (सौंप-, फेंक-, छोड़-, खो-) नौकर ने पैसे रख *दिए*। (पढ़-, कर-, धो-) वह *हँस दिया*। (रो-, मुस्करा-, चल-, छींक)	separation other beneficiary other beneficiary	accomplishment	
उठना	वह रो *उठा*। (बोल-, चिल्ला-, चौंक-)	suddenness		impulsive
पड़ना	लड़की गिर *पड़ी*। (हंस-, चौंक-, कूद)	suddenness accidental		
डालना	उसने सभी पेड़ काट *डाले*। (मार-, फाड़-, कर-, फोड़-)	hastiness	accomplishment	extremeness
बैठना	तुम क्या कर *बैठे* ? (मार-, कह-) वह उठ *बैठा*।	indiscretion suddenness		undesirability
निकलना	वह बढ़ *निकला*। (चल-, आ-)	unhindered progression		
मारना मरना	उसने सारा कमरा छान *मारा*। वह आखिर वहीं जा *मरा*। (आ-, लड़-)	labour		excitement disrespect
छोड़ना	यह क्या हालत बना *छोड़ी* है ? (कर-)	carelessness		disagreement

2.6 Conjunct Verbs

2.6.1 Defining a Conjunct verb

A conjunct verb is a combination of two verbs where both the verbs retain their own lexical meanings, e.g. ले जाना and ढूँढ निकालना. The first verb (ले) is in the form of a verb root and the second verb (जा) takes on the markers of aspect, tense and mood. Thus ले जाना is a combination two actions –'to take' and 'to go'. Similarly the conjunct verb ढूँढ निकालना also consists of two actions – ढूँढना 'to search for' and निकालना 'to take out'. Thus the conjunct verbs do not only consist of two verbs, but also two separate actions. This is technically called a *bipolar* construction where there are two poles of meaning.

Now compare this with another set of verb combinations like आ जाना 'to come' in a sentence like वह घर आ गया, which we have called *compound verb* (see 2.6.1). It also consists of two consecutive verbs आ and जा, but it does not denote two different lexical meanings or actions (आना and जाना 'to come' and 'to go'). This is technically called a *unipolar* construction.

For instance, in the sentence वह किताब ले गया, the combination ले गया is a conjunct verb but in the sentence वह आ गया, the combination आ जाना is a compound verb and not a conjunct verb because the verb गया loses its lexical meaning and only the lexical meaning of आना remains. Some of the important conjunct verbs of Hindi are:

ले जाना	आ बैठना	जा गिरना	कर दिखाना
ले आना	आ घेरना	जा घुसना	लिख भेजना
ले उड़ना	आ झपटना	जा बसना	उखाड़ फेंकना
ले डूबना	आ टपकना	सोच निकालना	
दे जाना	आ फँसना	खींच निकालना	
दे आना	आ लेटना	ढूँढ निकालना	

2.6.2 Distinctive Features

The surface structures of the conjunct and the compound structures are normally the same. Both are made up of two verb roots. See:

(1) वह आ गया (आ+गया) (conjunct verb)

(2) वह किताब ले गया (ले +गया) (compound verb)

Despite this similarity, there is a substantial difference in the internal structure and semantics of the compound and conjunct verbs as will be evident from the following distinctive features of the conjunct verbs:

(a) Independent Lexical Meaning: In the case of compound verbs only the first component has an independent lexical meaning and not the second component (intensifier) whereas in the case of conjunct verbs both the components possess independent lexical meanings and denote two separate actions, e.g.

compound verb : आ जाना (= आना)

conjunct verb : ले जाना (= लेना और जाना)

(b) Deletion of कर: There is normally an inherent existence of a conjuct particle कर in conjunct verbs which is sometimes overtly expressed in the surface structure and somes times remains unexpressed, e.g. ले जाना (ले कर जाना), दे आना (दे कर आना), कर दिखाना (करके दिखाना), ढूँढ निकालना (ढूँढ कर निकालना), लिख भेजना, लिख कर भेजना. It is, however, not possible to delete similar कर in compound verbs. Compare:

(3) लड़की चिट्ठी *दे गई/देकर* गई। (conjunct verb)

(1) वह आ गया/*आकर गया। (compound verb)

Some verb constructions, however, are used both in the sense of compound as well as conjunct verbs, which can be distinguished only through the context, e.g.

(4) वह खाना *खा गया।*

– उसने खाना खाया। (compound verb in this sense).

– उसने खाना खाया और चला गया। (conjuct verb in this sense)

(c) Negation: Compound verbs are not used in simple negative sentences (see 2.5.2), but the conjunct verbs can be used in negative sentences as well, e.g. लड़की चिट्ठी *नहीं* दे गई, वह किताब *नहीं* दे गई, वह किताब *नहीं* ले गया, उसने काम करके *नहीं* दिखाया. On the contrary, the negative version of sentence (1) is not acceptable *वह नहीं आ गया.

(d) Collocational Restrictions: Theoretically, a conjunct relationship between the two components of the conjunct verbs should have been possible but it is not so. The two components of the conjunct verbs accompany each other on the basis of their semantic compatibility. Any two components of an action which do not possess the required compatibility can not form a conjunct. For instance, we cannot have a conjunct like *ले पीना or *कर लिखना on the analogy of conjuncts like ले जाना or कर दिखाना.

(e) Conjunct Relationship: The relationship that exists between the two components of the conjunct verb can also be expressed through the conjunct और 'and'. This relationship can also be expressed by the component कर in constructions like वह आकर लेटा where it denotes the sequence of actions or events. (for further functions of कर see 1.5.2). This is the reason why the transformation grammar does not recognize the conjunct verb as a basic verb construction because it is a construction derived from a sentence conjoining two transformation processes. See :

वह आया |
+ | = वह आकर लेटा > वह आ लेटा
वह लेटा |

2.7 Causativisation

2.7.1 Defining Causativisation

Causative verbs in Hindi are mainly formed by adding a suffix -आ or -वा to the verb root and whenever necessary there are some morphemic or morpho-phonemic changes in them, e.g. उठना-उठाना-उठवाना, सोना-सुलाना-सुलवाना. Causative verbs are part of the main verb and not the auxiliary verbs. The causative verb forms (आ-, or वा-, etc.) denote that the person who is performing the action (called the *agent*) is doing so at the instigation of someone else, (called *causer* or *intermediate* agent). See-

(1) *लड़की* सो रही है। (agent)
(2) *नौकरानी* लड़की को *सुला* रही है। (causer or instigator)
(3) माँ *नौकरानी से* लड़की को *सुलवा* रही है। (intermediate agent)

The act of sleeping is actually performed by लड़की in all these three sentences (1-3) where it is called an agent (also sometimes called an active subject or सक्रिय कर्ता in Hindi). In sentence (2) नौकरानी is the *instigator* or *causer* at whose bidding the agent is performing the act of sleeping. Remember that despite being a causer or an instigator, नौकरानी is in some way or other a co-participant in the whole act (of sleeping). In sentence (3) माँ is a causer or instigator who causes or instigates नौकरानी (the intermediate agent) to make the child sleep. Remember that in this sentence the instigator (माँ) instigates the intermediate agent (नौकरानी) and not the agent (लड़की) and is, therefore, not a co-participant in the act of sleeping, because it's role is limited only to giving orders.

In sentence (2) the instigation from the causer to the agent is direct and is therefore called the *first causative* or *direct causative*. In sentence (3) the instigation from the causer to the agent is not direct but through an intermediary and is, therefore, called second causative, or indirect causative.

2.7.2 First Causative

First causative verbs are formed from both - the base intransitive and base transitive verbs. (The *base form* of a verb is the verb stem devoid of any prefix, suffix or infix, e.g. खा, पी, सो आ etc.) The essential morphological feature of the first causative is the addition of a prefix –आ after the verb root plus some other minor changes wherever necessary, e.g. उड़ना-उड़ाना, सुनना-सुनाना, and सोना-सुलाना etc. It may be noted that the first causative verbs are formed from verbs falling in the verb-classes 1(a) and 2(b) (see 2.7.6 (सोना, उड़ना, खाना, पहनना etc.) Verbs falling in the verb-classes 3(a) and 4 (a) are in a position to directly form the second causative forms (see 2.7.6 p. 79 काटना, बनाना; ख़रीदना, गाना)

The base intransitive and transitive verbs can form the following two types of causative sub-patterns (Caus. S Patterns):

Caus. Sub-pattern-1

Causer	Agent	Verb
{+gram. subject + co-participant}	(+ को)	{+First causative +Group (1(b)}
नौकरानी	लड़के को	सुला रही है।
Class – I (b)		
नौकरानी	*लड़के को*	*सुला रही है।*

Caus. Sub-Pattern-2

Instigator	Agent	Object	Verb
{+gram. Subject +co-participant}	(+ को)	{+को -animate}	{+First causative +Group (2(b)}
नर्स	मरीज़ को	दवा	पिला रही है।

Causative sub-pattern-1 derives from a base intransitive verb सो and, therefore, it has two animate participants: causer नर्स and an agent (मरीज़ को). On the other hand, the causative sub-pattern-2 is derived from a base transitive verb पी and, therefore, it has an additional participant (an inanimate object दवा) after which the use of को is not possible.

According to the verb agreement rule of Hindi, only an unmarked subject, and in its absence, an unmarked object can be the grammatical subject of a sentence, with which the verb would agree in number, gender and person. (An *unmarked noun* is the one which is not followed by any postposition like को, से, में, के लिए etc.) In both the above sentences the agents (लड़की and नर्स) are marked by the postposition को and are, therefore, unlikely to control the number, gender and person of the verb. Hence in these sentences only the causer the (माँ and नर्स) which are unmarked have the capacity to control the agreement pattern of the verb. It may be noted that in these sentences the causer (माँ, नर्स) not only instigates the agents (लड़की, मरीज़) to perform the action but also acts like a co-partner or helper in the execution of the action. It may be noted that this feature of co-partnership is absent in the causer of the second causative sentences.

The agent has two distinct features: <+ animate, + volition>. In other words, the agent is the one who is free in doing or not doing an action, i.e. he is not a mere patient or an experiencer of the action. He is the real doer or performer of the action in real life and is the logical subject in the first causative sentence (e.g *लड़की* सो रही है, *मरीज* दवा पी रहा है). The grammatical status of the agent (लड़की) remains unchanged in all the three sentences – the base sentence, the first causative and the second causative (sentences 1-3). On the other hand, the grammatical status of the causer/instigator (नौकरानी and माँ) changes in the first and second causatives respectively as in sentences (2-3). The causative sentence patterns 1 and 2 are supposed to contain two embedded sentences viz. लड़की सोती है and नौकरानी को प्रेरित करती है.

2.7.3 Second Causative

The first essential formal feature of the second causative in Hindi is the addition of a suffix -वा after the verb root plus some other minor changes wherever necessary, e.g. उड़ना, उड़वाना, सुनना-सुनवाना, सोना-सुलवाना etc. We noted earlier that only two of the four verb groups listed in 2.7.6 were capable of forming the first causative forms but in the present case, all the four base verb groups are capable of forming second causatives.

Causative verbs derived from the base transitive and intransitive verbs form three types of second causative sentence sub-patterns as follows:

Caus. sub-pattern -3

Instigator	**Intermediate**	**Active Sub.**	**Verb**
3) माँ	नौकरानी से	लड़के को	सुलवा रही है।

Caus. sub-pattern -4

Instigator	**Intermediate**	**Active Sub.**	**Object**	**Verb**
(4) डॉक्टर	नर्स से	मरीज़ को	दवा	पिलवा रही है।

Caus. sub-pattern -5

Instigator	**Intermediate**	**Object**	**Verb**
(5) मकान मालिक	मज़दूरों से	मकान	बनवा रहा है।
(6) साहब	बड़े बाबू से	चपरासी को	बुलवा रहे हैं।

In these three causative sentences also the instigator is the grammatical subject of the sentence because it is the only unmarked noun out of the three. Sub-pattern (3) is derived from the base intransitive verbs whereas the sub-patterns (4) and (5) are derived from the base transitive verbs. Hence the existence of an object is not possible in pattern (3) unlike that in sub-patterns (4) and (5). The object (दवा) in sub-pattern (4) is unmarked because the agent (मरीज़ को) before this is already marked. Since there is no agent in sub-pattern (5), the object according to the normal grammatical rules can be marked by को or may remain unmarked (see sub-pattern 34b).

Compared to the first causatives, the sub-patterns of the second causatives have three distinctive features: (a) The absence of co-participation on the part of the instigator, (b) the entry of an intermediate subject and (c) the integration of the intermediate subject and the agent).

(a) Absence of Instigator's Participation: The instigating subject in the first causatives are co-participants in the execution of the action as नौकरानी and नर्स play an active role in the action of sentence (2) and (4), but in the second causatives, the instigating subject has no material role to play in the execution of the action : his only contribution is to give directions to the intermediary or creating a situation wherein the agent himself or with the help of an intermediary accomplishes the action. For instance, sentence (3) postulates that the instigator subject (माँ) directs the intermediate subject नौकरानी that she should make the child sleep. She herself is not partaking in the action of instigating the child to sleep.

Similarly, the following sentences (8) and (9) indicate that the instigator subjects so directed or created a situation wherein the action of transfer or getting the photograph was accomplished through the help of someone:

(8) मैंने स्टेनो का तबादला करवा दिया।

(9) मैंने कल एक फोटो खिंचवाई।

(b) Entry of an Intermediate Subject: If the instigating subject is not himself accomplishing the act, it is necessary that there should be an intermediary who should receive directions from the intermediate subject and accomplish the action by himself or through the assistance of some agent, as नौकरानी, नर्स, मज़दूर and बड़े बाबू in sentences (3, 5-7).

It should be noted that the instigating subjects of the causative verbs (verb class 1b, 2b) and the agents (active subjects) of the second causative verbs (verb class 3b, 4a) have the capacity to become the intermediate subjects of the second causative verbs, e.g.

(2) *नौकरानी* लड़की को सुला रही है। (instigating subject)

(3) माँ *नौकरानी* से लड़की को सुलवा रही है। (intermediate subject)

(10) *मज़दूर* मकान बनवा रहे हैं। (agent/active subject)

(6) मकान मालिक *मज़दूरों से* मकान बनवा रहा है।(intermediate subject)

In contexts where the status of the intermediate subject is ambiguous, insignificant or irrelevant, it may remain unexpressed as in sentences (8-9) and the following sentence:

(11) मैं भी मकान बनवा रहा हूँ।

(c) Integration of Active and Intermediate Subjects: The roles of intermediate and active subjects are integrated into one in the causative sub-pattern (5). The base transitive forms of the sentence patterns (6-7) are respectively like this: मज़दूर मकान बना रहे हैं and बड़े बाबू चपरासी को बुला रहे हैं. In these sentences मज़दूर and बड़े बाबू are agents (active subjects) and, therefore, their roles as agents are intact in the causative sentences (6-7) too. On the other hand it performs the role of an intermediate subject also because it is marked by the intermediate marker से and is acting at the direction or inspiration of the instigator. The integration of these two roles can also be seen in the second causatives which are formed with verbs belonging to verb class 3c and 4b, because these base verbs do not form first causatives and directly form second causatives.

The transformational grammar postulates three embedded

sentences in the underlying structure of the second causatives in Hindi, as, for instance in sentence (3) माँ नौकरानी से लड़की को सुलवा रही है, the three embedded sentences will be: i) लड़की सोती है, ii) नौकरानी लड़की को प्रेरित करती है and iii) माँ नौकरानी को प्रेरित करती है.

An additional use of instrumental case is also possible in certain causative sentences which is necessarily inanimate and is used with the postposition से. This should, however, not be confused with the intermediate subject because the intermediate subject is always animate. See:

(12) माँ ने नौकरानी से बच्चे को चम्मच से दूध पिलवाया। (instrument)

A causative verb is basically a verb that causes or inspires someone to do something. Certain causative verbs, however, give an additional sense of '*to assist to do* or 'to compel to do'. This additional sense does not basically rest in the causative verbs but in the nature of the action and the context of the causative verb. For instance, in the sentence मैंने लड़के को हिंदी लिखवाई (as if by holding his hands) the implication is that of assisting the boy in writing but in the sentence मैंने यह बात पिताजी से भी कहलवाई the implication is not that of assisting the father in saying something. Similarly in the sentence मैंने हरकिशन से खाली कागज़ पर दस्तखत करवाए, the implication is that of goading someone to do something. But in the sentence हरकिशन दस्तखत ही नहीं करता था, मैंने उसे धमकी दी और खाली कागज़ पर उससे दस्तखत करवाए there is an additional element of compulsion or force which is due to the context of situation.

2.7.4 Some Misleading Causative Forms

(a) Transitive and Causative Sentences: The surface structure of some sentences formed with transitive and first causative verbs may superficially look alike, but they are not, e.g.

(13) पुलिस चोर को *पीट* रही है। (transitive)

(2) नौकरानी लड़की को *सुला* रही है। (causative)

One of the characteristics of a causative verb is that there must exist a base form of the causative verb in which the subject of the sentence (i.e.) action should be a logical subject (i.e. an agent) and overtly expressed in the sentence. For instance, in the sentence लड़की सो रही है, सुलाना is a causative verb and its base form is सोना). Here the logical subject लड़की is an agent (i.e. active subject) and is also expressed in the sentence. There is, however, no such base form of the transitive verb पीटना. If we consider पिटना as its base form merely on the basis of analogy, e.g. चोर पिट रहा है, there can be two objections: First, the logical subject of पिटाई (i.e. the police) remains unexpressed in the sentence and secondly if we consider चोर as the logical subject, his role in the action of पिटाई is not active but only that of an experiencer (i.e. patient). Hence पिटना is, in fact, a derived intransitive of पीटना and not a base intransitive verb (see 2.7.4d). The transitive verb पीटना itself is a base transitive verb because in sentence (4) which is derived from this, the logical subject पुलिस is an agent as well as overtly expressed in the sentence. The base transitive verbs of this category have been shown in the table of Causative Verb Groups (see 2.7.6) under the group 3(b). These verbs do not have any first causative forms, they straight away make second causatives, e.g. पीटना – पिटवाना.

A difference can also be seen between these two sentences on the basis of some distinctive structural restrictions. For instance, it is possible to transform the base intransitive forms of causative verbs into –ना-पड़ construction, e.g. लड़की को सोना पड़ा (acceptable), but this transformation is not possible in the case of the derived intransitive verb, e.g. *चोर को पिटना पड़ा.

(b) Ditransitive and Causative Sentences: There is also some misleading ambiguity between the surface structures of ditransitive and causative sentences, e.g.

(14) नर्स मरीज़ को दवा दे रही है। (ditransitive, i.e. two objects)

(4) नर्स मरीज़ को दवा *पिला* रही है। (causative)

In sentence (4) the base verb of पिलाना is पीना (मरीज दवा पी रहा है) and therefore पिलाना is its causative form. On this analogy it is not possible to conceive दिलाना as the base form of देना (14). The verb देना is basically a ditransitive verb having two objects, and, therefore, it is not possible to have its normal transitive form. Hence this is also a base verb like पीटना which does not have a first causative form and, therefore, it straightway makes the second causative, e.g. दिलवाना/दिलाना. Both these optional forms are that of the second causatives.

(c) Bidirectional Verbs: The semantic relationship that exists between the base transitive verbs and their causative forms (e.g. पीना - पिलाना) is sometimes likened with the bilateral relationship that exists between verbs like लेना – देना, e.g.

(14) नर्स मरीज़ को दवा *दे* रही है। (giving)

(15) मरीज़ नर्स से दवा *ले* रहा है। (taking)

लेना and देना are bidirectional verbs which express the two aspects of the same action (see sub-pattern 39a). Actions of this category necessarily require two participants in the sentence. Even though it is a single action, it is viewed differently through different angles and each one is given a different name, e.g. लेना-देना, बेचना-ख़रीदना, सौंपना-प्राप्त करना. This relationship is bidirectional and linear whereas the relationship that exists between the base and causative verbs is hierarchical. Hence the verbs लेना and देना cannot be said to be mutually derived verbs. Both of them are independent lexical verbs.

Similarly, पढ़ना-पढ़ाना (as some subject) and सीखना-सिखाना are also bilateral verbs. The only difference is that the process of exchange in these cases is abstract and not concrete, e.g.

(16) आशीष अध्यापक से भूगोल *पढ़ता* है। (taking)

(17) अध्यापक आशीष को भूगोल *पढ़ाता* है। (giving)

The action of studying and teaching is physically a single unit but it has two aspects or angles (one that of a teacher and the other that of the student). The relationship between these two is also bilateral and linear and both of them form independent lexical verbs and are not derived from each other. In the sentence, मैं आशीष को अध्यापक से भूगोल पढ़वा रहा हूँ, the form पढ़वाना is the directly derived second causative form of पढ़ना. (Remember that in the sense of studying in school etc. पढ़ना is a base intransitive verb and its both transitive forms are possible: मैं इसी स्कूल में पढ़ा. पिताजी ने मुझे इसी स्कूल में पढ़ाया. अमीर लोग अपने बच्चों को इसी स्कूल में पढ़वाते हैं. In the sense of reading some book, letter or some written material etc., पढ़ना is a base transitive verb whose only second causative form possible is – पढ़वाना.

(d) Derived Intransitive and Causative: Causative verbs are always formed from either intransitive verbs or transitive base verbs and not from derived intransitive verbs (2.8.4). *Base verbs* are those verbs which are not derived from any other verb. On the contrary, other verbs are derived from them. Base verbs anticipate an animate and active subject, e.g. ढोना, सोना, काटना etc. which require an animate subject to perform this action.

Derived intransitive verbs are derived from the base transitive verbs and denote actions which can be accomplished only through two characters in real life – a subject and an object but appear in the sentence in such a way as if they do not have any subject and the work is being accomplished on its own, e.g. धुलना, काटना, बनाना etc. (see verb group 3a):

(18) धोबी कपड़े *धो* रहा है। (base transitive)

(19) कपड़े *धुल* रहे हैं। (derived intransitive)

In Hindi the derived intransitive verb has the same form as the verb root before adding the causative suffixes or prefixes, e.g. धुल (-वा), बिक (-वा), पिट (-वा) etc. The derived intransitive form of the base transitive verb कर-ना is हो-ना, e.g. शुरू करना – शुरू होना. Some other exceptions are: टूटना – तुड़वाना, छूटना : छुड़वाना, फटना – फड़वाना etc.

It is necessary for the subject to be animate, active and overtly expressed in the base verbs. All these three features are absent in the derived verbs. Hence the relationship that exists between the derived intransitive verbs and the base verbs (कटना-काटना) cannot be said to be equivalent to the relationship that holds between the base and causative verbs (पीना – पिलाना). Infact, काटना is not derived from कटना, but कटना is derived from काटना.

Not all the intransitive verbs in Hindi make derived intransitives but those which make, their active subjects have the capacity to become intermediate subjects by being marked by the postposition से, e.g. धोना, उबालना, खोलना.

(18) धोबी कपड़े *धो* रहा है। (subject/agent)

(19) रामलाल धोबी से कपड़े *धुलवा* रहा है। (intermediate subject)

Transitive verbs whose subjects/agents have the capacity to become dative by being marked by को in causative sentences cannot make derived intransitive verbs, e.g. खाना, पीना, पहनना, लिखना etc. e.g.

(21) *बच्चे* ने खाना खाया।

(22) नौकर ने *बच्चे को* खाना खिलाया।

Verbs belonging to this category can normally make both the types of causatives - first as well as second., e.g. खिलाना - खिलवाना, पहनना - पहनवाना etc.

In Hindi there are as many as about ten verbs which do not change their forms in base transitive and derived intransitive - खुजाना, खोना, घबराना, जगमगाना, फहराना, बदलना, बुनना, रंगना, जगना, भरना and ढकना. Out of these, only the last six verbs are capable of forming the second causatives, e.g. गिलास *भर* गया (intransitive), मैंने गिलास *भर* दिया (transitive), मैंने गिलास *भरवा* दिया (causative).

2.7.5 Constraints on Causativisation

All Hindi verbs do not make causative forms. Normally only base verbs which demand logical subjects/agents are in a position to form causative verbs but here also not all such verbs have the possibility of causativisation. The possibility of causativisation depends on the inherent nature and functional possibilities of the action and not on the structure of the verb. Verbs like सोचना, कमाना, जानना, सौंपना, ऊँघना, चिल्लाना, मुस्कराना, हिचकना, अखरना etc. do not make causative verbs because the very nature of these actions suggest that there is no scope of getting these actions accomplished through instigation, though in a couple of cases, some artificial causative expression are devised through some other verbal devices, e.g.

(23) मैंने उन्हें *सोचने के लिए मजबूर किया*।

Similarly causative forms of a few verbs which are grammatically not feasible can be seen in occasional use because of false analogy, e.g. हँसवाना, कुतरवाना etc.

Interestingly, causative meanings of a few verbs are conveyed through independent words, e.g. जाना - भेजना - भिजवाना, रहना - रखना - रखवाना; आना - लेना/बुलाना - लिवाना, लाना - मँगाना - मँगवाना. See :

(24) नौकर बाज़ार *गया।*

(25) शीला ने नौकर को बाज़ार *भेजा।*

(26) मैंने शीला से नौकर को बाज़ार *भिजवाया।*

2.7.6 Semantic Classification of Causative Verbs

Based on causativisation, the base verbs of Hindi can be classified into four semantic groups:

Base Verbs

Intransitive				**Transitive**
Category 1				Causative 0,2
	सोना		सुलाना	सुलवाना
	बैठना		बिठाना	बिठवाना
	उठना		उठना	उठवाना
	उड़ाना		उड़ाना	उड़वाना
	निकालना		निकालना	निकलवाना
Category 2		खाना	खिलाना	खिलवाना
		पहनना	पहनाना	पहनवाना
		पीना	पिलाना	पिलवाना
		सुनना	सुनाना	सुनवाना
		देखना	दिखाना	दिखवाना
Category 3	(कटना)	काटना		कटवाना/कटाना
	(बनना)	बनाना		बनवाना
	(बिकना)	बेचना		बिकवाना
	(पिटना)	पीटना		पिटवाना
	(पकना)	पकाना		पकवाना
	(धुलना)	धोना		धुलवाना/धुलाना
	(खुलना)	खोलना		खुलवाना
	(होना)	करना		करवाना/कराना
Category 4		खरीदना		खरीदवाना
		गाना		गवाना
		लिखना		लिखवाना/लिखाना
		भेजना		भिजवाना
		देना		दिलवाना/दिलाना

Causative 1-2 denote verbs which can accept first and second causative verbs. Caus. 0,2 denote verbs that can form derived intransitives and second causatives.

Given below is a table of verb categories of causative verbs

Causative Verb Categories (Semantic Classification)

2.7.7 The Formation Process of Causative Verbs

The formation of causative verbs in Hindi normally involves one or more of the following four morphological processes–insertion of a vowel or a consonant, phonemic change, change of consonant and suppletion. In the pages that follow the main elements of this multilayered system are being given in brief.

This table is based on the form-based structure of the causative verbs and not on semantic and syntactic categories like base, derived, intransitive, transitive and first and second causatives. The first form mentioned in the table denotes the form unaffected by the process of causativisation.

Suffix etc.	First form	Second form	Third form	Morphophonemic change
1(-आ,) -वा	उड़-ना	उड़ा-ना	उड़वा-ना	
	चल-ना	चला-ना	चलवा-ना	
	पक-ना	पका-ना	पकवा-ना	
	पहन-ना	पहना-ना	पहनवा-ना	
	सुन-ना	सुना-ना	सुनवा-ना	
	निकल-ना	निकल-ना	निकलवा-ना	inversion
	कट-ना	काट-ना	कटवा-ना	,,
	घूम-ना	घुमा-ना	घुमवा-ना	ऊ - उ
	सूख-ना	सुखा-ना	सुखवा-ना	,,
	रुक-ना	रोक-ना	रुकवा-ना	ऊ - ओ
	खुल-ना	खोल-ना	खुलवा-ना	,,
	जाग-ना	जगा-ना	जगवा-ना	आ - अ

	माँग-ना	मँगा-ना	मँगवा-ना	आ - अ
	बैठ-ना	बिठा-ना	बिठवा-ना	ऐ - इ
	देख-ना	दिखा-ना	दिखवा-ना	ए - इ
	टूट-ना	तोड़-ना	तुड़वा-ना	consonant change
	बिक-ना	बेच-ना	बिकवा-ना	,,
	छूट-ना	छोड़-ना	छुड़वा-ना	,,
	फट-ना	फाड़-ना	फड़वा-ना	,,
(2) -ला, -लवा	कह-ना	कहला-ना	कहलवा-ना	,,
	खा-ना	खिला-ना	खिलवा-ना	आ - ई
	पी-ना	पिला-ना	पिलवा-ना	ई - इ
	सो-ना	सुला-ना	सुलवा-ना	ओ - उ
	दे-ना	दिला-ना	दिलवा-ना	ए - इ
(3) वा	खरीद-ना		खरिदवा-ना	(ई - इ)
	बुला-ना		बुलवा-ना	
(4) ϕ, -वा	बदल-ना	बदल-ना	बदलवा-ना	
	भर-ना	भर-ना	भरवा-ना	
(5) Supple-tion	जा-ना	भेज-ना	भिजवा-ना	
	रह-ना	रख-ना	रखवा-ना	
	आ-ना	बुला-ना/ले-ना	लिवा-ना	
	ला-ना	मँगा-ना	मँगवा-ना	

2.8 Voice

Voice has been basically defined and treated only as a *morphological unit* (i.e. at a word level) in traditional Hindi grammars. *Voice* is basically a part of a syntactic system. It is not only a language specific system but also a language universal system which has semantics as its primary base.

2.8.1 Morphological and Semantic Basis of Voice

Morphologically, voice is said to be a transformation of a verb which tells us whether the sentence is giving prominence to the subject or to the object or to the verb (*भाव*) (Guru 1920). It is on this basis that Hindi grammarians have traditionally provided for three voices: active voice, *passive* voice, and *impersonal voice* (भाव वाच्य). The basic verbal and formal criteria of the passive and impersonal voices in Hindi has been recognized as the addition of the suffix *-या जा-* after the verb root, e.g.

1. Active Voice	(1) नौकर दरवाज़ा *खोल* रहा है।
	(2) बच्चों ने गीत *गाए*।
2. Passive Voice:	(3) दरवाज़ा *खोला जा* रहा है।
	(4) नौकर से दरवाज़ा नहीं *खोला जाता*।
3. Impersonal Voice	(5) ज़मीन पर नहीं *बैठा जाता*।

In Hindi only transitive verbs are capable of forming sentences in the passive voice (e.g. sentence 3-4). Intransitive verbs can, however, form sentences in the impersonal voice (e.g. sentence 5). In the passive sentences the objects (दरवाज़ा and नौकर) are grammatical subjects. There is no object in sentence (5) and, therefore, it is called an *impersonal* voice. Here only the action of the verb (बैठा) is central or dominant.

At a *syntactic* level, the concept of voice is based on a different criterion, called the principle of *mutual dominance* between the subject and the object. It is also called the real world dominance *vs*. the grammatical dominance.

(a) *Real World Dominance* follows the principles of the *real* world in which, according to the laws of the real world, the status of the subject is superior while that of the object is subordinate. At this level the subject is called the logical subject and the object is called the logical object. For instance, in sentence (1) नौकर is a logical subject and दरवाज़ा is a logical object.

(b) *Grammatical Dominance*, in which the dominance of the subject and the verb is not measured on the basis of the facts of the real world but on the capacity of the subject and the object to influence the verb agreement of the sentence. In the case of grammatical dominance there is an additional dimension of the subject's viewpoint or his preferences. The speaker can verbally project the state of the real world the way he wants, in which the logical subject may become a logical object. For instance, in sentence (3-4) दरवाज़ा is a grammatical subject because it controls the verb agreement of the sentence. In sentence (3) the logical subject नौकर is omitted, and in sentence (4) it is followed by the postposition से as a result of which it forfeits its capacity to control the verb agreement.

Hence on the one hand we have the state of the real world and on the other hand the state of the grammatical world. The mutual relationship between the real world and the grammatical world is what is called **voice**. This difference is, however, evident in passive sentences in many ways, for instance the omission of the real world subject from the passive sentences, the marginalization of the subject by being marked by some postposition and the promotion of the real world object into a grammatical subject, etc.(see below 2.8.2 (a-b))

At a *sentence level*, the voice system in Hindi has been classified as under (Ravindranath Srivastava 1983):

1. Active Voice (1) नौकर दरवाज़ा **खोल** रहा है।
   (6) हम ज़मीन पर नहीं **बैठते**।
   (7) मैंने गिलास नहीं **तोड़ा**।
   (8) मैंने गलती **की**।
2. Passive Voice
   (a) Passive
   (3) (i) दरवाज़ा **खोला** जा रहा है।
   (ii) दरवाज़ा **खुल** रहा है।
   (5) ज़मीन पर नहीं **बैठा जाता**।
   (9) (i) गिलास (नहीं) **तोड़ा गया**।
   (ii) गिलास नहीं **टूटा**।
   (b) Incapabilitative
   (4) (i) नौकर से दरवाज़ा नहीं **खोला जाता**।
   (ii) नौकर से दरवाज़ा **नहीं खुलता**।
   (10) हमसे ज़मीन पर नहीं **लेटा जाता**।
   (11) (i) मुझसे गिलास नहीं **तोड़ा गया**।
   (ii) मुझसे गिलास नहीं **टूटा**।

(c) Unintended

(12) मुझसे गिलास टूट गया।

(13) मुझसे गलती हुई।

The following three observations need to be noted about the above classification:

(a) The division of the voice system shown here is binary (active and passive), and not tertiary as shown in traditional Hindi grammar– active, passive and impersonal. The distinctive feature of the passive voice is the *inactiveness* of the subject. As a result of this, there is no possibility of the object or the verb (as a notion) performing any active or dominant role in the sentence. Hence there is no need to have an exclusive category of impersonal voice (i.e. भाववाच्य). Therefore, both the conventional categories of passive voice (कर्मवाच्य) and the impersonal voice (भाववाच्य) have been merged into one as non-active voice (अकर्तृवाच्य) in the above classification. In this sense the Hindi अकर्तृवाच्य is the synonym of the English passive voice.

(b) The passive voice here covers both या-passives (i.e. passives formed by adding -या-जा) as well as derived intransitives (see 2.8.4), e.g.

(3a) दरवाज़ा *खोला जा* रहा है।

(3b) दरवाज़ा *खुल* रहा है।

Amongst the Indian grammarians it was Bajpei (1958) who for the first time pointed out the similarity between these two types of sentences and called both these sentences as अकर्तृक.

(c) The feature <±> intention of the grammatical subject has been for the first time accepted as a basis for the sub-classification of voice (2.8.4) and the unintentional sentences attributed to the grammatical subject (intentional) was for the first time accepted as a norm for the sub-categorization of voice and the unintentional sentences have been recognized as a separate category of the passive voice (e.g. मुझसे गिलास टूट गया, मुझसे गलती हुई).

2.8.2 The Semantic Basis of Voice

The voice system exists in almost all the languages of the world in one form or the other. The two universal features of passives accepted in the universal grammar are: (i) recognized to be the devaluation of the subject, and (ii) the promotion of the object.

(a) *Devaluation of the Subject*: At the level of morphology, the main criterion of passive transformation is the addition of -या जा- in the Hindi verb and at the level of the sentence the dominance of the real world object over the real world subject. In the universal voice system, the devaluation of the subject or the promotion of the object is the only cornerstone of passivisation (Keenan 1974). The demotion of the subject in passive sentences is effected through three ways in Hindi:

First, by deleting the real world subject, as in sentence (3) दरवाजा खोला जा रहा है, दरवाजा खुल रहा है.

Secondly, by placing a postposition after the real world subject thereby detaching it from the main grammatical stream of the sentence. It renders it functionally defunct for the purpose of verb agreement. e.g. sentence (4b) and (14-15):

(14) *बच्चों द्वारा* गीत गाए गए।

(15) इस भवन का उद्घाटन *मंत्री द्वारा* किया गया।

Thirdly, by giving an impression that the verb has no subject and the action is taking place on its own whereas in reality the real world subject is supposed to be performing the action, for instance in certain sentences made from derived intransitives (दरवाज़ा खुल रहा है, मकान बन रहा है).

(b) *Promotion of the Object*: Sometimes the demotion of the subject is accompanied by the promotion of the object into a subject, but this is not the necessary condition of passivisation. The promotion of the object is an independent, optional language process (Keenan 1975, Jagdish Jain 1977). It is not necessary that in the process of passivisation the object must be promoted to the status of a subject. In fact, there is no place for an object in the so-called impersonal sentences made from intransitive sentences, e.g.

(5) ज़मीन पर नहीं बैठा जाता।

(16) अब सोया जाए।

Besides, the object may sometimes even appear marked with the postposition को, e.g.

(17) सभी लोगों को यहीं बुलाया जाए तो अच्छा रहे।

Taking these two criteria as a basis for voice system, we shall examine the following three linguistic processes involved in Hindi voice system – incapabilitative sentences, derived intransitives and unintentional actions and present an overall classification of Hindi voice system.

2.8.3 Incapabilitative sub+से Construction and Passives

Mainly two types of sentence constructions can be obtained in Hindi by using the combination subject + से :

Incapabilitative : *नौकर* से दरवाज़ा नहीं खोला जाता/खुलता। (4)

Unintentional : *मुझसे* गिलास टूट गया। (12)

Incapabilitative sentences beginning with sub+से (4) has been treated as passive voice by most Hindi grammarians mostly because, like all other passives, the verb here also contains the passive marker -या+-जा and secondly by virtue of the subject being marked by the postposition से, it also gets detached from the main grammatical stream of the sentence. And again, it has the potentiality to promote the real world object into a grammatical subject. At a semantic level also there seems to be an element of indirectness in the performance of the action. Despite all these similarities, the subject plus+से sentences cannot be accepted as passive sentences in Hindi for the following reasons:

(a) Incapabilitative sentences with subject + को are acceptable only in negative sentences and not in positive sentences, e.g. नौकर से दरवाज़ा नहीं खोला गया is an acceptable sentence but *नौकर से दरवाज़ा खोला गया is not an acceptable sentence. There is as such no such restriction on the passive voice in the universal grammar. Even at the language specific level in Hindi this restriction does not apply on normal passive sentences where we can have both the positive and negative forms of the sentence, e.g. दरवाज़ा खोला गया (positive), दरवाज़ा नहीं खोला गया (negative). This leads to the conclusion that incapabilitative sentences in Hindi are not passives. If it were, it should have been acceptable both in negative and positive environments.

(b) Incapabilitative sentences with subject + को can also not be said to be the passive form of any active sentence, because the sense of incapability is not present in its active form. Secondly, the passive form of its so called active sentence already exists in the language. See:

Active voice:	नौकर ने दरवाज़ा खोला।	(- incapability)
Passive voice:	दरवाज़ा खोला गया।	(- incapability)
Independent sentence:	नौकर से दरवाज़ा नहीं खोला गया।	(+ incapability)

This leads us to the conclusion that the prefix -या जा -used in the incapabilitative sentences is part of the mood and not the voice (see 2.10.4).

(c) It is important to determine whether the sense of incapability expressed in the subject + से type sentences is inherent in the postposition से used after the subject or the verb form -या जा -or in their combined use. In the following two sentences *-नौकर से दरवाज़ा नहीं खोला जाता-* and *-नौकर से दरवाज़ा नहीं खुलता-* the sense of incapability is equally evident in both the sentences and, therefore, it will not be proper to say that the sense of incapability is because of the verb form -या जा-. On the contrary, there is a sense of incapability in the sentence मुझसे ज़मीन पर नहीं बैठा जाता but in the subject-less sentence *-ज़मीन पर नहीं बैठा जाता-* there is no expression of the sense of incapability. Hence in sentences like this the sense of incapability can be said to resting with the postposition से. (For the use of subject + से in the sense of unintentional activity, see 2.8.5) Hence it is not proper to consider subject + से sentences as passives.

2.8.4 Derived Intransitive and Passive Voice

We have already discussed about the nature, formation and

syntactic functions of derived intransitives in 2.7.4d. We have seen that the derived intransitives are derived from base transitive verbs (see 2.7.6) and they express actions which necessarily require the participation of two characters (the subject and the object) for their execution in the real world but occur in the sentences in such a way as if they do not have any subject (agent) and the action is taking place on its own, e.g. खुलना, धुलना, काटना, बनाना etc.

There are many common features between the sentences formed through the derived intransitives and those formed through जा- passives, namely: (**a**) in both the sentences the demotion of the real world subject is effected through a process of omission and the object is promoted to the position of the subject. For instance, the omission of the real world subject नौकर in the sentence दरवाज़ा खोला जा रहा है and the promotion of the real world object into a grammatical subject in the sentence दरवाज़ा खुल रहा है, **(b)** Both these sentences can be transformed into incapabilitative sentences by the use of the subject + से construction e.g. नौकर से दरवाज़ा नहीं खोला जाता, नौकर से दरवाज़ा नहीं खुलता. **(c)** In both these sentences there is a sense of indirectness in the execution of the action.

There are also some significant differences between the sentences formed through the derived intransitives and those formed through जा-passives, namely:

(a) The addition of the suffix -या जा- after the main verb in passive sentences is a grammatical device in Hindi for converting the verb into the passive form (e.g. पहनाया जा रहा है). On the other hand the (derived) intransitivisation is a lexical device which is achieved through a morphophonemic process. Grammatical device is a part of the auxiliary verb of the verb phrase while the lexical device is part of the main verb (see 2.3.6).

(b) Even when the subject is missing from the जा-passive sentences, it conveys the sense that the action is being executed by some agent (an active subject) (see 3.5.3a), though it's mention in the surface structure of the sentence is considered unnecessary or secondary. On the other hand, the intransitivised passive sentences lead you to believe that the action is taking place on its own without the help of any subject, that is, the sentence gives no indication of any actor or subject whereas in real world there does exist a subject or doer.

(c) Almost all or most transitive verbs can form जा-passives, but only a few transitive action verbs can have their intransitivised forms. For instance, transitive verbs like लिखना, पढ़ना etc. can not have their intransitivised forms. जा-passives can, however, be formed from intransitive verbs also (e.g. (5) ज़मीन पर नहीं बैठा जाता, (12) अब सोया जाए, but the intransitive verbs cannot form their derived forms (बैठना, > *बिठना), सोना > *सुलना)

(d) The object of the verb in जा-passives can sometimes be marked by some postposition, but the object (i.e. the grammatical subject) of the derived intransitive verb always remains unmarked, e.g. sentences like ऊपर वाले दरवाज़े को खोला जा रहा है, रामू को पीटा जा रहा है, सभी लोगों को यहीं बुला लिया जाए are acceptable but sentence like *ऊपर दरवाज़े को खोल रहा, *रामू को पीट रहा है are not acceptable.

(e) The real world subject can, however, appear in the sentence alongwith the postposition द्वारा in the जा-passive sentences (sentence 14-15), but it is not possible in the derived intransitive sentences (e.g. *नौकर द्वारा दरवाज़ा खुल रहा है).

Despite these formal differences, the derived intransitive verbs possess all the tenets of the passive voice: the demotion of the subject through the process of omission, the promotion of the object into the grammatical subject, the existence of the passive form and the indirectness of the meaning. Hence the derived intransitives can be accepted as a second passive in Hindi.

2.8.5 Unintentional Actions and Passive Voice

When an animate subject is followed by the postposition से and the verb is a derived intransitive in a non-negative (i.e. positive) environment), the action denoted is generally an unintended or unintentional one, e.g. मुझसे गिलास टूट गया (sentence 12), मुझसे गलती हुई

(sentence 13). (In negative environment the corresponding sentences denote incapability e.g. sentence 4b, 11b). An *unintentional* action is one which the animate subject does not do consciously but which gets done accidentally or by mistake (see sentence 42b).

Based on the transitivity structure, the unintended actions can be put into two categories: (a) involuntary force and (b) *natural force*.

(a) Involuntary force: It refers to actions which are performed by an animate subject but involuntarily or by mistake, e.g. (12) मुझसे गिलास टूट गया, चाकू से उँगली कट गई. Both मैं and चाकू here are involuntary force. Both employ the postposition से which technically stands for an instrumental case.

(b) Natural Force (Halliday 1970 :148): It refers to actions which take place on their own as a force of nature without human intention or intervention. (see sub-pattern 29d, 42b). See:

(18) *पानी से* कागज़ फूल गया।

(19) *हवा से* दरवाज़ा खुल गया।

(20) *धूप से* घी पिघल गया।

पानी, हवा and धूप in these sentences appear to be an instrumental case in the surface structure but technically they cannot be called instrumental case because behind an instrumental case there is an intention of an animate subject or agent which makes the action intentional and not unintentional. For instance, चाबी in sentences (21-22) is an instrumental case:

(21) मैंने इस *चाबी से* दरवाज़ा खोला।

(22) इस *चाबी से* दरवाज़ा खुल गया।

There is sometimes a structural confusion between the intended and unintended action in Hindi because it uses the postposition से both for intended and unintended action while in many languages there are different postpositions and markers for them. For instance, English uses the preposition *with* in the context of intended and *by* in the context of unintended, e.g.

The door was opened *with* this key. (intrument)

The glass was broken *by* the ball. (natural force)

Not all verbs can, however, make sentences involving intentional and unintentional actions. Only verbs denoting desirable and undesirable actions in real life can form sentences involving intentional and unintentional sentences, e.g. गलती होना, टूटना, फूटना, फटना, गिरना, चोट लगना, कटना etc. This is the reason why sometimes the active voice of the unintentional sentences becomes ambiguous, e.g.

(23) मैंने गिलास तोड़ दिया।

Sense (i) मैंने स्वेच्छा से गिलास तोडा।

(ii) मुझसे गलती से गिलास टूट गया।

Actions which are neither basically undesirable acts nor can they be executed without the will of the subject cannot normally make unintentional sentences, e.g. लुटना, धुलना, बिकना, सुलझना can not normally make unintensional sentences, e.g. *मुझसे मकान बिक गया.

Since an unintentional action is one of the actions denoted by the derived intransitives sentences, it has been included under derived intransitives.

2.8.6 Classification of Voice in Hindi

Based on the above discussion, the voice system in Hindi can be classified as follows:

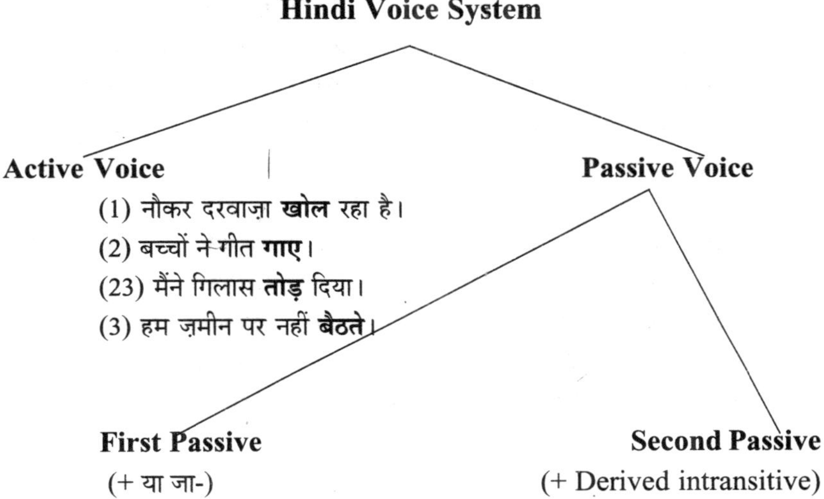

(3) दरवाज़ा **खोला जा** रहा है। (3b) दरवाज़ा **खुल** रहा है (intentional)
(14) बच्चों द्वारा गीत **गाए गए**। (12) मुझसे गिलास **टूट** गया (unintentional)
(5) ज़मीन पर नहीं **बैठा जाता**। (19) हवा से दरवाज़ा **खुल गया** (unintentional)

Note: The incapabilitative sentence subject + से is passive only at the level of structure and not meaning (see 2.10.4).

2.9 Aspect

2.9.1 Defining Aspect

Simply speaking, the form of a verb which gives us the perception of the beginning, the progress and the completion of an action or its habitual or non-habitual nature or periodicity is called *aspect,* e.g

(1) सूरज पूरब से *निकलता* है। (habitual nature, universal truth)
(2) बाहर बारिश ***हो रही*** है। (the continuity of the action)
(3) राघव देर से घर *लौटा*। (the completion of the action)

The verb of Hindi sentence (1) has three constituents: निकल + -ता + है. Out of these, निकल is a verb which denotes the action; -ता is an aspect marker (suffix) which gives the perception of its habitual or repetitive nature. The second component है is an auxiliary verb which denotes the present tense and is called the present tense marker.

In the following English sentence (4) the aspect marker -s is used to denote the habitual nature of the action. -ing is used along with the present tense marker *is*. In sentence (5) the suffix *-ed* is added to the verb denoting the perfective aspect.

The three corresponding sentences in English below also have their aspectual suffixes -s, -ing and -ed after the verb:

(4) The sun ris**es** from the east. (-s) habitual/simple present
(5) It is rain**ing** outside. (-ing) continuous/progressive
(6) Raghav return**ed** home late. (-ed) perfective

Aspect

Habitual	Continuous/progressive)	Perfective
-ता है (-s/-es)	रहा है (-ing)	-या/आ (-ed)
लौटता है (returns)	*लौट रहा है (is returning)*	*लौटा (returned)*

It may be remembered that aspect as such has not been included as an independent constituent or a grammatical category of a verb form in the traditional Hindi grammar. This constituent of the verb form has been supposed to be included indirectly in the tense. For example, according to Kamata Prasad Guru, tense is that form of a verb which tells about the time of the action and the status of its completion or non-completion, e.g. मैं जाता हूँ (present tense), मैं जाता था (imperfect past tense), मैं जाऊँगा (future tense). There has been a tradition of treating the aspect constituent of the verb as an overall part of the verb not only in Hindi but in almost all languages of the world. An independent concept of aspect as a separate grammatical category and its study started only three decades ago though its grammatical existence by some other name is found in German and Russian languages. Despite this the aspect is more fundamental, more ancient and more comprehensive in the languages of the world. It is, therefore, necessary to briefly examine the interrelationship between the aspect, tense and time.

2.9.2 Aspect, Tense and Time

Aspect and tense are the two dimensions of an action which exists only in the language and not outside the language. The tense outside the grammar is called *time* –the real world time. In the real world, every action takes place at a certain point on the surface of time. When we describe this action in the language in a time perspective, we consider the time of the utterance as the reference point and accordingly place the action into the artificial time divisions of present, past and future. It is artificial because time in the real world is a continuous and indivisible stream in which what is present today becomes tomorrow the next day today. This time of reference is called the *zero point of utterance* (Lyons 1977:682) and the time slabs divided on this basis are called the *grammatical tense* (2.11). This is not the real-world time but is a grammatical time perception which caters to the time related grammatical needs of the language. It is, therefore, possible that one single action may be seen in three different tense forms from three different reference points. For instance, while from the reference point of 1948 we could make an acceptable sentence 'पंडित जवाहर लाल नेहरू भारत के प्रधानमंत्री **हैं**.' but from the reference point of 1982 we will express the same fact like this 'पंडित जवाहर लाल नेहरू भारत के प्रधानमंत्री **थे**.'

It is not necessary that all actions should be necessarily assigned a time frame and assigned the reference points of present, past and future. Every action has its own *temporal constituency* or time territory which spreads from the beginning of the action up to its end. This is generally referred to as the internal temporal constituency of the situation. We may view an action with reference to its internal temporal constituency also. *The perception of this temporal constituency of the action is known as* **aspect.** This perception is unbound by time (काल निरपेक्ष) in which neither the zero point of utterance is important nor the time divisions. It only makes you aware of some stage of the accomplishment or un-accomplishment of the action and not of where did the action take place in the real world. It is another thing that because of the completion or non-completion of the action we mentally tend to associate it with the past and the present which can appear on the surface structure of time with or without the desired tense marker depending on the rules of the aspect and tense system of the language. For instance, the verb लिखी in the sentence रमेश ने चिट्ठी लिखी, the verb form लिखी denotes the sense of the completion of the action which we normally associate with the past tense. In Hindi, however, it is possible to have its tense-free usage (i.e. without है or था etc.) , but in sentence like रमेश चिट्ठी लिखता है or लिख रहा है, the use of the tense marker है, था etc. is mandatory. It for this reason that some linguists like Shrivastav (1973) consider लिखी as a tense-free aspect though some others (Guru,

Ashok Kelkar) consider it a tense-based marker and place it in the category of Simple Past.

2.9.3 Developmental Concept of Aspect

The notion of aspect has undergone some drastic changes during the last few decades. Comerie (1976:3) defines aspect as *the different ways of viewing the internal temporal constituency of a situatition.* This definition directly or indirectly underlines two statements:

(a) The aspect covers only the internal time space or *temporal territory* of the action starting from its beginning to the end. This means that any part of the action which falls beyond this internal territory is not a part of aspect.

(b) This interpretation of aspect is basically event based. In other words, the action or event should actually take place in the real world and not in the realm of probability, resolution, wish or imagination. The perception of the aspect is therefore, relevant only about those actions which are happening or which must have happened in the real world. Actions which have not happened in the real world or are still in the mind of the speaker (as a wish, probability or resolution) do not form part of the *aspect* (but of the *mood* (see 2.10). For instance, in the sentence शायद आज गाड़ी देर से आए the verb form आए is indicative of mood and not aspect, because the sentence does not denote an action of the real world.

Modern linguists now present the *developmental interpretation* of aspect. *Aspect* is now seen not in the context of an action or event but in the context of an action passing through some clear developmental stages (Johnson 1981:152). In these developmental stages of the event not only the actual internal 'temporal constituency' of the event but also the fringe zones immediately before and after the event are included which are likely to influence the aspectual perception of the event. For instance, see the different dimensions of the aspect:

-ने वाला है	(वह खाने वाला है)
-ने को है	(वह खाने को है)
-ने जा रहा है	(वह खाने जा रहा है)

The following diagram illustrates the linear development of the aspect and its three dimensions - *anterior*, *simultaneous* and *posterior*, in which the *simultaneous* represents the zero point of utterance time. It can be illustrated as follows:

The three dimensions of aspect

⊙ ————————→ ⊙ ————————→ ⊙

anterior simultaneous posterior

Based on these parameters, the aspects represented by the following markers have been included under auxiliary aspect markers: -ने को है, -ने जा रहा है, -ने लग, चुक and रख etc. though they do not follow the traditional norms of aspect.

2.9.4 The Time Texture of Aspect

The dimension of the aspect which we discussed above is linear in the sense that they go on adding segments quantitatively one after another. The aspect has yet another dimension which builds up the internal time texture

The time texture of the aspect indicates as to how the various segments of the action are connected with the time segments so that we have time related notions like duration, frequency and periodicity etc. which form the texture of the aspect i.e. whether the action is punctual or durative, whether it occurs only once or more frequently, whether it is a one-time action or frequentative, whether it is stative (denoting state) or process-based, whether it is related to the perception of an achievement or an accomplishment, etc. All these are the deep level features of the aspect which lend some depth and distinctness to the notion of aspect. This dimension of the aspect is not linear but hierarchical. For instance, the two aspect forms पढ़ता है and पढ़ा करता है have a basic semantic similarity (i.e. habitualness), yet a very precise semantic distinction or nuance differentiates the perception of these two forms. For instance the following five sentences basically denote a continuous aspect yet, there is a very subtle difference among the aspectual perceptions of each of them:

1. वह पढ़ *रहा* है।

2. वह पढ़ता *आ रहा* है।

3. वह पढ़ता *जा रहा* है।

4. वह पढ़ता *चला आ रहा* है।

5. वह पढ़ता *चला जा* रहा है।

The perception of the aspect is sometimes quantified or delimited by certain adverbs which accompany them. Such adverbs are called *aspect quantifiers*. For instance, adverbs रोज़, हमेशा, अक्सर, कभी-कभी have a strong tendency to be used with the habitual aspect –ता because these adverbs basically denote the expansion of time, e.g. सतीश रोज़ अंग्रेज़ी अखबार पढ़ता है. Aspect markers of this category are called *linear* adverbs because they occur in a *linear* sequence.

Punctual verbs, on the contrary, are often associated with adverbs which denote a specific point of time or moment, (इसी क्षण, तीन बजे etc.,) e.g. वह तीन बजे स्टेशन पहुँचा. Abverbs that quantify such verbs are called *punctual* adverbs. Similarly there are *frequentative* verbs like खटखटाना, बड़बड़ाना etc. in which the element of frequency is inbuilt in the format of the verb itself, but sometimes such verbs may give double meanings also, e.g.

मैंने *तीन बार* आपका दरवाजा *खटखटा*या।

Meaning 1 : three times at one time

Meaning 2 : at three different times

Sometimes the use of tense markers (है, था etc.) also makes some difference in the aspect. See:

(7) मैं पैदल स्कूल *जाता हूँ।* (habitual, frequent)

(8) प्यार अंधा *होता है।* (universal truth)

(9) मैं पैदल स्कूल *जाता था।* (past, frequent)

(10) वह अपनी पत्नी को बहुत *चाहता था।* (past, extension of state)

Despite the present tense marker है, the -ता है form in sentences (7-8) is free of any time boundary. Hence the verb form -ता है can take any meaning – habitual, class, universal, or axiomatic depending upon the context, e.g. sentence 7-8, but in the verb form -ता था of sentences 9-10, the time period is specified i.e. past. Hence no universal or axiomatic meaning can be derived from this verb-form –ता था.

2.9.5 Basic and Auxiliary Aspect Markers

(a) Basic Aspect Markers

(a) Habitual

-ता + रह-	वह पढ़ता रहता है।
-या + रह-	वह सोया रहता है।
-या + कर-	वह सोया करता है।

(b) Progressive

-ता + चल-	वह पढ़ता चलेगा।
-ता + जा-	वह पढ़ता जाएगा।
-ता + आ-	वह पढ़ता आ रहा है।
-ता + चला + आ-/जा-	वह पढ़ता चला आ रहा है।
	वह पढ़ता चला जा रहा है।

(c) Completive

-ϕ + चुक-	वह खा चुका है।
-ϕ + रख-	उसने खा रखा है।

(d) Inceptive

-ने + लग-	वह खाने लगा।

(e) Ingressive

-ने वाला (है)	वह खाने वाला है।
-ने को (है)	वह खाने को है।
-ने जा रह-	वह खाने जा रहा है।
-या चाह-	दस बजा चाहते हैं।

A common characteristic of the perfect, imperfect and continuous aspects mentioned above is that they are represented in the verb by some suffixes (—या, —ता, —रहा) which are attached to some verb-forms, e.g. खाया, देखा, जाता, जा रहा etc.) Aspect markers of this category are called the **basic aspect markers**. [रहा, however, is technically not a suffix, but loosely for the convenience of categorization it has been included under aspect markers]. The basic aspect markers occur as a last constituent of the verb phrase or just before the tense marker (है, था etc.).

(b) Auxiliary Aspect Markers

Not all the basic aspect markers are, however, able to express the various dimensions of the aspect. Some aspectual elements or characteristics are expressed through certain other markers which even while being a part of the verb phrase are distributionally different from the basic aspect markers, e.g. —या कर-, -ता रह-, -ने लग-, चुक- etc. (मैं उन दिनों पैदल स्कूल *आया करता* था, तभी बारिश *होने लगी*, मैं चाय पी *चुका* हूँ). Aspect markers of this category are called **auxiliary aspect markers.**

Auxiliary aspect markers are always used before the basic aspect markers or modal suffixes. Like the basic aspect markers, they can not be used as the last constituent of the verb phrase or before the tense markers. Seen aspectually, the auxiliary aspect markers qualitatively affect the meaning of the basic aspect markers or highlight some specific aspect of the completeness or incompleteness of the action.

In sentences where both the basic aspect markers and the auxiliary aspect markers express similar or almost similar aspects, it becomes sometimes difficult to comprehend the basic meaning even in the absence of auxiliary aspect markers e.g.

वह कई साल से *पढ़ रहा है* : वह कई साल *से पढ़ता आ रहा है।*

हम रोज़ पैदल *जाते थे* : हम रोज़ पैदल *जाया करते थे।*

However, in cases where there is a difference between the perception of the aspects as denoted by the basic aspect marker and that denoted by the auxliary aspect markers, the use of auxiliary aspect markers is inevitable, e.g.

(1) हम साथ *खाया करेंगे।* *(repetition + future)*

(2) *वह पढ़ता गया।* *(progressive + completion)*

(3) शायद वह तब तक पहुँच *चुका हो।* (completion + probablity)

(4) चल*ते रहो।* (continuity + imperative)

2.9.5 (a) BASIC ASPECT MARKERS (-या, -ता, रहा)

Basic aspect markers are those markers that are represented in the verb through some suffixes which are attached to some verb form, e.g. खाया, देखा, जाता, जा रहा etc.). The basic aspect markers occur in the sentence as the last constituent of the verb phrase or just before the tense marker (है, था etc.). See examples:

(a) Perfective Aspect (aspective suffix (0) रमेश **दौड़ा**.

(b) Habitual Aspect (aspective suffix -त-) सूरज पूरब से निकल**ता** है.

(c) Continuous Aspect (aspective suffix रह-) लड़का खेल **रहा** है.

[Where there is no need to show precise distinction among these aspects, these suffixes have been shown as -'या', -'ता', and 'रहा' respectively in the book for the sake of convenience.]

It is, however, important to remember that these suffixes do not necessarily represent only these designated aspects or functions. If you examine their use at the level of discourse and pragmatics, you may find that all these three aspect markers many a time deviate from their designated functions and transgress the areas of other aspects or moods. See:

a.

(1)	मैं अभी-अभी **आया**।	(perfective aspect)
(2)	(तुम रुको) मैं अभी **आया**।	(immediate future)
(3)	अगर बारिश **हुई** तो मैं नहीं आऊँगा।	(contingent mood)

b.

(4)	वह पैदल जा **रहा** है।	(continuous aspect)
(5)	वह कल पैदल जा **रहा** है।	(future)
(6)	*वह कल खाँस **रहा** है।	

c.

(7)	सूरज पूरब से निकल**ता** है।	(habitual)
(8)	तभी घंटी बजती है और दरवाजा खुल**ता** है।	(past)
(9)	अगर घंटी बजती तो मैं जरूर **जाता**।	(conditional mood)
(10)	अच्छा मैं चल**ता** हूँ।	(future/ continuous)

2.9.5 (b) AUXILIARY ASPECT MARKERS

As already mentioned, auxiliary aspect markers are always used before the basic aspect markers or the tense markers and are never used as the last constituent of the verb phrase or before the tense markers.

Given below is the functional classification of the auxiliary aspect markers of Hindi. This classification takes into consideration the classification presented by Ramanath Sahay (1978:20-33) based on the theory of aspect as propounded by Comerie (1976).

(a) Habitual

-ता + रह-	वह पढ़ता **रह**ता है।
-या+ रह-	वह **सोया रह**ता है।
-या+ कर	वह **सोया कर**ता है।

(b) Progressive

-ता चल-	वह **पढ़ता चलेगा**।
-ता जा-	वह **पढ़ता जायेगा**।
-ता आ-	वह **पढ़ता आ** रहा है।
-ता+चला+आ-/जा-	वह **पढ़ता चला जा** रहा है।

(c) Completive

-0 +चुक-	वह खा **चुका** है।
-0 +रख-	उसने खा **रखा** है।

(d) Inceptive

-ने लग-	वह खा**ने लगा**।

(e)Ingressive

-ने वाला है	वह खा**ने वाला** है।
-ने को है	वह खा**ने को** है।
-ने जा रह-	वह खा**ने जा रहा** है।
-या चाह	दस ब**जा चाह**ते हैं।

2.9.6 Major Auxiliary Aspect Markers

Aspect markers are semantically very sensitive, they often convey subtle meanings and nuances not generally expressed through simple lexical words. See, for instance, the following sentences:

(1) वह शराब *पीता रहता* है। : वह पीया रहता है।

(2) वह पैदल स्कूल *जाता* था। : वह पैदल स्कूल जाया करता था।

(3) गाड़ी छूटने वाली है। : गाड़ी छूटने को है।

(4) मैं खाना खा चुका हूँ। : *मैं खाना नहीं खा चुका हूँ।

(5) हम यहाँ कई सालों से पूजा *कर रहे* हैं। : हम यहाँ कई सालों से पूजा *करते आ रहे* हैं।

The linguistic behavior of some major auxiliary verbs and their subtle semantic roles in the sentence are being explained below:

(i) -या रह- : The -या component in the aspect marker –या रह denotes the resultant state of the event or action and the element रह gives the perception of a comparatively longer period or time expansion. Joined together, -या रह gives the sense of the event or action spreading over a longer period of time, e.g. मोहन दिन भर *लेटा रहता* है.

There are, however, certain collocational restrictions on the use of -या रह- with the main (i.e. lexical) verb. The use of -या रह is possible only in *state-ending* verbs. The *state-ending verbs* are those that denote actions which ultimately end in a state and not process. [Here the state-ending verbs should be taken as partially different from the state verbs of Lakoff (1966)* from the point of view of scope and coverage.

Contrary to this, verbs लिखना and दौड़ना etc. are process-ending verbs (see below) and not state-ending and so it is not possible to use या-रह along with this (sentence 4-5). See:

(1) मोहन दिन भर *लेटा रहता* है. (state-ending)
(2) दुकानें बहुत देर तक *खुली* रहीं . (state-ending)
(3) गीता हमेशा लाल साड़ी पहने रहती है. (state-ending)
(4) *वह दिन भर *लिखा* रहता है. (unacceptable) (process-ending)
(5) *लड़की अकसर *दौड़ी रहती* है. (unacceptable) (process-ending)

It should be noted that in such an environment if the state-ending verbs happen to be transitive, the verb form –या will change into –ए ending i.e. the verb form पहना will become पहने as in sentence (3). Similarly the verb पीया becomes पिए in the sentence वह हमेशा पिए रहता है.

Since the verb form -या रह- is associated with the perception of duration or time, it is possible to use a durative verb but not a punctual

---

*State-ending verbs can be basically state verbs as well as process verbs, but on the completion of the process or event it must end in a resultant state. बैठा, लेटे, सोना, खुलना, पहनना etc. are state-ending verbs, because after the first action of lying, opening or wearing, the stage of remaning lying, open or wearing continues (sentence 1-3).

verb. For instance, पाना, टकराना, अनुभव करना, समझना, पता करना etc. are *punctual* verbs and, therefore, they cannot be used with -या रह- e.g. वह कार से *टकराया *रहा*.

It is important to note that the verb construction made up of -या रहा can be interpreted in two ways depending upon the context or the intention of the speaker – a constituent of the verb phrase or an adjective phrase used as a complement. In the second case, a constituent हुआ can be optionally used after it, e.g. सोया (हुआ) and the function of रह is equivalent to a copula verb है (see sentence sub-pattern 14) :

Interpretation 1 वह x सोया रहता है.

Interpretation 2 वह x सोया (हुआ) x रहता है.

(ii) -ता रह- : The -ता constituent occurring in the auxiliary aspect marker -ता रह- gives the sense of repetition or infinity of the action or event and when it is combined with the durative रह-, it gives a perception of a frequentative time spread, as in the sentence वह दिन भर लिखता रहता है.

Here also, there are certain specific collocational restrictions for its usage in the company of certain lexical (main) verbs. The use of -ता रह- is possible only in the company of process-ending* verbs and not the state-ending verbs. The *process-ending verbs* are verbs which denote actions which remain process from the beginning of the action till its end and do not convert into a resultant state.

All such verbs are necessarily process verbs, but not all process verbs are process-ending verbs (e.g. पहनना). लिखना, डाँटना, देखना, हँसना, दौड़ना, रोना etc. are process-ending verbs. If a person does the action of weeping, writing or running for five minutes, he is doing this action every moment through out the five minutes and the moment the process stops, the action of weeping, writing or running comes to an end. In other words it does not end into the resultative state unlike the state-

*Process-ending verbs can be compared with Vendler's notion of 'activity', according to whom, activities are those processes that go in time in a homogenous way : any part of the process is of the same nature as the whole (1961:101)]

ending verb लेटना in which after the first action of lying, the resultant state of remaining lying continues. See:

(6) वह दिन भर लिख**ता** (*लिखा) रहता है। (process-ending)

(7) मैं आधे घंटे तक दौड़**ता** रहा। (process-ending)

A few verbs are capable of being used in both the categories of verbs: state-ending as well as process-ending, with some minor differences in their aspectual meaning and, can therefore, accept both the aspect markers -या रह as well as -ता रह, e.g.

(8) a- वह दिन भर **बैठा** रहता है। (state)

b- वह बार-बार **बैठता रह**ता है। (frequency)

(9) a- जग्गू हमेशा **पिये रह**ता है। (state)

b- जग्गू हमेशा **पीता रह**ता है। (frequency)

Some process-ending transitive verbs can be transformed into state-ending verbs. In such a situation it is possible to use the aspect marker -या रह along with them, e.g.

(10) आपका नाम सूची में लिखा (हुआ) रहेगा.

Please note that here 'लिखा' functions as a complementary adjective phrase in which the use of हुआ is only optional, for we can have the same sentence as 'आपका नाम सूची में लिखा रहेगा'.

(iii) -या कर- :

We had seen earlier that the habitual aspect marker -ता denotes an action which is repetitive in nature or continuous for an indefinite period, but when we have to highlight the habitual or repetitive aspect of the action as a nature or habit of the subject, we have to use another auxiliary aspect marker -या कर- . Compare:

(1) मैं पैदल स्कूल *जाता था।* (habitual/repetitive)

(2) मैं पैदल स्कूल *जाया करता* था। (extension of habit/repetitive)

Normally the characteristic feature of the habitual aspect is repetition, continuity and sequence, but the actions which are related to physical and mental state, the features of repetition, continuity or sequence can not be imposed as we do for the frequentative or process-based actions. Hence we shall have to add one more feature in the habitual aspect -the extension of the duration of the state which is different from the feature of frequency or repetitiveness. For instance, in the following sentences (3-4) the verbs चाहना and होना denote a longish extension of the state of चाहना and होना and not the frequency or the repetitiveness of the action:

(3) वह अपनी पत्नी को बहुत *चाहता था/चाहा करता था।* (used to)

(4) यहाँ एक मंदिर *होता था/हुआ करता था।* (used to)

In addition to the perception of the expansion of state, there is also an important perception of distance in time which is normally towards the past (but sometimes future also). In such contexts the aspect marker -या कर gives the perception of a state of period spread over a long time back (or sometimes *far distant in future*) which implies that this state or fact is not true in the present time. Compare:

(2) मैं पैदल स्कूल *जाया करता* था। (+ distant past + repetitive)

(5) यहाँ एक मंदिर *हुआ करता* था। (+ distant past + expansion of state)

(6) यहाँ एक मंदिर *हुआ करेगा।* (+ distant future + expansion of state)

It needs to be noted that in certain contexts both the aspect markers can replace each other without harming the meaning or intent, e.g. मैं पैदल स्कूल जाता था/जाया करता था, but in certain contexts there are certain collocational restrictions in their usage. Generally, in the context of an inanimate subject, the use of -या कर- in the present tense is rare or less appropriate, e.g.

(8) यह पंप पानी *खींचा करता* है। (- volition)

(9) आजकल वह कुएँ से पानी *लाया करता* है। (+ volition)

One important difference between the basic aspect marker -ता and the auxiliary aspect marker -या कर needs to be noted. The aspect marker -ता is capable of denoting the perception of a habitual action with reference to the present and the past, but the aspect marker –या कर is capable of denoting not only the perception of the past, present and future, but also of various moods, e.g.

(10) a- मैं ठंडा दूध *पिऊँगा।* (+ once, + future)

b- मैं ठंडा दूध *पिया करूँगा।* (+ repetitive, + future)

(11) a- काली स्याही *से लिखिए।* (+ once, + imperative)

b- काली स्याही से *लिखा कीजिए।* (+ repetitive, + imperative)

The sentences (10a) and (11a) which refer to single events when not bound by time and space can also denote the sense of repetitive action in an appropriate context, e.g. मैं अब से ठंडा दूध पिऊंगा and हमेशा काली स्याही से लिखिए.

(iv) – ता-, -आ/ जा- : As already mentioned above, the basic aspect marker 'रहा' indicates that the action is incomplete and is continuing (वह पढ़ रहा है). The auxiliary aspect marker –ता-, -आ/ जा- (वह पढ़ता चला आ/जा रहा है) also denotes the same perception but with two additional features. The first feature is the relatively longer period of the continued action from the starting time of the action to its reference time. Consequently, while it is possible to use durative adverbs along with these aspect markers, it is not possible to use punctual adverbs along with them. See:

(1) वह कई सालों से *पढ़ता आ रहा* है। (durative)

(1a) वह [*इस समय /*अभी] *पढ़ता आ रहा* है। (*punctual)

The second feature is inherent in the aspect markers आ- and जा-. Though in these two constituents there is the perception of the action taking place, continuing in the past, present and future, but even then our attention is focused on the action taking place some where in between the reference time and some earlier (past) point of time. Similarly in the aspect form –ता जा- our attention is focused on the action taking place on or after the time of reference (future). आ- is a past directional constituent and –जा is a future-oriented constituent. This is the reason why -ता आ- is compatible with past related adverbs (बहुत पहले से, घंटों से, विशिष्ट तिथि/समय/से, etc) and –ता जा is compatible with future oriented adverbs (तीन दिन\तक, कब तक, बाद तक etc.). Note the natural and unnatural usages of sentences (2) and (3):

(2) वह कई सालों से पढ़ता *आ* रहा है। (natural)

(2a) वह कई सालों से पढ़ता *जा* रहा है। (unnanatural)

(3) तुम कब तक *पढ़ते जाओगे* ? (nanatural)

(3a) तुम कब तक *पढ़ते आओगे* ? (unnatural)

(v) -ता चल-, -ता चला आ-/जा- : The existence of the constituent चल- in the auxiliary aspect markers here gives an additional depth and intensity to the perception of continuity and gradual progression. What is in focus here is the perception of the continuity of the process of reading for a longer period and its uninterrupted progress. That is the reason the use of durative adverbs denoting shorter periods appears incompatible in this context, e.g. *वह अभी कल से ही पढ़ता चला आ रहा है.

Contrary to this, in constructions like ऐसा होता चला आया है or लोग यहाँ फूल चढ़ाते चले आ रहे हैं there is an inherent indication of an elongated action or tradition even without the use of any durative adverb. In a sentence like वह बढ़ता *चला जाएगा* there is a strong perception of the action moving ahead more speedily and without interruption.

Similarly, in the sentence वह पढ़ता चला जा रहा है, the addition of चल gives the additional perception of speediness and uninterrupted progress. Needless to say, here also the aspect marker –ता चला जा- is future oriented.

The constituent चल- in the aspect marker –ता चल- also gives an additional perception of dynamic progression (वह पढ़ता चलेगा). The lexical verb चल is an inclusive verb. For instance, in the sentence चलिए there is a perception that both (the speaker and the hearer) should go.

vi) -चुक- : The auxiliary aspect marker -चुक - (वह खाना खा चुका है) and the basic aspect marker -या both in a way denote the completion of the action but in चुक the completion of the action is seen as the completion of a complete process consisting of a beginning, middle and end within the internal temporal constituency. In the basic aspect marker -या, the action is seen from outside its temporal constituency and as a complete single unit of events.

The aspect marker -या can also be used without the tense markers (है, था etc.) because it is not necessary for it to be linked to any reference time, e.g. उसने रेडियो खरीदा, but the auxiliary aspect marker चुक- demands a tense marker (है, था etc.) because it denotes that the action has taken place and ended even before the time of utterance and is thus remains linked to some reference time. For instance, वह खाना खा चुका है is a natural sentence. The sentence वह खाना खा चुका is relevant only when it is linked to some other sentence, वह खाना खा चुका तब मैं पहुँचा. If it is not linked with some sentence it may be taken differently as a metaphorical sentence, e.g. वह (तो अब) खाना खा चुका ! (=वह अब खाना नहीं खा पाएगा).

The use of चुक is not possible in negative, imperative and continuous sentences (sentence 1-3). Its negative use is possible only if the sentence occurs as a contextualized sentence (4). Similarly, the use of चुक is not permitted with a compound verb also (sentence 5). See:

(1) *मैं खाना नहीं खा चुका। (negative)
(2) *खाना खा चुको। (imperative)
(3) *मैं खाना खा चुक रहा हूँ। (continuous)
(4) अगर वह जा न चुकी हो तो उसे रुकवा लेना।(contextualized, negative)
(5) *मैं आपकी बात भूल जा चुका हूँ। (compound verb))

चुक does not accept the subject + ने construction, that is, if the aspect marker चुक is used, even the transitive verbs lose their capacity to use subject + ने construction e.g.

(5) मैंने खाना खाया - मैं खाना खा चुका हूँ।

(vii) रख- : The perception of the completion of the action denoted by चुक is only one phase of the process of the action. The auxiliary aspect marker रख represents the final stable status of the action and not the process. In the sentence मैंने यह फिल्म देख रखी है, the perception is not focused on any segment of the process (like completion) but on the resultative state of the film having been seen. This state is much closer to the stable state denoted by the perfect participle देखी हुई in a sentence like यह फिल्म *मेरी देखी हुई* है. Unlike चुक, however, रख can accept a ने-construction (उसने खाना *खा रखा* है).

The aspect modifier रख is normally used with transitive and not intransitive verbs. In the corresponding intransitive environment the use of चुक is more natural. See:

(1) मैंने यह फिल्म *देख रखी* है।
(2) मैं दिन में *लेट चुका* /*रखा हूँ।

(viii) -ने लग- : -ने लग- denotes the beginning of an action (वह खाने लगा). It is a positive aspect marker which cannot be normally used in negative and imperative environments (*वह नहीं खाने लगा, *खाना खाने लगो). Remember that sentences like अगर वह रोने लगे तो मुझे कहना are not simple negative sentences. They are highly contextualized and conditional sentences. Semantically their corresponding lexical verb is शुरु करना, but they do not have any negative or imperative restrictions, e.g. उसने खाना शुरू नहीं किया, खाना शुरू करो).

(ix) -ने वाला (है)/-ने को (है) : These two aspect markers denote the state of the action existing immediately before it starts e.g. गाड़ी *छूटने वाली* है, गाड़ी *छूटने को* है. Though technically they do not strictly fall within the internal temporal constituency of the aspect, yet the perception of the action is so close that one is likely to take it as the prior information of the action. A similar aspect marker, which is normally used in chaste Urdu, can be seen in constructions like चार बजा चाहते हैं, बारिश हुआ चाहती थी. These are highly stylized usages and are restricted to certain contexts only.

Here it is necessary to distinguish between the two constructions of -ने वाला है which are similar at the surface level but are different in their deep structure. See:

(1) साड़ी - फटने वाली - है। (NP x ADJ x VP)

= साड़ी फटने वाली किस्म की (यानी कमज़ोर) है।

(2) साड़ी - फटने वाली है। (SP x VP)

= साड़ी (खिंचने के कारण) फटने वाली है।

In sentence (1) it is possible to use an attribute in the adjectival phrase, as in कभी न फटने वाली, जल्दी फटने वाली etc, which is not possible in sentence (2). It is possible to insert particle ही in between ने and वाली, e.g. फटने ही वाली है which is not possible in sentence (1).

ने को है is a special construction of Hindi which is idiomatically more powerful than the construction ने वाला है in terms of showing urgency.

(x) ने जा रहा है: This aspect marker denotes the pre-beginning stage of the action which is generally referred to in relation to an animate subject, वह मेरा नाम काटने ही जा रहा था कि मैं वहाँ पहुँच गया.

2.10 Mood

2.10.1 Defining Mood

Language is not merely a means of conveying or receiving a message from one another. It is something more than this: it is communication *between people.* It is also a process of communication between two persons. It often expresses the emotions and attitudes of the speaker and he often uses it to influence the behavior of the hearer. This function of the language belongs to *mood.* The mood reflects the speaker's attitude towards the action and may manifest itself in many ways in the language - sometimes through the use of communicative devices like exclamations, interjections, apology, admiration and command and sometimes through the use of some special adjectives or adverbs. Mood can also be expressed at times through simple repetition of words, the change of voice or word-order etc. It is also a fact that modal expressions and devices at times communicate more than the words do. See:

(1) क्या लाजवाब कैच है ! (interjection)
(2) आप बुरा न मानें तो एक बात कहूँ। (aplogy)
(3) आपकी हाजिरजवाबी के क्या कहने। (admiration)
(4) आइए मेरे साथ चलिए। (polite command)
(5) हो सकता है शायद वह यहीं कहीं हो। (guess)
(6) To my regret he did not accept my offer. (sentence adverbials)
(7) Be careful of your clothes. (warning)

Actions which have not taken place in the real world and are lying in the mind of the speaker in the form of a wish, probability, conjecture, order etc. fall within the realm of mood and not aspect (cf. 29.1). *Aspect* tells us about the material status of the action whereas the *mood* tells us about the psychological state of the action. That is why Crowell calls mood the *psychological aspect* of the action. Mood thus denotes the stage of the action which the speaker sees or perceives mentally from his own angle. It is possible that this vision may have been inspired or influenced by his own vision, wish, imagination, resolution or conjecture etc. Hence the *mood* basically represents the speaker's attitude towards the action.

In the normal discourse or day-to-day interaction it is not difficult to identify words or areas where the speaker directly or indirectly displays or projects his individual attitude towards the action. He often uses some modal devices for this purpose such as the following:

(a) Intransitavisation: (where the subject of the sentence is down-graded or deleted from the sentence and the object is promoted as the subject (see 2.8.2.) e.g. पुलिस चोर को *पीट* रहा है > चोर *पिट* रहा है.

(b) Change in the theme or word-order (हम यहाँ रहते हैं > यहाँ हम रहते हैं. (change in word order).

(c) Projection of the subjective impression of the action e.g. खेल *फीका* था > मुझे खेल फीका *लगा.*

(d) Use of some special lexical words and expressions denoting some forms of mood (e.g. शायद, संभव है, हो सकता है, मैं चाहता हूँ कि, काश etc.)

(e) The modal auxiliaries (सक, पा, -ना है, -ना पड़. -ना चाहिए etc.) which may be distributionally different from the modal auxiliaries but are semantically related to the attitude or mood of the speaker because they ultimately reflect the speaker's attitude towards the action. For instance, in sentences like वह हिंदी पढ़ *सकता* है, उसे देर तक दफ्तर में *रुकना पड़ा* it is ultimately the question of the speaker's attitude whether he is looking at the relationship between the speaker and the subject as a duty, a capability or a compulsion.

2.10.2 Classification of Mood in Hindi

From the point of view of modal components inherent in Hindi verb phrases, the moods in Hindi can be placed in two categories- modal suffixes and auxiliary modal verbs which have the following sub-classes:

(A) Modal suffixes

1-Imperative

-ϕ, - ओ, - इए	पढ़, पढ़ो, पढ़िए।

2-Subjunctive

-ए	शायद वह भी आए।
	मैं चाहती हूँ कि वह भी आए।
	कल कोई न आए।
	मैं आऊँ?

3-Indefinite potential

-ता हो	शायद वह **आता हो**।
-या हो	शायद वह **आया हो**।
रहा हो	शायद वह आ **रहा हो**।

4-Definite potential

-ता होगा	वह यहीं काम **करता होगा**।
-या होगा	उसने यहीं काम **किया होगा**।
रहा होगा	वह यहीं काम कर **रहा होगा**।

5-Conditional

-ता...ता	अगर वह **कहता** तो मैं ज़रूर **आता**।
-या होता...-ता	अगर उसने **कहा होता** तो मैं ज़रूर **आता**।
-ता	काश, मैं भी आपके साथ **जाता**।
-या होता	काश, मैं भी आपके साथ **गया होता**।

6-Future

-एगा	वह **जाएगा**।

(B) Auxiliary Modal Verbs

1-Capabilitative

-सक	मैं हिंदी पढ़ **सकता हूँ**।
-पा	मैं आपकी लिखावट नहीं **पढ़ पाया**।
-या जा-	नौकर से दरवाज़ा **नहीं खोला जाता**। (incapability)
-ते बन	मुझसे **कहते नहीं बना**।

2-Compulsion

-ना है	उसे जल्दी **जाना है**।
-ना पड़	उसे जल्दी **जाना पड़ा**।
-ना चाहिए	उसे जल्दी जाना **चाहिए**।

2.10.3 Hindi Modal Suffixes

Hindi has five modal suffixes: (a) Imperative mood, (b) Subjunctive mood. (c) Indefinite potential mood, (c) Definite potential mood.

(a) Imperative Mood

The imperatives perform the directive function of the language, i.e. the imperative sentences direct the hearer to act in a certain way. The subject in the imperative sentence is always in the second person (आप, हम, तू etc.) but it overtly remains unexpressed in the sentence unless it is required to be specially mentioned or emphasized. Despite the overt omission of the subject, the information regarding the number-gender forms of the subject in the imperative sentences is achieved through their verb forms, e.g. (तू) आ, (तुम) आओ, (आप) आए.

All imperative sentences are linked with the present real-world context. For instance, we ask for water when we are thirsty, we welcome the guest only when we see him before us in the real context. Sentences other than imperatives do not have this restriction. To direct the actions of others, as in the imperative, is called the*directive function* of the language. It is, however, not necessary that the directive function of the language is performed through imperative sentences alone. Some other sentence forms when connected with the proper context are also capable of performing this function. For instance, a non-imperative sentence like मुझे बड़ी प्यास लगी है uttered by a guest before the host has the same imperative force as good as saying - Please give me some water. Similarly, the non-imperative interrogative sentence आपका पता क्या है has the same force of imperative as आपका पता क्या है?

Unlike English, Hindi has three regular and two extended

imperative forms:

पढ़ ϕ suffix (impolite form)

पढ़ो -ओ suffix (familiar form)

पढ़िए -इए (polite form)

The imperative forms पढ़, पढ़ो, पढ़िए denote an immediate compliance of the order or request whereas the -ना verb-form indicates a somewhat remote compliance, i.e. at some subsequent time. In some situations the use of न suffix serves to mitigate the bluntness of the order. In such situations the use of ज़रा is also common, e.g. ज़रा यह किताब पकड़ाना, ज़रा इधर आना. The modal suffix -इएगा also indicates a subsequently later compliance of the request but with some additional element of politeness. See:

(1) ये कपड़े धो दो। < +immediate>

(2) ये कपड़े धो देना। <-immediate, -respect>

(3) ये कपड़े धो दीजिएगा। <-immediate, +respect>

There is, however, a constraint on the formation of imperative sentences. Only verbs having the feature +volition can generate imperative sentences. Non-volitional stative verbs cannot generate proper imperative sentences. Hence while we can have an imperative sentences like बाहर निकलो, इधर आइए etc., we can not have sentences like *अच्छे लगो, *यह बात जानो, *जवाँ होवो, *छींको etc. because they are not acceptable sentences.

(b) Subjunctive Mood

The information regarding the subjunctive mood in Hindi is conveyed by the verbal suffix -ए, e.g. आए, रखे, जाए etc. The Subjunctive Mood reflects the speaker's view about the action which is to take place in future, which he expresses in the form of a wish, desire, probability, indirect order, request or petition etc. e.g.

(1) शायद/हो सकता है वह भी आए। (probablity)

(2) मैं चाहता हूँ कि वह भी साथ चले। (wish)

(3) भगवान् आपको सुखी रखे। (desire)

(4) कल कोई छुट्टी न ले। (indirect order)

(5) राधा से कहो जल्दी तैयार हो जाए। (indirect order)
(6) मैं अंदर आ जाऊँ ? (permission)

Remember that in sentences (1-2 and 5) the information regarding the probability, wish and indirect order, is not only conveyed by the verb form -ए but also by the main clause हो सकता है, मैं चाहता हूँ, राधा से कहो and the adverbial शायद. Secondly these clauses anticipate or demand a that-clause and it is necessary to use the modal suffix -ये after these verbs. If we remove the modal suffix or the first clause confirming the mood element, it will be difficult to determine their modal value in the absence of the proper context, because the modal suffix -ये is the same in all the clauses. See:

(हो सकता है कि)	वह भी आए	(probability)
(मैं चाहता हूँ कि)		(wish)
(उनसे कह दो कि)		(indirect order)

The portion of sentences shown within the large brackets in the left are called performative elements in the Speech Act Theory because it is these elements which inform us as to what roles the sentence plays in the real world (i.e. whether it is performing the function of providing information, expressing a wish, or probability, or asking questions etc.) In addition to these regular modal usages, the use of -इ ending subjunctive form is obligatory in complex sentences beginning with ताकि, जिसे, कहीं, मानो/जैसे etc. e.g.

(7) कागज़ पर लिख लो *ताकि/जिससे* याद रहे। (purpose)
(8) वह ऐसे बात करता है जैसे—मानो यहाँ का डिप्टी *हो।* (imagination)

In clauses beginning with जो and अगर/यदि etc. the use of the subjective form is optional, e.g.

(9) हम उन्हीं को बुलाएँगे जो हमारे कुछ काम *आएँ/आएँगे।* (restriction)
(10) अगर वह बुलाए तो मत जाइए/जाइएगा।(condition)

(c) Indefinite Potential Mood

Information regarding the indefinite potential mood is denoted through the verb suffixes -ता हो, -या हो or रहा हो, e.g. करता हो, सुना हो or आ रहा हो etc. The indefinite potential mood denotes the sense of an indefinite probability or supposition of an action occurring in its habitual, continuous or complete stage. Please remember that this realization was future centric in subjunctive, but in indefinite potential it is verb-centric. In both the situations there is a lack of certainty of the action taking place. See:

(1) शायद वह यहीं काम **करता हो**। (habitual, potential)

(2) संभव है डॉक्टर भी आ **रहा हो**। (continuous, potential)

(3) हो सकता है आपने भी उसका नाम **सुना हो**। (perfective, potential)

(4) ईश्वर करे वह ठीक हो **गया हो**। (perfective, probablity)

(5) अगर रेडियो चल **रहा हो** तो बंद कर देना। (continuous, condition)

(6) यदि पानी भर **चुका हो** तो बता देना। (perfect, condition)

(7) मुझे ऐसा आदमी चाहिए जो काम से न **डरता हो**। (habitual, condition)

(8) ऐसा धमाका हुआ जैसे भूचाल **आया हो**। (perfect, imagination)

(9) वह ऐसे बात करता है जैसे काटने आ **रहा हो**।(contnuous, imagination)

(d) Definite Potential Mood

The definite potential mood in Hindi is denoted by the verb suffixes -ता होगा, -या होगा and रहा होगा, e.g. करता होगा, सुना होगा, हो रहा होगा etc. The definite potential mood gives the sense of the definite possibility of the action being in the completed, habitually continued or perfective stage. See:

(1) वह यहीं काम **करता होगा**।

(2) आपने उसका नाम **सुना होगा**।

(3) वहाँ इस समय बारिश हो **रही होगी**।

It may be noted that there is an element of definiteness evident in these sentences with the result that the element of doubtfulness that was present in the indefinite potential is removed. Hence the use of doubt markers like शायद, हो सकता है and संभव है etc. can not be used in such sentences, e.g.

(4) हो सकता है वह यहीं काम करता हो (*होगा).

In the definite potential verb forms, होगा is a modal element and not a tense marker. It is proved by the fact that the use of होगा remains the same both in relation to the past as well as the present, e.g.

जब डॉक्टर वहाँ **पहुँचा** तो वह सो रहा होगा।

जब डॉक्टर वहाँ **पहुँचेगा** तो वह सो रहा होगा।

Contrary to this, there is an element of futurity in the -गा constituent in the sentence वह बड़ा होकर डॉक्टर होगा.

(e) Conditional Mood

The sense of conditionality in the conditional mood in Hindi comes through the two suffixes -ता and -या, e.g. जाता, कहाँ होता etc. The conditional mood provides a situation which is opposite to that of the reality even though they are related to each other through a cause and effect relationship. Besides the modal suffix -ता also denotes the sense of the wish of the speaker which has not been materialized or which is not likely to materialize. See:

अगर वह कहता तो मैं ज़रूर **आता**। (condition)

अगर तुमने पहले कहा होता तो काम हो **जाता**। (condition)

काश, मैं भी आपके साथ **जाता**। (wish)

काश, मैं भी आपके साथ **गया होता**। (wish)

The sentence तुमने कहा इसलिए काम हुआ shows a cause and effect relationship. Since the first action did not take place, therefore, the second action also did not materialize. To describe the imagined situation of the cause and effect relationship is the objective of the sentences (1, 2). The sentence (1) envisages the incomplete stage of the supposed action while the sentence (2) envisages the complete stage of the action.

The sentences (3-4) also contain two elements: immaterialized wish and the actual action. An imaginary description of these contradictory situations accomplished according to the wishes of the speaker is the objective of the sentence.

A difference between the habitual aspect marker -ता (2.9.6) and the conditional aspect marker -ता needs to be noted here. After the use of the aspect marker -ता, it is obligatory to use a tense marker like है, था etc. (e.g. मैं जाता हूँ), but in the case of the conditional aspect marker -ता cannot accept any such tense marker (*काश मैं भी आपके साथ जाता हूँ).

2.10.4 Auxiliary Modal Verbs

Hindi has the following classes of modal auxiliary verbs:

(i) सकना, पाना (capabilitative),

(ii) -या जा- (incapabilitative)

(iii) -ते बन,

(iv) -ना है, -ना पड़, -ना चाहिए (Verbs of Obligation)

(v) -ना चाहिए

(i) सकना, पाना : सकना denotes that the action for which it has been used does not encounter any obstacle in its execution. In Hindi the auxiliary verb सक performs three functions:

a. capability (1) वह हिंदी बोल **सकता** है। वह नहीं चल **सकता।**

b. permission (2) अब आप जा **सकते** हैं।

c. possibility (3) आज बारिश हो **सकती** है।*हो सकता है* कि वह न आए।

पाना denotes only the sense of *capability* (मैं हिंदी नहीं बोल **पाता**), and not of permission or possibility. There is, however, an additional sense of the speakers's attitude or view in पाना, e.g. in the sentence मैं आपका काम नहीं कर पाया the auxiliary modal verb पाना has the force of saying - मैं चाहता था, मैंने कोशिश की, लेकिन खेद है मैं आपका काम नहीं कर पाया.

सका can be used both in the positive as well as negative environments (e.g. वह हिंदी बोल सकता है, वह हिंदी नहीं बोल सकता) sentence 1), but there is a restriction on its unconditional or unqualified use in the perfective tense (e.g. *वह चल सका), but perfective use in the negative and half negative sentences is, however, possible as in the following sentences:

(1) वह नहीं चल **पाया/सका।** (negative sentence)

(2) वह चल **सकता** है/(*वह चल पाता है) (full positive)

(3) क्या तुम साहब से मिल **पाए/सके?** (half-negative)

(4) काश, मैं भी आपके साथ चल **पाता/सकता !** (half-negative

The transitivity structure of सकना can be subject-centric as well as object-centric. In other words it can be used both in the active as well as passive constructions, e.g. मैं आपका काम नहीं कर सका/आपका काम नहीं किया जा सका. Their imperative forms, however, can not be formed

(*बाहर बैठ सको, *काम कर पाओ).

(ii) -या जा- (incapabilitative)) The modal suffix -या जा- can form two types of incapabilitative sentences: (see also 2.8.5 for unintentional subject + से -construction)

(1) नौकर से दरवाज़ा नहीं **खोला जाता**। (-या जा-)

(2) नौकर से दरवाज़ा नहीं **खुलता**। (derived intransitive)

In Hindi -या जा- is basically a passive marker suffix (e.g. काम पूरा कर **लिया जाएगा**) and, therefore, sentence (1) is traditionally treated as a passive sentence but the construction mentioned in sentence (1) is not a passive sentence (see 2.8.3). Semantically it is a modal construction. One characteristic of this construction is that it is acceptable only in a negative environment and not in full positive environment (e.g. *नौकर से दरवाज़ा **खोला गया**). Their contextualized usage in certain sentences which are not fully positive sentences is possible, e.g. (3) क्या तुमसे दरवाज़ा **खोला गया** ?

(iii) -ते बन: Like पाना, ते बन is also used in only negative or semi-negative sentences, but here the action does not materialize despite the willingness or effort of the subject and the subject has no control over the impeding elements of the action. For instance, in the sentence मुझसे कहते नहीं बना, the subject seems to have tried to say something but was unable to do so because of hesitation or some other uncontrollable obstacles. The modal auxiliary –ते बन requires a subject + से sentence. In certain metaphorical usages we do find a positive use of -ते बन, but here it does not denote the sense of capability, e.g. उसकी हालत देखते बनती थी.

(iv) Modal Verbs of Obligation- ना है, -ना पड़ and -ना चाहिए : All these three modal auxiliaries require subject + को sentencs. In all these three modal auxiliaries there is some element of obligation or compulsion on the subject to perform the action, e.g.

सुनील को डॉक्टर के पास *जाना* है।

सुनील को डॉक्टर के पास *जाना पड़ा*।

सुनील को डॉक्टर के पास *जाना चाहिए*।

(a) -ना है: The sense of obligation or compulsion in -ना है is usually internal and implies a tacit approval or consent of the subject, e.g. जल्दी जाना है, राधा को बैंक से पैसे निकालने हैं, मुझे पत्नी को पैसे भेजने हैं।

(b) -ना होगा denotes an additional sense of work accomplishment or definiteness, e.g. मुझे कई काम करने होंगे. This difference will be clearer if you consider these structural restrictions:

(1) राधा को बैंक से पैसे *निकालने हैं* लेकिन वह नहीं निकालेगी।

(2) राधा को बैंक से पैसे *निकालने होंगे* (*लेकिन वह नहीं निकालेगी)।

In some usages of -ना था, the underlying perception is that the action did not take place in the past which it should have. Thus in the positive meaning of this class of sentences underlies a negative meaning. Similarly in the negative meaning of this type of sentences underlies a positive meaning. See:

(3) राधा को बैंक से पैसे निकालने थे (i.e. उसने नहीं निकाले)।

(4) राधा को बैंक से पैसे नहीं निकालने थे (i.e. लेकिन उसने निकाले)।

In usages of this type it is much closer to the meaning of -ना चाहिए था (see sentence 8-9). Sometimes -ना था is used in the meaning of -ना है, e.g.

(5) मुझे आज जल्दी जाना था (= जाना है), क्या मैं चला जाऊँ ?

(v) -ना पड़: The modal auxiliary ना पड़ denotes an external compulsion on the subject to perform the action, e.g. मुझे कल जल्दी घर लौटना पड़ा (though I did not want to), हमें बिना चीनी के चाय पीनी पड़ रही है, कल मुझे देर तक दफ़्तर में रुकना पड़ा।

Like the modal auxiliary suffix -ना होगा, the -ना पड़ suffix also presumes the sense of accomplishment or inevitability. This will be evident from the following structural constraints: कल मुझे देर तक दफ़्तर में रुकना पड़ा *लेकिन मैं नहीं रुका।

The modal verbs -ना है and -ना पड़ basically demand an animate subject and are used with only such verbs (actions) on which the subject has a control or has the volition to do or not do, e.g. खाना, जाना, पढ़ना, लिखना, बैठना etc. Verbs which denote actions which are not basically in the control of the subject, i.e. in which the subject is not free to do or not do the action at his will can not in normal circumstances accept the -ना है and -ना पड़ constructions, e.g. चिढ़ना, ऊबना, चौंकना, अफ़राना, घबराना,

छूटना, डरना, डूबना, थकना, सहमना, सूझना etc. See:*मुझे चौंकना है. *अब आपको थकना पड़ेगा, *अब आपको डरना चाहिए।

(vi) -ना चाहिए : The modal suffix -ना चाहिए conveys the sense of obligation in various ways and can be used with reference to both animate and inanimate subjects. In the context of the animate subjects the sense of obligation is conveyed in the form of duty or advice and its compliance or non-compliance depends on the discretion of the subject, e.g.

आपको गरीबों की सेवा *करनी चाहिए।*

तुम्हें पुलिस को खबर कर *देनी चाहिए।*

The use of -ना चाहिए is not possible with reference to actions on which the subject does not have a control or freedom to do or not to do the action, e.g. *आपको थकना चाहिए, *इन्हें घबराना चाहिए), but in certain negative or contextualized sentences the use of -ना चाहिए is possible, e.g. आपको इतनी जल्दी **नहीं चिढ़ना चाहिए**, ऐसे मौकों पर **नहीं घबराना चाहिए**, आपको इस तरह **नहीं डरना चाहिए**.

In relation to the inanimate subjects the modal verb -ना चाहिए denotes the relationship of cause and effect or a resultant action, e.g. अब पेट्रोल का चूना बंद **हो जाना चाहिए**, अब इसमें से आवाज़ नहीं **आनी चाहिए**।

In certain contexts an additional dimention of the speakers wish is manifest in sentence, e.g.

बहुत ठंड हो गई है, अब तो धूप निकलनी चाहिए।

2.11 Tense

2.11.1 Defining Tense

Simply speaking, the form of the verb which denotes the perception of the time of the occurrence of the action vis-a-vis our own concept of the past, present and future is called *tense*. Seen in this perspective, *tense* is not 'time' but a *time perception.* This perception exists only in our mind and not outside it. This perception of time may or may not match with the time of the real world.

Thus *tense* is thus a grammatical category, which has no existence outside grammar. *Time,* on the other hand, is a physical or logical category, which is related to the real world. Time in the real world is like a stream of flowing water – continuous, dynamic and indivisible. Society has, for its own practical convenience, divided time into some artificial segments like present, past and future, presuming *now* as the zero point of reference. The society has also given them some calendar labels like year 1971, May 1971, Monday, Tuesday etc. It is important to note that the value of the calendar time is context free and unchangeable. It denotes the specific date or time whenever it is uttered. For instance the date March 5, 2008 will denote the same time, date or year whenever it is uttered. Contrary to this, the value of temporal adverbs like *today, tomorrow* or *day-after-tomorrow* etc. will be relative to the point of time when the statement was uttered. In other words, its value is relative to the point of time when the sentence was uttered. Similarly, the word *tomorrow,* will signify 2nd January 2008 if the sentence was uttered on 1st January 2008, because the determination of their values is possible only after taking the time of the utterance as the central point. The value of the temporal adverbials like के पहले, के बाद etc. is also relative to the time of utterance but they are not dependent on the point of time of the utterance but on some other point of time mentioned or inherent in the utterance. See:

(1) वह *5 मई 1983* को आया।
(context free)

(2) वह *कल* आया।
(in relation to the time of utterance)

(3) वह *दफ़्तर बंद होने के एक घंटे बाद* आया।
(in relation to some other reference point)

Generally we divide *time* into three segments – present, past and future. The segment prior to the present is called the *past* and the segment that follows the present is called the *future*, e.g.

(4) सुधीर इस कॉलेज में पढ़ता है। (present)

(5) सुधीर इस कॉलेज में पढ़ा। (past)

(6) सुधीर कल देर से आएगा। (future)

The perception of time denoted by these verb forms and the actual time of the action are the same in these sentences, but now look at the following sentences in which the perception of time denoted by the verb forms and the actual time do not coincide.

(7) बैठक सोमवार को है।

(the verb form is present but the time perception is future)

(8) वह कल अमरीका जा रहा है।

(the verb form is present, but the time perception is future)

(9) कमीज़ का दाम 900 रुपए होगा।

(the verb form is future but the time perception is present)

(10) रुकिए, मैं अभी आया।

(the verb form is past, but the time perception is future)

(11) अगर वह आया तो।

(the verb form is past, but the time perception is future)

(12) बारिश होने वाली है।

(the verb form is present, but the time perception is future)

Besides this, the tense can also link the time of the action with some other reference point. This reference time can be the point of time of the utterance or any other point of time mentioned or inherent in the utterance. For instance, in sentence (4) the grammatical tense stands in relation to the time of utterance and in sentence (5) the grammatical tense stands in relation to the point of time of the action मेरे वहाँ पहुँचने तक. The time of utterance remains unexpressed in the sentence. See:

(4) मोहन सोया हुआ है।

(time of utterance unexpressed)

(5) *जब मैं वहाँ पहुँचा* तो मोहन सोया हुआ था।

(another point of time expressed)

Sometimes the speaker places himself either before or after the event on the time surface from where he sees the event occurring in the past or the future, as in sentence (6) the past has been recalled on the time surface of the future and in sentence (7) the present has been recalled on the time surface of the past:

(6) तब आप पाएँगे कि आपका सब कुछ लुट **चुका** है।

(7) मैंने उसे बताया काम कैसे होता है।

The above instances lead us to certain basic assumptions about the notion of the tense:

(a) Tense is not time, but a perception of time. It is only a time frame for indicating the time reference. It is subjective in nature and not objective, and it's basis is not the real world but the psychic world of the speaker.

(b) The perception of tense is the result of a mixed process. In this process the time of the event, the point of time of the utterance and the reference time all play important roles. Tense is the grammatization of the relations between the time of event and the reference time.

(c) At the *structural* level, *tense* is a category of verb forms, but at the level of semantic structure it is a syntactic category. It is often influenced or constrained by some other temporal constituents, like temporal adverbs/adverbials as in sentences (1-2), any temporal event or action mentioned or inherent in the utterance, as in sentences (3-6,7) and aspect. For instance, in sentence (9) the use of पी है (i.e. mood + tense) is controlled by the reference time of अभी-अभी and in sentence (10) the use of पी थी is controlled by the reference time of कल भी. See:

(8) मैंने चाय *पी।*

(9) मैंने अभी-अभी चाय *पी है।*

(10) मैंने कल भी चाय *पी थी।*

(d) It needs to be noted that the semantic range and the linguistic manifestation of the *future tense* is much larger compared to the present and the past tenses. See:

-एगा	वह *जाएगा।*
-रहा है	वह कल अमरीका जा *रहा है।*
-है	बैठक सोमवार *को है।*
-या	रुकिए मैं अभी *आया।* अगर वह *आया* तो।
-ता है	बस, अभी *आता हूँ।*
-वाला है	बारिश होने *वाली है।*
-को है	बस जाने *को है।*

2.11.2 Joint Classification of Aspect and Tense

The formation of Hindi tense markers is as follows:

Tense constituent	*number-gender suffix*	*Tense*
ह-	-ए, एं, (है, हैं	Present
थ-	-आ, इ- ई, ईं, (था, थे, थी, थीं)	Past

The tense markers and modal markers that are used after the aspect markers are as follows:

Tense	है	:	चलता है	चला है
	था	:	चलता था	चला था
Mood	हो	:	चलता हूँ	चला हूँ
	होता	:	चलता होता	चला होता
	होगा	:	चलता होगा	चला होगा

The semantic fields of tense and aspect are so closely interlinked that there has been a tradition of presenting their verb forms together and, therefore, we tend to consider देखा है (has seen) as a single category whereas the constituent देखा represents aspect and the constiuent है represents the tense. Similarly we tend to consider past continuous as a single unit (खा रहा है). We are presenting below a joint classification of tense and aspect verb forms:

(a)	Present Habitual	सोता है
	Present Continuous	सो रहा है
	Present Perfect	सोया है
(b)	Past Habitual	सोता था
	Past Continuous	सो रहा था
	Past Perfect	सोया था
(c)	Perfective	सोया

The verb form सोता, however, expects a tense marker -ता in the context of habitual aspect without which its use in normal situation is not possible. It's tense-less usage is, however, possible in two situations: *one* in conditional sentences as in sentence (1) and *second* historical past (as in sentence (2):

(1) अगर वह चलता तो अच्छा होता। (conditional sentence)

(2) हम रोज़ पैदल जाते और बाग में फूल तोड़ते। (historical past)

□

Chapter-3

SENTENCE PATTERNS

3.1 Defining the Sentence Patterns

A *sentence* is a concrete and definite construction made up of various phrases. A *sentence pattern* is an abstract frame made up of the slots of these phrases from which we can generate innumerable sentences by inserting appropriate words in the appropriate slots. The sentence has a concrete and definite entity. The sentence pattern is an abstract and symbolic frame. The number of words used in a sentence is limited but the number of words that can be used in the sentence pattern or frame is unlimited. For instance, हम अखबार पढ़ रहे हैं is a sentence. The sentence pattern (or frame) of this sentence is subject x object x verb which is made up of three components. Innumerable sentences can, however be made by replacing these components with the appropriate words, e. g. मैंने खाना खाया, वह कुछ किताबें खरीदेगा.

Some of the major features of the sentence patterns are as follows:

(a) Phrase level component: Every component of the sentence pattern has a specific place of use in the sentence which is called a *slot*. Every slot represents a phrase. No component below the level of a phrase is considered relevant for the purpose of sentence patterns. Hence in a sentence हम अखबार पढ़ रहे हैं only phrase level components like वर्मा जी, मेरे बड़े भाई or इस कमरे में रहने वाले सभी लोग etc. can be used.

(b) Syntagmatic Relationship: Every sentence has a definite distribution system and their various components are related to each other in grammatical relationship, like subject, object, adverb, verb etc. A relationship like this is called a *linear* relationship or *syntagmatic* relationship. A linear relationship like this is possible only up to a certain practical limit, e.g.

(1) हम/ अखबार/ पढ़ रहे हैं।

(2) आज/ हम/ बहुत देर से/ अपने कमरे में/ अखबार/ पढ़ रहे हैं।

Needless to say, it is adverbs which are ultimately the main instruments of extending the length of the sentence patterns and in normal circumstances has the capacity to occur at any place before the verb. In unusual and contextualized instances there may be a change in the normal distribution system of the sentence patterns. (e.g. अखबार ही तो पढ़ रहे हैं हम) but in the context of sentence patterns only the normal and basic distribution system is accepted as a matrix.

(c) Paradigmatic Relationship: Just as the components of the sentence pattern are related to each other in a linear or syntagmatic relationship, they are also related to each other in a vertical relationship called *paradigmatic* relationship. Paradigmatic relationship exists between words of the same class and thus can be used in each other's place (slot) in the sentence pattern. For instance, in the sentence हम अखबार पढ़ रहे हैं, all the words that can be used in the place of हम (like वर्मा जी, मेरे बड़े भाई) are supposed to be in paradigmatic relationship). Similarly, अखबार can be replaced by किताब, पत्र, पत्रिका etc. All words capable of being used in the same slot form a word-class. It may have many structural classes like noun-class, adjective-class, adverb- class, verb-class etc. The number of words of any word-class can be unlimited and, therefore, an unlimited number of sentences can be generated from a given sentence pattern by inserting appropriate words in appropriate slots.

These two aspects of syntagmatic and paradigmatic relationship between the different constituents of the sentence pattern can be illustrated as follows:

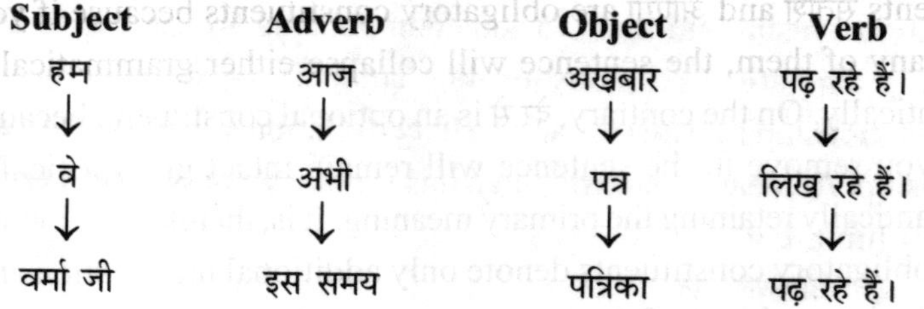

(d) Surface and Deep Structure: Both the above dimensions of the sentence patterns are basically dependent on the surface structure. It has a third dimension, too – the semantic component, which is related to the internal structure of the sentence. Normally the kernel structure of the sentence patterns is determined on the basis of the surface structure of the sentences. The deeper or interior differences that appear on the basis of the semantic component or the deep structure are sub-classified as sub-patterns. For instance, all the following four sentences fall under the sentence pattern subject x object x verb, but on the basis of the deep structure and the semantic components they make four different sub-patterns:

(3) हरी/ पानी/ पीता है। (sub-pattern 34 a)
(4) विजय/ कार चलाना/ जानता है। (sub-pattern 35a)
(5) रंगनाथ/ जाने की/ सोच रहा है। (sub-pattern 36)
(6) मजदूर/ हड़ताल/ कर रहे हैं। (sub-pattern 37a)

Sub-patterns of the sentence-patterns in this book have been determined on the basis of the componential analysis of the features appearing in each slot configuration. This will also give us an idea as to how a set of features which are outwardly similar but different at the deeper level have the capacity to generate different types of sentences.

(e) Obligatory and Optional Constituents: The constituents of a sentence pattern are of two types - obligatory constituents and optional constituents. *Obligatory* constituents are the essential constituents of the sentence and thus cannot be removed from the sentence. If it is removed, the sentence will collapse either grammatically or semantically. For instance, in the sentence सतीश देर से आएगा both the constituents सतीश and आएगा are obligatory constituents because if you remove any of them, the sentence will collapse either grammatically or semantically. On the contrary, देर से is an optional constituent, because even if you remove it, the sentence will remain intact grammatically and semantically retaining the primary meaning. It is, therefore, obvious that the obligatory constituents denote only additional information and are not the integral part of the sentence pattern. In a majority of cases this type of additional information is conveyed through adverb phrases.

In the context of sentence patterns, the constituents are sometimes also classified in a different way as *nuclear constituents* and *peripheral constituents.* Nuclear constituents are those that are *semantically* basic or central constituents of the sentence but are loosely used in the place of obligatory and optional constituents.

3.2 Kernel Sentences

Sentence patterns which have all the slots as obligatory constituents are called *kernel* sentence pattern (also sometimes loosely called *basic sentence* patterns). The kernel sentences have the inherent capacity to generate all the types of sentences in use in the language. The number of kernel sentences is limited in any language. An infinite number of sentences can be generated in that language by adding any number of optional constituents or taking recourse to transformation processes.

In order to understand the syntax of any language it is necessary to look into the kernel sentence patterns of that language. The nature and the number of kernel sentences may vary from language to language. Even for determining the kernel sentences different parameters are used. Despite this, the following criteria are supposed to be fundamental for determining the kernel sentences of the language:

(a) Only *obligatory constituents* of a sentence can find a place in the kernel sentence patterns (and not the optional constituents). मोहन अख़बार पढ़ता है is a kernel sentence, but मोहन रोज़ अख़बार पढ़ता है is a derived sentence and not a kernel sentence, because it contains an optional constituent रोज़ which can be done away with.

(b) Only *simple sentences* are included under the kernel sentences and not the complex or compound sentences. Similarly contextual sentences like negative, interrogative, imperative, passive sentences etc. are not included under the kernel sentences because all such sentences can be derived or transformed from the kernel sentences.

(c) Only *complete sentences* are acceptable as kernel sentences and not the sentence fragments or minor sentences.(see 1.3)

(d) In fact only the nature or the potential of the verb is accepted as a base for determining the verb pattern because it is actually the verb which mostly controls the whole pattern of the sentence and its various characters or participants (subject, object etc.). For instance, the verb मरना (int.) demands only one character (subject), the verb मारना (tr.) demands two characters (subject, object) and the verb देना (ditransitive) demands three participants (subject, object, ablative). These three verbs generate three different kinds of kernel sentences.

3.3. Derived Sentence Patterns

The *kernel* sentences are context-free sentences, i.e. they are free from the constraints of the tense, aspect, mood and voice etc. It is from these kernel sentences that various types of other live contextual sentences are generated. There are three processes or devices of generating various sentences from the kernel sentences:

(a) By expanding the length of the phrase: Any phrase can be expanded by adding modifiers or attributes, e.g.

(1) लड़की / सुंदर/ है। (subject x complement x verb)

> आपकी बड़ी वाली लड़की/ तीनों बहनों से सुंदर/ है।

(b) By adding optional constituents: The sentence can be expanded by adding optional constituents (phrases). These optional constituents are normally adverbs (adverbials) and make the sentence lively and meaningful.

(c) By transformation process: The transformation grammarians hold that a kernel sentence can be transformed into many types of contextual sentences by applying some specific rules, e.g. negative sentence, interrogative sentence, causative sentence, imperative sentence, passive sentence, subjunctive sentence etc. So much so that even the tense, aspect and mood can also be obtained through the application of some transformation rules. See:

(3)सुरेश अंग्रेजी समझता है।

> सुरेश अंग्रेजी समझ सकता है। (सक- transformation)

> सुरेश अंग्रेजी नहीं समझता। (negative transformation)

> क्या सुरेश अंग्रेजी समझता है ? (interrogative transformation)

3.4 Feature Analysis

3.4.1 Feature Analysis and its Methodology

Features are those distinctive characteristics of an entity or an object which distinguish it from other corresponding entities or objects. For instance, if we choose to mark the distinctive features for a *boy* we might start with the feature <+animate, +male, +young>. and for the girl the features might be <+animate, +female, +young>. Such an analysis is usually called *feature analysis* or *componential analysis*.*

The hypothesis behind the feature analysis is that all the constituents of the sentences are made up of certain features or characteristics that mark them and that all the sentences of the language can be converted into certain limited number of feature patterns. Thus every sentence pattern is a configuration of features and once a feature pattern of a sentence is evolved, a number of cognate sentences can be formed or generated by changing or adding the necessary features. The desired combination of the features in various slots of the sentence pattern is called a *configuration* of the features. Thus a similar feature configuration has the capacity to beget similar types of sentences in that language. A sentence pattern may also have a sub-pattern (see sentence-sub pattern)

*The method of componential analysis was first used for the description and comparison of kinship terms, e.g. Goodenough (1956), Loucebury (1956, Wallace & Atkins (1960). Later Lamb (1964), Nida (1964), 1975, Weinreich (1963, 1966) and Kartz & Fodor (1963) used this methodology in the transformational grammar to establish the relationship between semantics and syntax.

3.4.2 Classification of Features and Categories

The *features* are always marked on the slots of the sentence patterns thus suggesting that all phrases capable of occurring in that slot broadly share the same set of features. The term *categories* normally refer to the grammatical and functional categories like subject, object, complement, verb etc. occurring in a slot.

The features can sometimes also be classified as *overt* and *covert* depending on whether they relate to the surface structure or the deep structure of the sentence, called **overt** features and **covert** features. Grammatical features like number, gender, tense, aspect etc. are *overt* features because they are mostly visible through their markers on the surface structure of the sentence, e.g. boy*s*, hous*es*, wish*es* etc. Features like +human, +animate, +concrete, +count etc. are called *covert* features, because they do not display any visible markers and are related to the real world or semantics. Such features are sometimes also called *inherent* features.

The analysis of Hindi sentence patterns which is being presented from Chapter 4 to 6 below in Part-2 contains the following categories and features:

Noun-based Features

(a) *Function-based categories*: containing slots for subject, agent, instigator, को-subject, natural force, patient, unintentional force, object, indirect object, phrasal object, complement, object complement, dative, ablative, source, recipient, donor, co-participant, associative, co-adverbial, complement and verb etc.

(b) *Relation-based categories*: containing slots for ±class, ±sub-class, ±member, ±class inclusion, ±identifier, ±identified, ±possessor, ±possessed, ±master, ±property, ±prior state, ±changed state, ±mutuality.

(c) *Semantic and inherent features*: ±animate-inanimate, ±concrete-abstract, ±male-female, ±concrete, ±active, ±volition, ±definite, ±natural phenomena, ±social phenomerna, ±phyacal, ±notion, ±feeling, ±knowledge, ±skill, ±fact, ±relationship, ±blood relationship.etc. (The inherent features are very crucial in interpreting the internal structure of the sentence and forming sub-patterns of the sentence.)

Verb-based Features

(a) *Functional Category*: Intransitive, transitive, ditransitive, linking verb, existive, instrument-based, location-based, manner- based, purpose related, manner related, object complement based, co-participant.

(b) *Grammatical/structural Features*: Semantic/inherent features: ±lexical, ±bi-directional, ±stative, ±mental, ±appearance, ±visual, ±guess, ±experience, ±audio, ±touch, ±process, ±conscious, ±resultative, ±resolution, ±dramatisation, ±conventional.

(c) *Grammatical/structural Features (overt features)*: ±aspect, ±mood, ±tense (present), ±inversion, ±कर (activisation), ±infinitive (-ना)

(d) Relational Features: ±class, ±member, ±sub-class, ±class inclusion, ±identifier, ±identified, ±possessor, ±possessed, ±property, *prior position, changed position.

Semantic/inherent features: ±human, ±animate, ±concrete, ±active, ±volition, ±definite, ±natural event, ±social phenomenon, ±physical, ±feeling (मनोभाव), ±knowledge, ±fact, ±skill, ±relation, ±blood relation.

Verb-related Features

(d) Transitive, intransitive, ditransitive, linking verb, existential, instrumental, vocational, temporal (time-related), manner-related, purpose-related.

3.4.3 Some Major Features Explained

(a) Agent: An agent (in case grammar) is a grammatical category akin to the traditional notion of the *subject* with the difference that an agent is the one who performs an action at his discretion or on his own volition, that is, he is free to do or not do the action, e.g. to eat, drink, purchase, dance etc., e.g.

(1) The traveller *bought* the ticket.

(2) The traveller *died*.

The *traveller* in both the sentences is traditionally a subject of the sentence but while in sentence (1) the traveller performed the action at his own discretion or on his volition, in sentence (2) the traveller (i.e. the subject) has no control over the action (death) and is not virtually a subject. It it is called an *experiencer* in case grammar.

The *subject*, on the other hand, does not necessarily have the volition to act or not act. For instance, in the sentence the *traveller bought the ticket*, the traveller is a tradional subject as well as an agent, but in the sentence *the traveller died*, the traveller may be the subject in the traditional sense but is not an agent, because he does not have the volition to die or not die. An action on which the subject has a control is called a *controllable* action. The one who controls the action and is free to do or not do the action is called an *agent.*

There are some other restrictions also. Verbs like नाचना, पीटना, खरीदना etc. are *controllable actions* and, therefore, their subjects are called agents. Remember that sentences having agents can be transformed into *volitional* sentences, but not others like घबराना, मारना etc, e.g.,

(1) राधा को *नाचना* पड़ा. (controllable action)

(2) *राधा को *घबराना* पड़ा. (not within the control of the subject) (for details see sub-pattern 29b)

The subject which is not the agent is labelled differently, e.g. *experiencer* (see 5.1.4), *को-subject* (see 5.2), *force* (natural/unintended) (see sub-pattern-28b,c, 30, 42a and 2.8.5)

(b) Co-participant: Some verbs expect some obligatory constituent or participant in the sentance apart from the usual subject and the object, in order to complete their meaning, e.g. से लड़ना and से सहानुभूति होना etc., as in these sentences:

(3) राधा *शंकर* से लड़ती है,

(4) मुझे *रामलाल* से सहानुभूति है।

These participants have been called *co-participants*, because their participation in the action is a pre-requirement without which the action can not take place. In a broader sense, they are part of the case system - dative, ablative, source etc. because they are used at the expectation of the respective verbs (see sub-patterns 23, 33, 39, 40, 41)

(c) Co-adverbial: Like the co-participants, some verbs also require an adverbial, called *co-adverbial*, as an obligatory constituent of the sentence in order to complete the meaning of the verbs, like रहना, रखना and तराशना, e.g. the co-adverbials गाँधीनगर में, गैरेज में and पैसे-पैसे के लिए in the following sentences:

(5) प्रताप *गांधीनगर में* रहता है।

(6) मोहन गाड़ी *गैरेज में* रखता है।

(7) वह *पैसे-पैसे के लिए* तरस रहा है।

The co-adverbials are basically inanimate in nature.

(d) Object + का: Some complex verbs (2.5) in Hindi demand a marked object, i.e. object + का, as in the following sentences:

(8) *लोग आपकी प्रशंसा* कर रहे थे।

(9) मोहन को *फुटबाल का* शौक है। :

The words आपका and फुटबाल का in the above sentences are objects in the deep structure even though the regular Hindi object markers like को or zero marker are not used after them. Such a marker has been simply called object + का or का-object. Since such का-sentences (see 5.1) are basically intransitive in nature, the *object + का* in such sentences have also been called का-object. (see 5.3.2 b, 5.3.3b)

□

PART-2

APPLICATION

Chapter-4

COPULA SENTENCE PATTERN

4.1 Defining a Copula Sentence Structure

A copula sentence consists of a subject, a complement and a copula verb (also called a *linking verb*). The complement may be a noun (nominal), an adjective (adjectival) or an adverb (adverbial). The linking verb is so called because it links the subject with the complement of the sentence and defines certain relationships between them. (*Copula* is a Latin word meaning 'to link') For instance, the following Hindi sentences are copula sentences:

(1) मोहन अध्यापक है।

(2) राधा सुंदर है।

(3) पिताजी घर में हैं।

The basic sentence pattern of this sentence is thus represented as: NP x Complement x LV (where LV stands for Linking Verb). Despite the presence of the complement and the linking verb in the sentence, if the subject of the sentence happens to be marked by any postposition, like को etc., the sentence will not be called a copula sentence, e.g. मोहन **को** बुखार है, मेरे **पास** एक नई कार है.

Three word-classes that can occupy the position of complements in a copula sentence are – noun, adjective and adverb, on the basis of which they derive their names also:

(a) Nominal Copula Sentence: : NP x NP x LV

(1) मोहन अध्यापक है।

(b) Adjectival Copula Sentence: : NP x ADJ x LV

(2) राधा सुंदर है।

(c) Adverbial Copula Sentence: : NP x ADV x LV

(3) पिता जी घर में हैं।

The *nominal copula sentence* contains both the subject and the complement as noun phrases. The complements of the copula sentences are linked to the subjects in certain special relationships. For instance, in sentence (1) both the subject and the complement of the sentence refer to the same person or entity and are thus called *co-referents*. For instance, both मोहन and अध्यापक in sentence (1) above are the same person and not different entities.

In *adjectival copula sentences* the relationship between the subject and the adjectival complement is that of a modifier and modified at a sentence level. For instance, in sentence (2) राधा is the subject and सुंदर is its attribute or modifier.

In *adverbial copula sentences*, the complement of the sentence denotes the presence or existence of the subject around a certain specific location, as for instance, in sentence (3) the adverbial complement घर में indicates the existence of the subject पिताजी at some location. In addition to these grammatical relationships between the subject and the complement there are various other semantic and intrinsic relationships between them, e.g. class-member relationship, whole-part relationship, class inclusion relationship, identifier-identified relationship etc. which will be dealt with subsequently under relevant sentence patterns.

Normally one of the forms of होना *'to be'* is used as a linking verb in copula sentences, e.g. था, होता, हुआ etc. Nevertheless, quite a few other verbs at times may also occupy this place, though in a limited number, e.g. ठहरना, निकालना etc. may also occupy this position, e.g. जग्गू चोर *निकला*. These type of linking verbs are, in fact, a sort of idiomatised verbs and are different from other regular lexical verbs like देखना, पढ़ना etc. because in copula sentences their lexical, grammatical and functional values are different. (see 4.3.1, 4.3.2).

Copula sentences in Hindi are a three-unit constructions in which all the three units must appear overtly, otherwise the sentence may collapse if any constituent is removed, e.g. *राधा .... है, *राधा सुंदर ...., *...........है. In certain languages (like Bangla, Sanskrit, Latin and Russian etc.) the copula verb remains unmarked on the surface structure and the sentence remains a two-unit structure, e.g. मोहन अध्यापक (Bangla), but in its underlying structure, the existence of copula remains present. That is the reason why it becomes necessary to add the copula verb in other tenses in their surface structure, e.g. मोहन अध्यापक छीलो (मोहन अध्यापक था).

Another feature of the Hindi copula sentences is that in some negative present tense sentences the copula verb is sometimes optionally deleted in Hindi, e.g.

(1) इस कपड़े का रंग पक्का नहीं (है)।

(2) मैं इतना गरीब नहीं (हूँ) कि आपका पैसा न चुका सकूँ।

There has been a tradition of restricting the copula sentences to nominal, adjectival and adverbial copula sentences only. Some modern linguists like Halliday (1967, 1970) include under copula adverbs even such sentences as represent time, location and manner and call them *relational sentences*. Seen this way, any adverbial phrase, which is an obligatory constituent of the sentence is capable of forming a copula sentences, e.g.

(1) पैसे अलमारी **में** हैं। (locative adverb)

(2) बैठक सोमवार **को** है। (temporal adverb)

(3) यह पानी पीने **के लिए** है। (purpose)

(4) यह सारा झगड़ा आप ही **के कारण** है। (reason)

(5) लड़की हाथ में बैग **लिए हुए** थी। (manner)

4.2 Linking Verbs

As we have noted, the verb that links the subject and the complement of a copula sentence is called a *linking verb*. For instance in the sentence राजेश डॉक्टर है (Rajesh is a doctor), है is a linking verb that links the subject (राजेश) with the complement (doctor). The word copula is basically used for the verb *to be* but the term *linking verb* includes a few other verbs also which perform analogous functions, like the verb बना (वह डॉक्टर **बना**), निकलना (जग्गू चोर **निकला**), रहना (वह बीमार **रहता** है, etc.).

At the lexical level, however, the Hindi linking verbs can be grouped into two classes – (a) Linking verbs that are derived from the verb root *हो* (e.g. होना, होता etc) and (b) Linking verbs that are derived from other verb roots like **बन**, लग etc.

From the functional point of view, however, the following three inflectional forms of *हो* in Hindi are more relevant for our purpose: (a) stative *हो*, (b) non-stative *हो* and (c) stative *होता* है which can be illustrated as follows:

Linking Verb है

Stative हो	Non-stative/inflectional हो	Stative होता है
अनिल नाराज़ होता है/होगा	अनिल नाराज़ है	कौवा काला होता है

4.3 Types of Linking Verbs

4.3.1 Stative *हो*

The stative linking verbs (see 4.3.1) denote the *state* of the subject as it is whereas the non-stative verbs denote the change of state or beginning of the change/action. For instance, The verb नाराज़ होना in the sentence अनिल नाराज़ है is a stative verb and अनिल नाराज़ हुआ is non-stative. It is non-stative because it suggests a change of state i.e. from no-anger to anger. In Hindi there is a single form, but in English there are two different words *be* and *become* to denote the stative and non-stative forms.

The linking verbs may be both - aspective as well as non aspective. Aspective linking verbs can attach the aspect markers after them e.g. होता है, बनता है, बने etc. Non-aspective linking verbs like है and था can not attach the aspect or mood markers,

Non-lexical verbs like है and था (4.3.1) do not carry any lexical meaning and only perform their usual grammatical functions in the sentence (see 4.3.1b). The lexical linking verbs either do not denote any lexical meaning and simply perform their grammatical functions or abandon their normal lexical meaning and express some unique meaning or nuance, e.g. निकलना, ठहरना etc. (जग्गू चोर निकला, वह बड़ा तीसमारखाँ बनता है). The first is called the normal linking verb and the second is called the idiomatised linking verb.

At the grammatical level Hindi has four forms of हो to denote the stative information:

Tense:	है (present)	(1) अनिल नाराज़ है।
	था (past)	(2) अनिल नाराज़ था।
Mood	हो	(3) शायद अनिल नाराज़ हो।
	होता	(4) (अगर) अनिल नाराज़ होता।
	होगा	(5) अनिल (अब भी) नाराज़ होगा।

These five verb forms share a few common features - they denote a state (and not action) in these forms; they are used as main verbs and not auxiliary verbs, they are the finite verbs of the sentence and, therefore, they can not append intensifiers (like जाना etc.), the forms हो, होता, होगा here denote the mood and not the aspect, no lexical verb can be used before it and if it is used it no longer remains a linking verb but becomes an auxiliary verb, e.g. जाता है, जाता था, जाता हो etc. See

(6) ऊँट एक जानवर होता है। (*हुआ, *हो रहा है)

(7) वह दिन में दफ़्तर में होता है/था। *(हुआ, *हो रहा है)

It is important to note that the intensifier जाना can not be used with this type of intensifier (e.g. *ऊँट एक जानवर हो जाता है, *वह दिन में दफ़्तर में हो जाता है).

4.3.2 Non-stative (inflectional हो) हो

In order to denote the dynamic or non-stative information, (i.e. change of state) , the copula verb हो has 12 forms, out of which six are formed through aspectual suffixes and three through modal suffixes. Out of these the last (13) is a non-copula imperative form:

Aspect :	होता (incomplete)	(8) अनिल नाराज़ होता है।
	हो रहा (continuous)	(9) अनिल नाराज़ हो रहा है।

	हुआ (complete)	(10) अनिल नाराज़ हुआ।
Mood :	हो (subjunctive)	(11) (शायद) अनिल नाराज़ हो।
	होगा (future)	(12) अनिल नाराज़ होगा।
	हो/होवे/होइए/होइएगा (imperative)	(13) नाराज़ न होइए।

(non-copula)

The characteristics of all the above six verb forms (8-13) is that instead of giving information about the state of the subject, they provide information about the change of the state (called the inchoative), (b) except for the verb-form (9) it is possible to use the intensifier जाना wherever necessary, e.g. अनिल नाराज़ हो जाता है/हो गया, शायद अनिल नाराज़ हो जाए/जाएगा etc.

There is, however, a difference between the aspective sentences (9-10) and the modal verb-forms (11-12). It is possible to use the auxiliary verbs (है, था, होता, होगा) after the aspective verb-forms, e.g अनिल नाराज़ होता है/था/हो/ होगा. Contrary to this, it is not possible to add any auxiliary verb form after the modal suffixes (11-14) (*अनिल नाराज़ हो गयाहै). It is important to note that the surface structures of the modal (mood based) sentences (11-12) may appear the same and the only distinctive feature may be the presence or absence of the stative and non-stative feature, e.g.

5, 12 अनिल नाराज़ होगा = अनिल अभी तक नाराज़ होगा (*हो जाएगा)।
अनिल यह सुन कर नाराज़ होगा = हो जाएगा।

4.3.3 Stative होता है

The verb form होता है in Hindi has a dual function in the sentence. It shows a state of an action as well as a change of state. See the following sentences:

(1) उसे देखकर अनिल नाराज *होता है*। (non-stative, or change of state)

(2) कौवा काला *होता है*। (stative)

Remember that both the above sentences have the same verb-form -*होता है* but they differ in their semantic structures. The verb-form *होता है* as in नाराज़ होता है does not indicate a *state* but the *change of state* i.e. from being in a normal state to becoming angry. On the other hand, the verb-form होता है in the sentence कौवा काला *होता है* is stative, i.e. the verb forms cannot vary like *कौवा काला हुआ/*हो रहा है*/होता था, or *कौवा

काला हो जाता है. etc. whereas in sentence (1) we can generate varied tense and aspectual forms like अनिल आज नाराज़ हुआ/होगा/हो रहा है etc. Another difference is that the non-stative होता है can be used with an intensifier like जाना etc., e.g. अनिल नाराज़ हो गया etc.).

The sentences of the type कौवा काला होता है has, therefore, been termed as *stative होता है*.

(a) The Subclassification of Stative होता है:

There are two broad classes of Hindi stative sentences – (a) Universal stative sentences, and (b) Generalized stative sentences –

(a) Universal Stative sentences express universal and absolute truth about the entire class and not only about any specific member and is, therefore, not bound by any limits of time or space e.g.

(i) Class inclusion: (when a class becomes a member of a larger class the smaller class is supposed to be a part of a bigger class, e.g.

(1) ऊँट एक जानवर होता है।

(2) वैष्णव हिंदू होते हैं।

(ii) Generic : When a tendency or quality becomes a characteristic of the whole class it is called a generic characteristic, e.g.

(1) कौवा काला होता है।

(2) समुद्र का जल खारा होता है।

(3) पहाड़ी लोगों की नाक़ चपटी होती है।

(4) *समुद्र का जल खारा होता है।

(5) *बलबीर की नाक चपटी होती है।

(6) भाषा एक व्यवस्था होती है।

(7) साल में बारह महीने होते हैं।

(8) हाथी के एक सूँड होती है।

(9) पानी पीने के लिए होता है।

(10) शेर जंगल में होता है।

(iii) Unique Nouns

(11) सूरज गरम होता है।

(12) पृथ्वी गोल होती है।

(b) Generalised/Contextualised Stative Verbs

(13) जग्गू हमेशा पिए हुए होता है।

(14) सतीश शाम को घर में होता है।

4.3.4 Human Relation Marker हो

The linking verb हो also at times serves to denote a type of social or family relationship between two entities, e.g. वह आपका कौन होता है, इस रिश्ते से आप मेरे साले हुए (subpattern 5a) etc. In sentences such as this, the subject and the complement have to be human beings. There is, however, a restriction on the use of continuous tense.

4.3.5 Lexical Linking Verbs

Apart from the non-stative हो there are also quite a few other lexical verbs which along with their usual meanings also function as linking verbs e.g. बजना, रहना, लगना, सिद्ध होना, दिखाई देना, प्रतीत होना etc. See:

(3) सुधीर बड़ा आदमी बन गया है। (change of state)

(4) वह बिल्कुल अंग्रेज़ लगता है। (appearance)

(5) जगदीश बीमार रहता है। (duration)

(6) वह चोर सिद्ध हुआ। (confirmation)

At the deeper level, these are normal stative sentences – सुधीर बड़ा आदमी है, वह अंग्रेज़ है, जगदीश बीमार है, वह चोर है. In these sentences when the lexical semantic elements of बनना, लगना etc. are added, these sentences acquire some special nuance or meaning, e.g.

जगदीश बीमार है + durarion = जगदीश बीमार रहता है।

4.3.6 Eccentric Linking Verbs

Special linking verbs are the ones which completely abandon their lexical meanings and acquire a weird or eccentric meaning which may or may not have any relation with their actual meanings. At times they may represent some ghost *semantic structure* (Chafe 1970: 70) and acquire an idiomatic tone, e.g. निकालना, बनना, रहना etc. See:

(7) जग्गू चोर निकला। (unexpected)

(8) वह बड़ा तीसमारखाँ बनता है। (pride)

(9) खेल फीका रहा। (perception)

One characteristic of such verbs is that they largely express or represent the personal viewpoint or preferences of the speaker.

4.4 The Feature Analysis of Copula Sentence Patterns

Sub-pattern-1 है[1] (identification)

NP (subject) <+identified, +definite >	**NP (complement)** <+identified, +definite, +inversion>	**Linking verb** है[1] **(identified)** <-aspect, -lexical, +stative>
(1) रफ़ी	मेरा ड्राइवर	है।
(2) मेरे घर का नंबर	के-131	है।
(3) रामलाल	मोटा वाला आदमी	है।
(4) मैंने जिस लड़की को बुलाया	वह मेरी बहन	थी।

COMMENT: (SP-1)

In this sub-pattern the subject is a known element and the noun complement is an unknown element in which the unknown element (मेरा ड्राइवर) is the identification of the known element (रफ़ी). The known element which is being identified is called *identified* and the unknown element which provides the identification of the known element is called an *identifier*. The linking verb है performs the function of identification. The identification may be functional (related to his function), e.g. रफ़ी मेरा ड्राइवर है or formal (based on form), e.g. रामलाल मोटा वाला आदमी है.

All proper nouns are supposed to be definite nouns, e.g. सतीश, राम, अशोक etc. Besides, by using definitive modifiers like यह, वह, मेरा, उसका, वाला one can convert an indefinite noun into a definite one, e.g.

ड्राइवर (indefinite noun)	>	मेरा ड्राइवर (definite noun)
मकान (indefinite noun	>	यह मकान (defnite noun)
आदमी (indefinite noun)	>	मोटा वाला आदमी (definite noun)

Sub-pattern-2 है[2] (class-member)

NP (subject) <+member, +definite >	**NP (complement)** <+class, -definite, +inversion>	**Linking verb** हैं[2] (class-member) <-/lexical, -aspect, +stative>
(1) मेरे पिता जी	अध्यापक	हैं।
(2) भारत	एक कृषिप्रधान देश	है।
(3) उसका रोना	ढकोसला	था।
(4) बिना टिकट यात्रा करना	जुर्म	है।

COMMENT: (SP-2)

The relationship between the subject and the complement in this sub-pattern (SP-2) is that of a member and the class. मेरे पिताजी is a definite entity which is a member of the class of teachers. In this sub-pattern the complement does not answer the question *who* or *which one*, but *what*. मेरे पिताजी क्या हैं? अध्यापक हैं. In this sub-pattern the relationship between the subject and the complement is that of a member and the class. मेरे पिताजी is a definite entity who is a member of the class of teachers. Here the complement does not answer the question *who* or *which one*, but *what*: मेरे पिताजी क्या हैं? अध्यापक हैं.

Sub-pattern-3 हो[1] (class inclusion)

NP (subject) <+member (sub-class), -definite >	**NP (complement)** <+class, -definite, -inversion>	**Linking verb** हो[1] (class-inclusion) <-lexical, +ता aspect, +stative>
(1) ऊँट	एक जानवर	होता है।
(2) वैष्णव	हिंदू	होते हैं।
(3) नर्सें	स्त्रियाँ	होती हैं।
(4) (पहले) सैनिक	राजपूत	हुआ करते थे।

COMMENT: (SP-3)

(a) *Class-member relationship:* In this sentence also the relationship between the subject and the noun complement is that of a member and a class but the member (subject) is itself a sub-class and not a specific member. The linking verb होता है denotes the merger of a sub-class inclusion.

From the viewpoint of features this sub-pattern can be said to be derived from the sub-pattern -2 (class members) with the difference that it has an additional feature of universal truth or class inclusion. Many languages have a common sentence pattern for the two sentences -*my father is a teacher* and *camel is an animal,* but in Hindi an additional verb-form होता है is used in such cases, e.g. ऊँट एक जानवर *होता* है. (see 4.3.3)

(b) *Unstressed* एक. ऊँट एक प्रकार का जानवर होता है is equivalent to saying ऊँट एक जानवर है. In such a case ऊँट remains unstressed in the sentence. In corresponding English sentences it is rendered as *a kind of animal*.

Sub-pattern-4 A है[3] (demonstrative)

NP (subject) demonstrative pronoun <+indication>	**NP (complement)** indicated object <+definite, +concrete, +non-present>	**Linking verb** है[1] (indication) <+present, -lexical, +stative>
(1) यह	कलम	है।
(2) वह	रंगनाथन का मकान	है।
(3) ये	आपके रुपए	हैं।
(4) ये	मेरे बड़े भाई	हैं।

Sub-pattern-4 B रह[1] (demonstrative)

NP (subject) demonstrative pronoun <+indication>	**NP (complement)** indicated object <+definite> +inversion	**Linking verb रह[1]** **(indication)** <+stylistic, + inversion, +या aspect +stative>
(1) ये	आपके रुपए	रहे।**
(2) वो	आपका मकान	रहा।**
(3) यह	आपका भाई	रहा।**

**After inversion these sentences will be : (1) ये रहे आपके रुपए, (2) वो रहा आपका मकान, (4) वह रहा आपका भाई।

COMMENT:

(a) *Difference between the demonstrative and class-member based sentences*: The demonstrative sentence यह कलम है and the class-member sub-pattern वह डॉक्टर है (sub-pattern-1) seems to be similar on the surface structure, but they are qualitatively different from each other in their deep structure.

(b) *English-Hindi demonstrative paradigm*- In the demonstrative sub-patterns only demonstrative pronouns (usually यह/ये, वह/वे, वो) are used and not the personal pronouns. It is a coincidence that Hindi has the same set of paradigms for demonstrative as well as personal pronouns (यह, ये, वह, वे). In English however, there are separate paradigms for demonstrative pronouns. Hence a Hindi sentence वह डॉक्टर है may give two meanings:

वह डॉक्टर है।	He is a doctor.	sub-pattern 2
	That is the doctor.	sub-pattern 4a

(c) The second NP of this sub-pattern is definite and generally concrete, but at times it is possible to extend its figurative use, as in यह तुम्हारी करतूत है, or कैसा चमत्कार है.

(d) *Phrase Inversion* -An inversion of phrases in also possible in such constructions, e.g.

ये आपके रुपए रहे > ये रहे आपके रुपए>

Sub-pattern-5 A हो[2] (relation)

NP (subject)	**NP (complement)**	**Linking verb हो[2]** (relation)
<+identified, +definite	<+identified, +definite +human± ±relation/blood relation>	<+'-ता'aspect, +stative>
(1) रामलाल	मेरा बड़ा भाई	होता है।
(2) वह	मेरा बॉस	होता है।
(3) वह	आपका कौन	होता है?
(4) कभी राधा	चंपा की सहेली	होती थी।

Sub-pattern-5 B लग[1] (relation)

NP (subject)	**NP (complement)**	**Linking verb लग[1] (relation)**
<+ identified, +definite, +human >	<+identified, +definite +human, +relation/ blood relation>	<+stative -'रह' aspect>
(1) साधना	मेरी बहन	लगती है।
(2) रमेश	तुम्हारा साला	लगा।
(3) वह	मेरा कुछ नहीं	लगता।

COMMENT: (SP-5)

(a) *Normal vs. Blood Relationship*: Both these sentence sub-patterns are derived from the earlier mentioned sub-pattern -1 (रफ़ी मेरा ड्राइवर है). Only two features distinguish them from the another, i.e. +human, +kinship. These two features closely delimit the area of identification to certain social and blood relationships only. The sub-pattern 5a हो[2] can accept both the social as well as blood relationships whereas in 5b लग only blood relationship is permissible, e.g.

रामलाल मेरा बड़ा भाई होता/लगता है। (sub-pattern 5 a)
वह मेरा बॉस होता है/*लगता है। (sub-pattern 5 b)

(b) *Basic Relationship:* The use of लग-relationship is not normal with reference to a mother, father, husband, wife and other basic relationships (*वह मेरा पिता लगता है), but it is used to refer to the derived or distant relationships. The sentence वह मेरा भाई है indicates that the brother is real, but in the sentence वह मेरा भाई लगता है it gives the meaning of a cousin brother.

(c) *Structural Restrictions*: The linking verb लग does not normally accept the continuous tense marker -य रह (*रामलाल मेरा बड़ा भाई हो रहा है, though some aspect forms are permissible in certain usages, e.g. इस रिश्ते से आप मेरे बहनोई हुए/लगे) In certain contexts. वह तुम्हारा क्या लग रहा है actually reads as यह तुम्हारा क्या लगता है ?

Sub-pattern-6a हो[3] (change of state)

NP (subject) prior state	**NP (complement)** changed state	**Linking Verb** हो[3] (change of state) <+process, -conscious, +lexical, +aspect, -stative>
(1) चंपा	युवती	हो गई।
(2) रमेश	बड़ा आदमी	हो गया।
(3) ये लोग	यहाँ के नागरिक	हो गए हैं।
(4) मानव-संस्कृति	अमानव संस्कृति	होती जा रही है।

Sub-pattern-6 B बन[1] (change of state)

NP (subject) prior state	**NP (complement)** changed state	**Linking Verb बन[1]** (change of state) <+process, +conscious, +lexical, +aspect -stative>
(1) चंपा	नर्स	बन गई है।
(2) रमेश	बड़ा आदमी	बन गया है।
(3) ये लोग	यहाँ के नागरिक	बन गए हैं।
(4) मंत्री	राजा	बना।

COMMENT: (SP-6)

Natural and conscious change of state : Normally the linking verb हो in this context denotes a natural growth or development while in the case of बन it denotes an element of conscious effort on the part of the subject. See:

(1) a - चंपा युवती हो गई (natural change of state)
*चंपा युवती बन गई (subject's effort impossible)
(2) a- चंपा नर्स बन गई है (subject's efforts are important)
चंपा नर्स बन गई है (subject's efforts are not important)
(Eng. Champa grew into a young lady.)

Sub-pattern-7 रह[2] (duration)

NP (subject) <+ identified/member>	**NP (complement)** <+identified/class>	**Linking verb रह[2]** (duration) <+lexical-रह aspect+stative>
(1) मैं	(कुछ दिनों) इस समिति का अध्यक्ष	रहा।
(2) सतीश	यहाँ का छात्र	रह चुका है।
(3) आप	(जीवन भर) क्लर्क के क्लर्क	रहेंगे।

COMMENT: (SP-7)

(a) *Time Perception:* This sub-pattern is also derived from the sub-pattern 1-2. In these sentences there is a relationship of identifier and identified. Only the time element differentiates it from one another.

For instance, if we add the time element, in the sentence मैं इस समिति का सदस्य हूँ, the sentence it will be: मैं कुछ दिनों इस समिति का अध्यक्ष रहा. This sub-pattern normally expects a durative adverb like कुछ दिनों, जीवन भर, कुछ समय etc.

(b) *Structural Restrictions*: There is a restriction on the use of continuous tense रह in this sub-pattern *वह यहाँ का छात्र रह रहा है।

Sub-pattern-8 सिद्ध हो (Proving)

NP (subject) <+member>	NP (complement) <+class, +quality addition>	Linking Verb **सिद्ध हो** (confirmation) <+lexical, -कि,+stative, +aspect>
(1) वह	कुशल अध्यापक	सिद्ध हुआ।
(2) हेमा	एक सफल पत्नी	सिद्ध होगी।
(3) यह नुस्खा	रामबाण	साबित हुआ।

COMMENT: (SP-8)

(a) *Proof and quality addition:* There is a relationship of class and member between the subject and the complement. The additional feature of the verb of this sub-patttern is confirmation or reinforcement and that of the complement is quality addition, i.e. not only a teacher but an efficient teacher. In other words, only such nouns can occupy the place of the noun complement which basically represnt the quality or which can be associated with some adjectives. See:

(1) a - वह कुशल अध्यापक सिद्ध हुआ।
b- *वह अध्यापक सिद्ध हुआ।

(2) a- हेमा एक सफल पत्नी सिद्ध होगी।
b- *हेमा एक पत्नी सिद्ध होगी।

It is only because of the epithets like कुशल and सफल that the phrase acquires the quality of an adjective.

Sub-pattern-9 दिखाई दे - class

NP (subject) <+member>	**NP (complement)** <+class,-definite,+form based>	**Linking verb** <+appearance, +visual, -estimate, +lexical, -कि, +aspect, +stative>
(1) वह	पुलिस अफ़सर	दिखाई देता/लगता है।
(2) आपकी लड़की	बंगालन	दिखाई देती/लगती है।
(3) वह	तपेदिक का मरीज़	नज़र आता है।
(4) वह लड़का	(बिल्कुल) राजेश खन्ना	दिखाई देता/लगता है।

COMMENT: (SP-9)

(a) *Visual Appearance*: There is a class and member relationship of between both the NPs - the subject and the complement, and therefore this sub-pattern is also supposed to be derived from the sub-pattern -2. We get a sentence like वह पुलिस अफ़सर दिखाई देता है by adding the visual feature दिखाई देता है/लगता है. There is a form-based feature of resemblance in this sub-pattern. Linking verbs used in this pattern are the ones which represent the features <appearance, +visual, +guess>, e.g. दिखाई देना, नज़र आना, लगना, प्रतीत होना etc. (See also sub-pattern 16 a, b, c.)

(b) *Conjecture-based and form-based appearances*: The appearance may be of two types- (1) visual appearance based and (2) guess-based. This sub-pattern accepts only sentences which are based on visual appearance and not the ones based on guess. The basic feature of verbs like दिखाई देना, नज़र आना etc. are visual appearance whereas the verb लग shares the features of both -- the visual as well as guess. Note the structural difference between the two:

(i) The appearance based on *guess* is a mental experience and, therefore, like other mental experiences it can be expressed through a कि-clause whereas it is not possible in the case of visual appearance. See the difference:

1) *लगता है* वह पुलिस अफ़सर है। <guess>

1b)* दिखाई देता है कि वह पुलिस अफ़सर है। <visual>

(ii) Since the sentence वह पुलिस अफ़सर लगता है is marked by both the types of features, the sentence वह पुलिस अफ़सर लगता है can express both the types of meanings:

1. मेरा ख्याल है वह पुलिस अफ़सर है। <+guess, - visual>

2. वह शक्ल सूरत से पुलिस अफ़सर दिखाई देता है। <- guess, + visual>

The sense of visuality is inherent in the verb दिखाई देना and, therefore, there is no need to mention the visual markers like देखने में etc. (*वह देखने में पुलिस अफ़सर दिखाई देता है).

(c) *Objective and Subjective Expressions*: Verbs like लगना, दिखाई देना basically require three participants whose third participant is the experiencer + को and in this form it constitutes the sub-pattern 25 and 26:

(5) *मुझे* वह पुलिस अफ़सर लगता है/दिखाई देता है।

In the corresponding copula sentences the experiencer +को normally remains omitted and is mentioned at a surface level only when the opinion or view of the the experiencer is needed to be mentioned, .e.g *मुझे* वह तपेदिक का मरीज़ लगता है/नज़र आता है।

Sub-pattern-10 A निकल (unexpected)

NP (subject) <+identified/member>	**NP (complement)** <+identifier/class>	**Linking verb निकल** (unexpected) <+usage, +stative>
(1) जग्गु	चोर	निकला।
(2) शेखर	छुपा रुस्तम	निकला।
(3) राधा	मेरी पत्नी की सहेली	निकली।
(4) आज के बच्चे	माँ-बाप के भी गुरु	निकलते हैं।

Sub-pattern-10 B निकल[2]

NP (subject) <+member +human, -first person>	**NP (complement)** <+class,+satire, +big>	**Linking verb बन[2]** (think big) <+convention, -या aspect, -mood, -नहीं-, + stative>
(1) वह	बड़ा तीसमारखाँ	बनता था।
(2) आप (तो)	बड़े सिद्धांतवादी	बनते थे।
(3) शीला	बड़ी आदर्शवादी	बन रही है।
(4) ये लोग	बड़े पैसे वाले	बनते थे।

Sub-pattern-10 C आ

NP (subject) <+member+human, -first person>	**NP (complement)** <+class, +satire, + कहाँ का>	**Linking verb आ** (challenge) <+convention, +exclamation, +या aspect, -no- +stative>
(1) आप	कहाँ के नवाब	आए !
(2) वह	आपकी कहाँ की बहन	आई !
(3) तुम	कहाँ के लाट साहब	आए !

Sub-pattern-10 D ठहर

NP (subject) <+identified/member>	**NP (complement)** <+identifier/class>	**Linking verb ठहर** (pre conception)
(1) आप तो	साहब	ठहरे।
(2) हम तो	आपके नौकर	ठहरे।
(3) मैं तो	तुम्हारी सौतेली माँ	ठहरी।

COMMENT: (SP-10)

(a) *Analogous stylistic features:* All the above four sub-groups share similar stylistic features. They are all very closely related to the immediate contexts. They mostly use some special or idiomatic linking verbs in which they abandon their regular lexical meanings and acquire some slightly different menings.

(b) These sentences have strong semantic and structural restrictions of use, e.g. छुपा रुस्तम *निकला*, साहब *ठहरे*. The change in the verb-form is also restricted, e.g.

* मैं बड़ा तीसमारखाँ बनता हूँ।

* आप कहाँ के तीसमारखाँ हैं।

(c)The subject of ठहर normally requires the use of तो after the subject (मैं *तो* तुम्हारी सौतेली माँ ठहरी।)

Sub-pattern-11 है (as member)

NP (subject) <+member, +definite>	**ADJ (complement)** <-definite>	**Linking verb** है (member) <-aspect ,-lexical, +stative>
(1) राधा	सुंदर	है।
(2) चिड़िया	ज़िंदा	है।
(3) मेरा संदूक	लकड़ी का	था।
(4) यह खिलौना	मोम का बना हुआ	है।
(5) खिड़की	टूटी हुई	थी।
(6) यह किताब	मेरी लिखी हुई	है।
(7) यह पेन	सस्तेवाला	है।
(8) यह साड़ी	कभी न फटने वाली	है।
(9) घास पर चलना	मना	है।

COMMENT: (SP-11)

(a) *Modifier-Modified Relationship*: The relationship between the subject and the complement in this sentence pattern is that of an NP and Adj. The linking verb है here is only stative i.e. it only denotes the state (e.g. लड़का बीमार है and not the change of state as in लड़का बीमार *हो गया* (it in fact pertains to another sentence pattern 13A). It will be evident that most of the adjective complements in the adjective slot are adjectival participles (मोम का बना हुआ, टूटी हुई, सस्तेवाला etc.).

(b) *Participle and pseudo participle forms*: The words मना and निषिद्ध in the sentences घास पर चलना मना है and यहाँ धूम्रपान *निषिद्ध* है functionally belong to the same word-class but the word मना has some structural restrictions. मना, for instance, is not a derived participle form just as the word निषिद्ध is. Secondly the past participle निषिद्ध can be used as an adjective in combinations निषिद्ध कार्य, but it is not possible to have a combination like *मना काम. Therefore, there has been a tradition of accepting मना as an inseparable component of the complex verb *मना होना।*

(c) *Past Perfect Participles*: (Sentences 4-6) represent three types of adjectives:

1. यह खिलौना मोम से बना है > मोम से बना हुआ खिलौना
2. खिड़की टूट गई > टूटी हुई खिड़की
3. मैंने किताब लिखी > मेरी लिखी हुई किताब

It is important to note that at times such past participle forms can also be fallacious which can be clarified only through the context, as बना in sentence (4):

4. खाना बन रहा है: sense 1: खाना बन गया है।
sense 2: खाना बना हुआ है।

It is in the sense 2 only that this sentence is covered under the present sentence pattern:

Sub-pattern-12 (class)

NP (subject) <+ member, - definite>	ADJ (complement)	ADJ (complement) <-lexical,+ता aspect,+stative>
(1) कौवा	काला	होता है।
(2) समुद्र का जल	खारा	होता है।
(3) पहाड़ी लोगों की नाक	चपटी	होती है।
(4) सूरज	गरम	होता है।
(5) पृथ्वी	गोल	(होती) है।

COMMENT: (SP-12)

(a) *Generic Features*: The features and tendencies defined in the adjective complements represent a generic information, tendencies or qualities of a whole class or genre and not any particular member of the class. It is like a universal truth about the class as a whole, as in the sentence कौवा काला होता है. It is, therefore, also possible to use any inclusive adjective like सभी, हर etc. before the NP, e.g. सभी कौवे काले होते हैं. If the subject of these sentences were to be non-generic or specific as, for instance, in the sentence बलबीर की नाक चपटी है, we could not have an appropriate generic sentence like.*बलबीर की नाक चपटी होती है.

(b) *Unique Nouns*: Some nouns like चाँद, सूरज, पृथ्वी, ईश्वर etc. are unique nouns because they do not have any other members in their class. For instance, there is only one sun, one earth and one God with no other members of the class. They can not also be technically called

Proper Nouns. Such nouns are, therefore, referred to as unique nouns.

(c) *Universal Features*: The adjective complement in this sub-pattern describes the generic and universal features of the subject, e.g. सूरज गरम होता है. In certain cases, however, होता है also gets omitted, e.g. सूरज गरम है, पृथ्वी गोल है etc.

(d) *Generalization*: Sometimes it is possible to resort to some type of generalization of the features instead of their univresalization particularly in relation to some adverbial constituents of the sentence, e.g.

जग्गू *हमेशा* पिए हुए होता है।

पहले वह बहुत शरीफ़ होता था।

Sub-pattern-13 A हो (Change of state)

NP (subject)	**ADJ (complement)**	**Linking verb हो (change of state)** <+process -effort, +lexical, +aspect, -stative>
(1) लड़का	बीमार	हो गया (= हुआ)।
(2) लोग	बेचैन	हो रहे हैं।
(3) मेरा बाहर जाना	मुश्किल	हो गया है।
(4) साहब	सख़्त मिज़ाज का	होने लगा है।

Sub-pattern-13 हो (Change of state)

NP (subject)	**ADJ (complement)**	**Linking verb बन** <+process, +effort, +lexical +aspect, -stative>
(1) लड़का	शरीफ़	बन गया है।
(2) हम लोग	यहीं के	बन गए हैं।
(3) आपके लड़के	पैसे वाले	बन गए हैं।

COMMENT: (SP-13)

(a) *Change of state*: The linking verb हो (हो गया) is the non-stative or dynamic counterparts of the stative linking verb है (लड़का बीमार है

>लड़का बीमार हुआ). It does not denote the *state* but the *change of state.* It does not denote *to be* but *to become.* In Hindi हो and बन in such situations are generally accompanied by some intensifier, like जाना, e.g. हो जाना, बन जाना.

(b) *Difference between बन and हो*: Despite the similarity between बनना and होना, there is a slight difference between the two. हो basically denotes the automatic or natural change of state in which the role of the subject is minimal (हो जाना) whereas बनना generally denotes a change of state in which there is some contribution or initiative on the part of the subject.

Sub-pattern-14 रह (duration)

NP (subject)	**ADJ (complement)**	**Linking verb रह (duration)** <+lexical, -'रह' aspect, +stative>
a-(1) रमेश	बीमार	रहता है।
(2) ऐसे लोग	भयभीत	रहते हैं।
(3) सभी दुकानें	(इतवार को) बंद	रहती हैं।
(4) वह	अवाक्	रह गया।
b-(5) मैं	(रात भर) जगा	रहा।
(6) वे लोग	(यहाँ) लेटे	रहते हैं।
(7) वह	(दिन भर) सोया	रहता है।

COMMENT: (SP-14)

(a) *Time Perception*: This pattern is also derived from the sub-pattern 11. In the sentence रमेश बीमार है (sub-pattern 11) the condition of the subject was expressed in terms of certain point of time but in the sentence रमेश बीमार रहता है, the element of time duration stands extended. Compare मैं इस समिति का अध्यक्ष रहा (sub-pattern 7).

(b) *Time and Space Participle*: The sentences of this sub-pattern anticipate adverbs/adverbials denoting time or space (हमेशा, रात भर, इतवार को etc. In sentences where they are not specifically mentioned in the sentence they are insinuated through the context.

(c) *State-ending Past Participles*: The complements given in sentences (5-7) are modifiers which are made up of past participles. This can be explained in two ways:

(5a) मैं x जगा (हुआ) x रहा। (subject x complement x LV)

(5b) मैं जगा रहा। (subject x verb)

According to the first interpretation (जगा is a complement and according to the second interpretation it is an adverb in which -रह is a habitual aspect marker (see 2.9.5.a). It may be noted that the past participle forms of all kinds of verbs can not be used in the place of जगा. Only past participle forms of state-ending verbs (see 2.9.5) can be used in its place and not even process ending verbs. खुलना, बैठना, लेटना, सोना, जागना etc. are state-ending verbs and verbs like लिखना, खाना, देखना, रोना etc. are process-ending verbs. The past participle forms of the process-ending verbs can not be used in the position of a complement e.g.*मोहन लिखा/देखा रहता है. (For the corresponding adverbial form (जग्गू पिए हुए था see sub-pattern 20)

Sub-pattern-15 (सिद्ध हो)

NP (subject) ±	**ADJ (complement)** <value judgement>	**Linking verb सिद्ध हो** (confirmation) <+lexical, -कि, +aspect, +stative>
(1) यह दवा	कारगर	सिद्ध हुई।
(2) हमारी सारी दौड़-धूप	बेकार	साबित हुई।
(3) मेरा नौकर	बिल्कुल निकम्मा	सिद्ध हुआ।

COMMENT: (SP-15)

Value Judgment: Semantically this sub-pattern is also derived from the sub-pattern 11 and is the counterpart of the nominal sub-pattern. In this sub-pattern only such adjectives are used which need to be evaluated or proved. These adjectives provide a token of testing or evaluation. These adjectives also provide a value judgment (see 2.3.3), as for example यह दवा कारगर सिद्ध हुई, but a sentence like यह दवा खट्टी सिद्ध हुई is not natural because it does not need valuation. Some other synonyms of this category are साबित होना, प्रमाणित होना etc.

Sub-pattern-16 (दिखाई दे (seem-class)

NP (subject)	ADJ (complement)	Linking verb दिखाई-दे class <+appearance, +visual, -guess, +lexical, -कि-clause , +aspect, +stative>
(1) लड़की	सुंदर	दिखाई देती है।
(2) वह	अमिताभ-जैसा	लगता है/दिखाई देता है।
(3) आप	कुछ कमज़ोर	नज़र आ रहे हैं।

COMMENT: (SP-16)

(a) *Visual Semblance*: This sub-pattern is also semantically derived from the sub-pattern 11 because the sentence लड़की सुंदर दिखाई देती है is obtained from the sentence लड़की सुंदर है by the addition of the semantic component visual semblance. This sub-pattern is a counterpart of the nominal sub-pattern (9) - only an adjective has been substituted in place of a noun (see sub-pattern 9).

(b) *Form-based Semblance*: In this sub-pattern only such adjectives can be used which share the feature <+ semblance, +visual, +guess>, e.g. दिखाई देना, नज़र आना, प्रतीत होना, लगना etc.

(c) *Mental and Visual Experience*: As has been explained in the sub-pattern (9b), the resemblance can be of two types: one based on mental experience and the other based on visual experience. In this sub-pattern only sentences which express visual resemblance, are included and not those which express guess or mental experience. The verbs दिखाई देना and नज़र आना basically express visual experience, but the verb लगना is capable of expressing both visual as well as mental experience. This distinction can be brought out more clearly with the help of कि-clause because the mental experiences can be expressed through a कि-clause whereas pure visual experiences can not be expressed through a कि-clause. See:

(1) लड़की सुंदर दिखाई देती है। (visual)

(1a) *दिखाई देता है कि लड़की सुंदर है। (mental)

(4) लड़की सुंदर लगती है। (=beautiful to look at) (visual)

(4a) लगता है लड़की सुंदर है। (=I guess) (mental)

(d) *Experiencer + को*: Verbs like लगना, दिखाई देना etc. have the capacity to be used in a subject + को sentences also e.g. (मुझे लड़की सुंदर लगती है) but here it basically expresses the subjective view of the experiencer. On the contrary the present sub-pattern basically projects an objective view. (see sub-pattern 9c).

Sub-pattern-17 A (निकल)

NP (subject)	**ADJ (complement)**	**Linking verb** निकल (unexpected) <+usage (रूढ़), +stative>
(1) आम	सड़े हुए	निकले।
(2) उनका कहना	सच	निकला।
(3) (इनमें से) कोई न कोई	जाना-पहचाना	निकल आता है।

Sub-pattern-17 B (बन)

NP (subject)	**ADJ (complement)**	**Linking verb** बन (बड़ा समझना) <+usage (रूढ़), -या aspect, -mood, +stative>
(1) रामू	बड़ा होशियार	बनता था।
(2) आप	बड़े चालाक	बनते थे।
(3) तीनों लड़कियाँ	बड़ी शरीफ़	बन रही थीं।

Sub-pattern-17 C (ठहर -)

NP (subject) **+तो**	**ADJ (complement)**	**Linking verb** ठहर (pre-supposition) <+covention, -या aspect, +stative>
(1) आप तो	नाजुक	ठहरे।
(2) हम तो	पराए	ठहरे।
(3) सिल्विया तो	आपकी चहेती	ठहरी।
(4) मैं तो	नासमझ	ठहरा।

Sub-pattern-17 D (रह)

NP (subject)	ADJ (complement) <+presumption, +value judgement>	Linking verb रह <+presumption, -रह aspect, +stative>
(1) खेल	फीका	रहा।
(2) आपका आना	बेकार	रहा।
(3) पार्टी	ऐसी ही	रही।
(4) वे	अच्छे	रहे।

COMMENT: (SP-17)

(a) *Value Judgment*: The sentence sub-patterns 17a, 17b, 17c are respectively the adjectival counterparts of the nominal sub-patterns 10a, 10b, and 10c. For explanation of their features see (4.3.6) and sub-pattern 10. The sub-pattern 17d does not have any nominal counterpart because only an adjective can replace this position and amongst them also only adjectives which can convey the sense of value judgement, e.g. अच्छा, बेकार, फीका, सुंदर, सुखद etc. Sentences like *पार्टी आयोजित रही, *वे पथभ्रष्ट रहे are not possible. The use of the aspect marker like रह is not possible in this sentence. (*खेल फीका रहा है).

Sub-pattern-18 A (locative)

NP (subject)	ADV (complement) <+location/direction>	Linking verb हो।
(1) सतीश	घर में	है।
(2) मेरा घर	दुकान के पीछे	है।
(3) किताब	यहीं कहीं	होगी।
(4) उनकी पहुँच	बहुत दूर तक	है।
(5) मेरी नज़र	आप पर	थी।

Sub-pattern-18 B (adjectival locative)

NP (subject)	ADV (complement) <+adjectival, -concrete>	Linking verb हो।
(6) सतीश	संकट	में है।
(7) आप	किस उधेड़बुन में	हैं?

(8) मैं	जल्दी में	हूँ।
(9) मरीज़	ख़तरे से बाहर	है।
(10) ऐसी साड़ी	चलन में नहीं	है।

COMMENT: (SP-18B)

(a) *Locative as Adjective*: The locative adverbs as in sub-pattern (18a) are made up of concrete nouns (e.g. घर में, दुकान के पीछे) or locative adverbs (e.g. कहाँ, किधर etc.). In sub-pattern 18b, however, the adverbials are made up of such noun words as convey the sense of adjectives. Consequently the adverbials like संकट में, उधेड़बुन में, खतरे से बाहर etc. indirectly serve as adjectives qualifying the noun and do not provide any locative or topographical meaning. See:

(1) सतीश *घर* में है। (locative)
(2) सतीश *संकट* में है। (attributive)
(3) ऐसी साड़ी *दुकान* में नहीं है। (locative)
(4) ऐसी साड़ी *चलन* में नहीं है (attributive)

(b) *Structural Features*: Some structural features are significant in both the types of sentences: (i) Some cognate questions can be posed in both the types of sentences (e.g. सतीश कहाँ है? -घर में) Such a type of questions is not possible in the case of the second category of senences.(e.g *सतीश कहाँ/किसमें है? *मरीज़ कहाँ है? --*खतरे से बाहर (ii) It is possible to have an inversion or theme shift in the case of, say, घर में लड़का है, दुकान में ऐसी साड़ी नहीं है, but it is not possible to invert the sentence in the other category of sentences (i.e. *संकट में लड़का है, *खतरे से बाहर मरीज़ है). Hence even when these sub-patterns (18a and 18b) are similar at the surface structure, they are different in their deep structures.

Sub-pattern-19 A (event-based)

NP (subject) <+event >	**ADV (complement)** <+time>	**Linking verb** हो
(1) शादी	सोमवार को	है।
(2) दीवाली	दूसरे महीने	है।
(3) स्वागत भाषण	भोजन से पहले	था।

Sub-pattern-19 B (natural/social phenomena)

NP (subject) <+time and space, +inversion>	ADV (complement) <+abstract, +natural/social phenomena>	Linking verb हो (existive)
(1) आज	गर्मी	है।
(2) यहाँ	बहुत उमस	है।
(3) आजकल	बहुत महँगाई	है।
(4) चारों ओर	बेईमानी	है।

COMMENT: (SP-19A)

(a) *Phenomena-based Sentences*: The sub-pattern (19a) anticipates the existence of some natural or social phenomenon occurring as the subject of the sentence. These phenomena may occur at any point of time or place and occur in the sentence as a subject e.g. marriage, examination, meeting, birthday, festival, inauguration etc. Non-phenomenal events can not occur as subjects of the sentence, e.g. *लड़का कल है, *सत्य आज है. etc.

(b) *Future Perception*: A sense of future in the sub-pattern (19a) is inherent as in the event, as in the sentence शादी सोमवार को है (= होगी). The verb है of the sub-pattern 19b does not have this intrinsic sense (*सर्दी सोमवार को है). This characteristic can be seen only in the context of sentences which are event based or phenomenal.

(c) *Changed Word order*: The temporal adverb in sentence (19b) has occurred in the first slot of the sentence because it is the theme of the sentence about which some new information is being given. This changed word-order is the natural word-order of this sub-pattern (गर्मी आज है) is the unusual word-order.

Sub-pattern-20 (Adverbial Relationship)

	NP (subject)	ADV (complement)	Linking verb हो
A-class	(1) यह किताब	विदेशियों के लिए	है। <+ beneficiary>
	(2) यह चपरासी	आपके लिए	है।

B-class	(3) पानी	पीने के लिए	है। <+ purposive>
	(4) सभी प्राकृतिक चीज़ें	भोग के लिए	हैं।
C-class	(5) मोहन	अपने परिवार के साथ	है। <+ associative>
	(6) उसका झगड़ा	हमारे साथ (नहीं)	है।
	(7) यह मूल्य	बिक्रीकर के अतिरिक्त	है।
D-class	(8) यह सब झगड़ा	आपकी वजह से	है। <+ causal>
	(9) यह प्रेमभाव	गांधीजी के कारण	था।
E-class	(10) हम	आराम से	हैं। <+ manner >
	(11) सभी बच्चे	अच्छी तरह	हैं।
	(12) लड़की	हाथ में बैग लिए हुए	थी।
	(13) दुकानदार	शराब पिए हुए	था।
	(14) मैं	एक नौकर रखे हुए	हूँ।
	(15) मैं	अपनी इज़्ज़त बनाए हुए	हूँ।
	(16) सरला	लाल साड़ी पहने हुए	है।
	(17) वह	रोब जमाए हुए	है।
	(18) शेखर	लड़की की कलाई पकड़े हुए	था।

COMMENT: (SP-20)

(a) *Adverbials as Complement*: Sentences of this sub-pattern have adverbials as complements of the sentence. These adverbial complements ultimately define the nature of the relationship between the subject and the linking verbs and identify as many as five major functions of these sub-patterns: beneficiary, purposive, causal, manner and inclusive-exclusive. Sub-patterns which cater to the beneficiary normally make use of adverbs like के लिए, के वास्ते, के हेतु (3) etc. Sub-patterns that indicate the inclusion or exclusion of the subject or compliment normally have adverbs like के साथ, के अतिरिक्त etc. (5, 6, 7) Causal sentences (8, 9) may have adverb phrases के कारण, की वजह etc. The adverb of manner may appear in many forms: से, -ये हुए etc. (10 - 18) etc.

(b) *Beneficiary and Purposive Adverbials*: Unlike other adverbial phrases, the adverbial phrases of this sub-pattern (20) are the obligatory constituents of the sentence and function as the complements of the sentence as shown in the sub-pattern (18). The adverbial phrases of both the sub-patterns (18, 19) make use of the postposition के लिए, but it needs to be noted that both the sentences have important structural and semantic differences. It should, however, be remembered that in generic or generalized sentences it is possible to use होता है instead of है in such cases, e.g. पानी पीने के लिए होता है (see 4.3.3).

(c) *Inclusive/Exclusve Adverbials*: Some important indicators of such adverbials are के साथ (सहित, समेत, से, के अतिरिक्त etc.) There are sentences where the agents or the co-agents in the sentence share equal status which can be determined through transformation process, e.g.

(5) मोहन अपने परिवार के साथ है।

> मोहन और उसका परिवार साथ हैं।

(d) *Manner Adverbials*: The participles used in the place of the complements are perfective participles and are always ए-ending and indeclinable, i.e. their endings do not change according to the gender and number of the subject, as for instance पिए हुए, लिए हुए, रखे हुए, बचाए हुए etc. as shown in sentences (12 to 18). These participles should be treated as different from the ones which are used as adjectival participles because the forms of adjectival participles may change according to the gender and number of the grammatical subject. See:

लड़की थकी हुई है।

लड़का थका हुआ है।

हम थके हुए हैं।

It needs to be noted that sometimes because of false analogy the declinable forms of even adverbial participles are seen to be in use, e.g. लड़की लाल साड़ी *पहनी* हुई थी.

(e) *State-ending and process ending*. The past participle normally gives information about the manner or state of the action. Hence the perfect participle forms of only the state-ending verbs (2.9.7i), and not the process ending verbs *मैं किताब लिए हुआ था (2.9.7ii) are used in the place of the complement. The generalization of this type of sentences is also possible by making use of the stative होता है (4.3.3) and durative रह (sub-pattern 7), e.g.

(13a) यह दुकानदार हमेशा शराब पिए हुए *होता है।*

(16a) सरला आजकल हमेशा लाल साड़ी पहने हुए *रहती है।*

□

Chapter-5

SUBJECT + को SENTENCE

5.1 को-Sentence Patterns

5.1.1 Defining a को-sentence Structure

A certain class of sentences in Hindi require the use of को after the subject. Such sentences are normally referred to as sub+को sentences or simply को-sentences). For instance, complements like बुखार, नींद, दुख, जल्दी etc. in the following sentences anticipate the use of a postposition को after the subject.

(1) सुधीर को *बुखार* है।

(2) बच्चों को *नींद* आ रही है।

(3) मुझे इस बात का *दुख* है।

(4) मोहन को *जल्दी* है।

In other cases, the use of को after the subject is because of the expectation (requirement) of the lexical verbs (आना, मिलना, चाहिए, लगना) e.g.

(5) स्मिथ को हिंदी *आती* है।

(6) सरला को आपकी चिट्ठी *मिल* गई।

(7) रमन को एक तौलिया *चाहिए*।

(8) मुझे वह लड़का धूर्त *लगता* है।

In all the above sentences the को-construction is determined and controlled by the lexical verbs. Other Hindi sentences in which the postposition को occurs after the subject where the postposition को occurs after the subject also include the modal verbs of obligation, but their construction is not controlled by the complements or the lexical verb but by the modal markers -ना है, -ना, नड़, -ना चाहिए). Hence, they are generated through modal transformation and are themselves base sentences. See:

(9) सुशील बाज़ार जाता है। > सुशील को बाज़ार *जाना है*।
> सुशील को बाज़ार *जाना पड़ता है*।
> सुशील को बाज़ार *जाना चाहिए*।

The use of subject + को in all these three sentences is because of the requirement of the modal markers -ना है, -ना पड़ and -ना चाहिए and not because of the lexical verb (जाना). Consequently, any number of lexical verbs that can be used in the place of जाना may be innumerable. In other words, any lexical verb that denotes an action which is in the control of the subject can be used in its place. Such a verb is also called a *volitional* verb. A *volitional* verb is the one on which the subject has a control i.e. the subject is free to do or not to do the action or do it at his (own) volition, e.g. मरना, घबराना, ऊबना etc. These denote actions on which the subject has no control.(see 3.3.3a)

Thus the types of Hindi sentences that can be called को-sentences can be classified as follows:

1. Complement based (1) सुधीर को *बुखार* है। (complement)
(2) मोहन को फुटबाल का *शौक* है। (phrase object)
(3) रमेश को लड़कियों से *नफ़रत* है। (co-agent)
2. Object based (4) सीता को *मकान* चाहिए।
3. Object complement based (5) राधा को नौकर *चोर* लगता है। (object complement noun)
राधा को नौकर *होशियार* लगता है। (object complement adj)
4. Object +के पास/के/में (6) मोहन *के पास* तीस रुपए हैं। (possession)
(7) सुशीला *के /की* तीन बहनें हैं।
(8) शीला *में* प्रतिभा है।

5.1.2 को-sentence vs. copula sentence

Some linguists consider को-sentences as a part of the copula sentences and not an independent class of sentence patterns (see 3.4.2). One of the reasons for the misunderstanding is that both the copula and the को-sentences share the same copula verb (है, था etc.) as their finite verbs. We hold that the को-sentences in Hindi form an independent class of sentence pattern different from the copula sentences. Both have significant structural and semantic differences as shown below:

(a) The deep and surface level subjects of the copula sentence (1) are the same whereas they are different in the को-sentences (2). See:

(1) सुधीर डॉक्टर था। (copula sentence)
(2) सुधीर को बुखार था। (को-sentence)

Sudhir in sentence (1) is both an underlying as well as a surface level subject whereas in sentence (2), सुधीर is only an underlying subject and बुखार is a grammatical subject. The criterion of a grammatical subject is that its verb always agrees with the number and gender of the subject.

(b) In को-sentences the complements (बुखार etc.) or the verbs are the controlling constituents of the sentence and the lexical words capable of being used in this slot can be listed or the rules formulated. For instance, we can formulate a rule that nouns belonging to the physical state or diseases etc. (e.g. बुखार, जुकाम, भूख etc.) can be used in the slot of the complement. No such rules can be formulated in the case of copula sentences.

(c) In equational copula sentences the subject and the complements are co-referent in the sense that both of them refer to the same person or object whereas in the case of को- sentences they always refer to different persons or objects. For instance, in the sentence मोहन को बुखार है, मोहन and बुखार are two different entities. They are not co-referent.

5.1.3 को-sentences in other languages

A regular provision of forming sentences by using the dative case marker (को) after the logical subject is a typical characteristic of

Hindi and other Indian languages (Marathi, Tamil, Malyaalam, Kannada etc.) – a feature not often seen in English and other European languages. In Bangla, however, in a similar sentence structure generally the relative suffix –er (का) is used instead. See:

सुधीर **को** बुखार है।	= को-sentence	(हिंदी)
सुधीर **ला** ताप आहे।	= को-sentence	(Marathi)
सुधी**रुक्कु** जुरम।	= को-sentence	(Tamil)
सुधी**रन्नु** पनियाणु।	= को-sentence	(Malyalam)
सुधीर **निगे** ज्वर दिदे।	= को-sentence	(Kannada)
सुधी**रेर** ताप आछे।	= को-sentence	(Bengali)

This structure in English is mostly expressed through a possessive have-sentence, e.g. Sudhir *has* a fever. Though corresponding forms for all types of Hindi को-sentences are not available in the European languages, but for certain specific sentences an indirect sentence construction is often used in Russian, Spanish, German, French and Romanian. The logical subject in Russian, Spanish and Romanian occurs in the first slot as a dative which is called an experiencer in case grammar. See:

Russian:	*M'ne nr'avista* doma.
Spanish:	*Me* gusta la casa.
Romanian:	*Imi* place casa.
Hindi:	मुझे मकान पसंद है।

In French and German the experiencer occurs as the last constituent of the sentence which is the proper place for the dative. See:

French :	La maison *me* plait.
German :	Das haus gefallt *mir.*

Despite this partial similarity, an indirect construction is not generally possible in these languages to match the Hindi को-sentences. In Romanian, however, the use of indirect constructions is comparatively more common where the dative form (to me) comes first in the sentence, e.g.

Mi-e foame/sete/sete/frig. मुझे भूख/प्यास/ठंड/लग रही है।
Imi pare rau/bine मुझे दुख/खुशी है।
Mi-e rusine मुझे शर्म आती है।

5.1.4 Different opinions on को-sentences

As seen above, को-sentences in Hindi is a peculiar construction and has been a subject of analysis by many modern linguists. Yamuna Kachru (1970) treats it as different from the regular subject x object x verb type of sentence. She calls it a dative x subject x verb (सुधीर को बुखार है।) As against this, Olphen (1970) calls it an indirect construction and places it in the category of subject x object x verb. As per the case grammar of Fillmore, which is based on semantics, the construction of the को-sentence is depicted as follows: E x O – (E = Experiencer, O = Object).

Halliday (1970:153) has enumerated three types of clauses: action clauses, relational clauses and mental process clauses. The को-sentences of Hindi belong to the mental process clause. The mental process class includes activities which are related to the consciousness of a person. The place of activity of this class of process is not the outer world but the conscious mind of the person. Some outer element overpowers the consciousness of the person and the person only reacts to it or gives his reaction. In this process the person does not do any thing nor does anything happens to him. He only expresses his mental experience.

Halliday calls the experiencer a *processor* and the outer element an (action) a *phenomenon.* For instance, in the following sentence मुझे is a processor and अपना घर is a phenomenon:

(1) मुझे अपना घर पसंद नहीं। [processor x phenomenon x verb]

Mental process sentences in which the phenomenon does not occur as a normal phrase but as some fact or a कि-clause is called a *metaphenomenon*, as for instance, the sub clause कि मैं पार्टी में नहीं आ सका

(2) मुझे दुख है *कि मैं पार्टी में नहीं आ सका*।

Halliday includes the following four categories of verbs under the mental process verbs which to an extent covers the area of को-

notion in Hindi (see 5.3) :

1. Perception देखना, सुनना, दिखाई देना
2. Reaction पसंद आना, अच्छा लगना
3. Cognition विश्वास करना, मालूम करना, जानना
4. Verbalization कहना, बोलना

5.2 को-Subject

The subject of a को-sentence is called a को-subject. It is the logical subject of the sentence and not a grammatical subject. The presence of the postposition को after it prohibits it to become the grammatical subject of the sentence and hence it loses the capacity to control the verb agreement of the sentence. The को-subject is the deep structure subject of the sentence and is called the *experiencer* or *recipient* in case grammar. As an experiencer, the subject takes an abstract object (as बुखार in the sentence सुधीर को *बुखार* है and as a recipient it takes a concrete object in the sentence as in the following sentences:

(1) सुधीर को *बुखार* है।	(abstract object)	(E O)
(2) मोहन को *तीस रुपए* मिले।	(concrete object)	(R O)
(3) लड़के के पास दस रुपए हैं।	(concrete object)	(R O)

Two inherent features of the को-subject are: its animate status and lack of volition:

(a) *Animate Status:* The nouns occurring in the slot of the को-subject should be animate and sensuous because the को-sentences express only such experiences, concepts, emotions, sentiments and abstract activities which belong only to a living being. The को-subject is normally an animate noun but sometimes some other words representing the overall dimension or consciousness of an animate noun are also used as को-subjects, e.g. मन, दिल, जान etc. (मेरे मन को बड़ा दुख हुआ, आपकी जान को खतरा है. Other parts of the body which do not represent the total consciousness or personality can not become the को-subjects. Compare:

(1) *राम को* दर्द हो रहा है।   (the total being or consciousness)

(2) *राम के सिर में* दर्द हो रहा है।   (only a specific part of the being)

It is important to note that though the inanimate noun does not have the capacity to become a को-subject, but in certain contexts or in extended meanings, the personification of an inanimate noun is possible, e.g.

(3) इस *कार को* बहुत पेट्रोल चाहिए।   (*कार* personified as animate)

(4) *देश को* तुम जैसे लोगों की ज़रूरत है।   (*देश* personified as animate)

(b) *Lack of Volition*: The को-subject can not be the agent (i.e active subject) of the को- sentence because it lacks all the important feature of *volition* i.e., the option to do or not to do the action. The को-subject does not itself perform any action but is itself the experiencer or recipient of the action. The subject thus has no control over the action. On the contrary, some external force gets over him. Besides, the use of such verb-forms or sentence constructions which basically express the activeness or volition of the subject is also not permissible, e.g. the use of the verbs of obligation like -ना पड़ etc. See:

(5) स्मिथ को हिंदी आती है।/*स्मिथ को हिंदी आनी पड़ी।

(6) सुधीर को बुखार है।/*सुधीर को बुखार होना पड़ता है।

5.3 को-Notion

A notion or concept that requires the use of a subject + को in the formation of a Hindi sentence is called a को-*notion*, for instance the notion or concept of बुखार, आना, दुख, पसंद, जरूरत etc. as shown in the following sentences:

(1) सुधीर को *बुखार* है।   (बुखार)

(2) बच्चे को *भूख* लगी है।   (भूख)

(3) पिता जी को *गुस्सा* आया।   (गुस्सा)

(4) मेरी पत्नी को यह मकान *पसंद* है।   (पसंद)

(5) आपको कितने पैसे की *ज़रूरत* है?   (ज़रूरत)

These notions or semantic elements express themselves through a complement or a verb which are respectively called को-complement and को-verbs. Hence the को-notions include both- the को-complements as well as को-verbs.

Some of these notions are expressed in Hindi only through को-sentences while some others may accept both को- as well as non-को-sentences. Nevertheless a workable classification of the को-notions is possible on the basis of some broad semantic features, as given below:

The Semantic classification of को-notions

Physical Experience	Mental Experience	Emotions	Liking/habit	Abstract human activity
बुखार	आना	दुख	पसंद	1. ज़रूरत-class
प्यास	मालूम होना	गुस्सा	शौक	2. उपलब्ध-class
नींद	याद आना	आशा	दिलचस्पी	3. लाभ/हानि-class
		नफ़रत	आदत	4. काम-class
				5. स्वीकार्य-class
				6. बधाई-class

5.3.1 Physical Experience

को-sentences form a natural sentence pattern for the expression of a physical experience, state or diseases, e.g.

(1) सुधीर को ... बुखार, खाँसी, तपेदिक, आराम, दर्द, तकलीफ़ है।
(2) शीला को ... प्यास, भूख, ठंड, गर्मी, चोट लगी।
(3) राम को ... नींद, पसीना, हँसी, छींक, रुलाई, होश आया/आई।

All these को-notions or concepts are used as noun complements in the को-sentences and not as adjective complements. When used as an adjective complement these notions are expressed as adjectival copula sentences, e.g. शीला भूखी है, सुधीर बुखार से पीड़ित है.

The को-notions representing physical experiences are different from other को-notions in three ways :

(a) *Structural Autonomy*: The को-notions expressing the physical experiences are autonomous or self-contained in themselves, i.e. they do not require any other constituent (phrasal object or any other extension) for the completion of their meaning. See 3.5.3). On the contrary, notions expressing a wish or emotions require yet another constituent like phrasal object etc. to complete their meaning, e.g. फुटबॉल in sentence (5). Compare

(4) मदन को चोट लगी। (physical experience)

(5) मोहन को फुटबाल का शौक है। (wish/liking)

(b) *Restriction on the use of कि-clause (that-clause)*: The use of that-clause or its nominalisation is not permissible in this class of को-sentences which express physical experiences whereas it is possible in the context of other को- notions. See:

(6) मुझे पार्टी में न जाने का दुख है। > मुझे दुख है कि मैं पार्टी में न जा सका।
(expresses emotion)

(7) मदन को चोट लगी। (*मदन को लगी कि चोट है।)

(c) *Inability to form Active Verbalization through –कर*: को notions denoting physical experiences are not capable of undergoing कर-transformstion. whereas other को-notions are capable of being verbalised through the verbalizer *–कर* . See

(8) सीता को दर्द है। (>* सीता दर्द करती है।

(9) राधा को मुझ पर विश्वास है। > राधा मुझ पर विश्वास करती है।

A list of some important को-notions denoting physical experiences are being given below:

(अपच, आघात, आराम, उबकाई, उबासी, कँपकँपी, कष्ट, कै, खाँसी, खुमारी, गर्मी, चोट, छींक, जलन, जाड़ा, ज्वर, टट्टी, ठंड, डकार, तकलीफ़, तड़पन, तृप्ति, थकान, थकावट, दर्द, दौरा (पड़ना), धक्का, नींद, पसीना, पेशाब, प्यास, बीमारी, बुखार, बेहोशी, भूख, मज़ा, मर्ज़, मूर्च्छा, मौत, राहत, रुलाई, रोग (हर प्रकार के जैसे, मलेरिया, तपेदिक, जुकाम, कैंसर आदि), हँसी, हरारत, हिचकी, होश आदि)।

5.3.2 Mental Experience

The notion of knowledge and perception is expressed in Hindi both through को-sentences and normal verb-based sentences. Some mental verbs like (जानना, समझना etc.) require the normal verb-based sentences whereas verbs like मालूम होना, पता होना, आना, दिखाई देना, सुनाई देना, विदित, याद होना require को-sentences. Similarly some को-complements also anticipate को-sentences, e.g. जानकारी, इल्म, समझ, अक्ल, भ्रम etc. See:

(1) स्मिथ हिंदी जानता है। (verb-based sentence)
(2) स्मिथ को हिंदी आती है। (को-sentence)
(3) रमेश को यह बात मालूम है। (को-sentence)
(4) राम को इस बात की जानकारी है। (को-sentence)

Four characteristics of the को-notions belonging to the mental experience need to be noted:

(a) *Skill versus Fact-based Knowledge*: From the point of view of the sentence structure, Hindi makes a distinction between two types of knowledge - (i) skill-based knowledge and (ii) fact-based knowledge. *Skill-based* knowledge is the one which is acquired through some training or practice, e.g. language learning, dance, music, swimming, motor-driving etc. Verbs of this category require a को-verb and a को-sentence. *Fact-based* or *information-based* knowledge is the one which is not needed to be learnt through training. For this category of knowledge the verbs used in Hindi are the को-verbs मालूम होना, पता होना etc. (see sub-pattern 24). A third category of verbs denoting knowledge is जानना which can be used with both the types of verbs, < + knowledge> as well as <-knowledge>. See:

(2) स्मिथ को हिंदी आती है। <+को, + knowledge, -skill>
(*स्मिथ को हिंदी मालूम है।)
(3) रमेश को यह बात मालूम है। <+को, + knowledge, -skill>
(*रमेश को यह बात आती है।)
(4) रमेश हिंदी जानता है। <- को, +knowledge, ±-skill>
(5) रमेश यह बात जानता है। - do -

(b) *Object vs. phrasal object*: Unlike the को-notions denoting physical experiences, the को-notions denoting knowledge or perception require either a regular object or a phrasal object for the completion of its meaning (see 3.5.3 d), e.g.

(6) उन्हें ये *सब बातें* याद हैं। (object)
(7) मोहन को *इन बातों की जानकारी* नहीं है। (phrasal object)

In sentence (6) *ये सब बातें* is a regular object of the verb याद हैं. In sentence (7) *इन सब बातों की* is the phrasal object.

The postposition *का*, and, in some special usages, में may also occur together (as a collocation) as part of the phrasal object for the completion of the meaning. In similar sentences where the noun is not followed by the postposition का or any other postposition, its status in the sentence is equivalent to an object. In many instances the object or the phrasal object forms similar categories. The difference is only that of a language specific system of expression. For instance, ये सब बातें in sentence (6) is an object and in sentence (7) the same object is a phrasal object. The unmarked object and not the marked object in a Hindi sentence controls the agreement of the verb. Some notions belonging to the mental perceptions require a regular object while some require a phrasal object.

(c) कि-*clause* :) Some objects of mental experience are capable of being expressed through a that-clause, e.g. पता, मालूम, ख्याल, etc. (उन्हें याद है *कि परसों आप नहीं आए थे.*) the objects of आना, सुझाना, कंठस्थ होना etc. can not be expressed through कि-clause. It is because these are factive verbs and not non-factive verbs (see 3.5.3 f).

(d) *Active verb Transformation* : Some को-notions relating to the mental experience or perception can undergo an active verb transformation, e.g.

(6) इन्हें ये सब बातें याद हैं > वे सब बातें याद करते हैं।

(7) मोहन को इन सब बातों की जानकारी है > मोहन इन सब बातों की जानकारी रखता है।

Some important को-notions relating to knowledge and perception are given below:

अंदाज़ा, अक्ल, अनुभव, आना, आभास, इल्म, एहसास, कंठस्थ, कंठाग्र, ख्याल, ज्ञात, ज्ञान, जानकारी, जान पड़ना, तजुर्बा, दिखाई पड़ना, दीखना, पता, परख, पहचान, प्रतीत होना, बोध, भान होना, भ्रम, भ्रांति, मालूम, याद, लगना, विचार, विदित, समझ, सुनाई देना, सूझना, स्पष्ट, स्मरण।

5.3.3 Emotions

Emotions and mental experiences like दुख, गुस्सा, जोश, खुशी, आशा, उत्सुकता, डर, नफ़रत, दया etc. which are either temporary or are results of some reaction are typically expressed through को-sentences in Hindi, e.g.

(1) सेठ जी को *नौकर पर* गुस्सा आया।

(2) मुझे *आपका काम न कर पाने का* दुख है।

(3) यह *सुनकर* मोहन को गुस्सा आया।

All these emotions are either momentary or are reactions of some stimuli. Emotions or qualities which are not momentary or temporary and are the part of the human qualities or characteristics do not require को-sentences in Hindi, e.g. साहस, उत्साह, प्रतिभा and धैर्य etc. It is, however, important to note that some emotions like प्यार, सहानुभूति etc. can not be said to be momentary or completely temporary (मुझे तुमसे प्यार है, उन्हें हमसे सहानुभूति है, but since they arise as a reaction of some stimuli, they are also expressed through को-sentences in Hindi even though some of them have the capability to be expressed through different sentence patterns, e.g. मैं तुमसे प्यार करता हूँ, वे हमसे सहानुभूति रखते हैं.

Some emotions have the capacity to be expressed in both the contexts - temporary as well as permanent, even though with some difference in the shade of the meaning, but both of them require two different sentence patterns, e.g. मैं तुमसे प्यार करता हूँ, वे हमसे सहानुभूति रखते हैं.

Some emotions have the capacity to be used in both the contexts-permanent as well as temporary, but both require two different sentence patterns. See:

(4) यह *सुनकर* मोहन को जोश आया। (momentary, reaction)

(5) मोहन में *जोश* है। (permanent, inborn quality)

Emotion-based को-sentences have three major characteristics:

(a) *Completion of meaning:* The को-sentences denoting physical experiences are self-contained from the point of view of complements, but the emotion-based sentences को-sentences directly or indirectly need another constituent for the completion of their meaning. These additional constituents are normally a *phrasal object*, a co-agent or stimuli, e.g.

(2) मुझे *आपका काम न कर पाने का* दुख है। (phrasal object)

(1) सेठ जी को *नौकर पर* गुस्सा आया। (co-agent)

(5) मुझे उस *लड़के से* नफ़रत है। (co-agent)

(3) *यह सुनकर* मोहन को जोश आया। (stimuli)

Sometimes these notions also seem to occur without the phrasal objects or co-agents in real life sentences, but in fact their phrasal objects or co-agents remain inherent in their deep structure or contexts. For instance, the sentences मुझे दुख है or मुझे डर है are incomplete from the point of view of communication unless the hearer is already aware of the reason or context of डर or दुख etc.

(b) *Phrasal object and that-clause* : There is a class of को- notions expressing emotions (see 2.5.3d) which anticipates a phrasal object. The phrasal object can also appear in the form of a noun infinitive (nominalisation) or a that-clause, e.g.

(6) मुझे इस बात का दुख है। (infinitive)

(2) मुझे *आपका काम न कर पाने का* दुख है। (nominalisation)

(7) मुझे दुख है कि मैं आपका काम नहीं कर पाया। (that-clause)

Here we should not confuse between the phrasal object + का and the modifier. See:

(8) राम को *मलेरिया का* शक है। (phrasal object)

(9) राम को *मलेरिया का* बुखार है। (modifier)

The modifier is the optional constituent of the sentence and can not be expressed through a that-clause (*राम को बुखार है कि उसे मलेरिया है. Most of the का+ phrasal objects can be expressed through कि- clause, e.g. राम को शक है कि उसे मलेरिया है।

Most of the verbs of this class are factive verbs but some verbs are non-factive verbs. Verbs like दुख होना and खुशी होना are factive verbs. Hence the truth value of these verbs remain unchanged even if the facts of the main clauses are negated, For instance in both the following sentences the truth value of the fact that *the vehicle has been broken* remains the same, e.g:

(a) मुझे दुख है कि *आपकी गाड़ी टूट गई।*

(b) मुझे दुख नहीं है कि *आपकी गाड़ी टूट गई।*

On the contrary, verbs like विश्वास होना, होना, यकीन होना are non-factive verbs. Hence if the main clause of this verb is negated, the truth value of this clause also stands negated. For instance the truth value of the sentence मुझे विश्वास नहीं कि आपकी गाड़ी टूट गई is perceived as 'the vehicle did not in fact break'.

(c) Co-agent: Some को-notions require or need to complete the cycle of their meaning, e.g. नफ़रत, प्रेम, घृणा, दया, सहानुभूति, ईर्ष्या etc. (मुझे उस *लड़के से* नफ़रत है)। These co-agents can be compared with those agentive verbs which require the presence of a co-agent to complete their lexical meaning, e.g. लड़ना, मिलना, पूछना, कहना, e.g. वह शत्रु से लड़ा, मैं डॉक्टर से मिला। (Sub-pattern (3).

The co-agents can not be expressed through a that-clause. (*मुझे नफ़रत है कि उस लड़के से), but some को-notions have the capacity to accept both - the phrasal object as well as the co-agent. In such instances the phrasal object can be expressed through a that-clause in which the co-agent is generally the subject of that-clause, e.g.

(10) मुझे नौकर पर *चोरी का शक* है। (मुझे शक है कि नौकर ने चोरी की)।

(11) सीता को मुझसे शिकायत है कि *मैंने उसकी चिट्ठी का जवाब नहीं दिया*।

The co-agents of some को-notions also occur as stimuli in the form of a separate adverbial or a clause, e.g.

(12) *ड्राइवर को देखकर* शीला को गुस्सा आया।

(13) *जब मैंने उसकी यह हालत देखी* तो मुझे बड़ी ग्लानि हुई।

(d) Active Verb Transformation: Some को-notions of this category can undergo active verb transformation (e.g. सेठ जी को नौकर पर *गुस्सा आया* > सेठ जी ने नौकर पर *गुस्सा किया*, राधा को शेखर से प्यार था > राधा ने शेखर से प्यार किया). Such an active verb transformation is not possible in relation to some other notions (e.g. *यह सुनकर उसने जोश किया, *ऐसी बातों से साहब बहुत *झुँझलाहट करते हैं*।)

A list of some important को-notions denoting emotions is being given below:

अंदेशा, अचंभा, अनुभूति, अनुराग, अफ़सोस, अभिमान, अरुचि, आनंद, आशंका, आशा, आश्चर्य, आस, आसरा, आस्था, इत्मीनान, इश्क, ईर्ष्या, उत्कंठा, उत्सुकता, उतावली, उम्मीद, ऐतराज, कुढ़न, कौतूहल, क्षोभ, खार, खीझ, खेद, गम, गरूर, गर्व, गिला, गुमान, गुस्सा, ग्लानि, घबराहट, घमंड, घिन, घृणा, चिंता, चिढ़, झेंप, डर, डाह, तमन्ना, तरस, ताज्जुब, ताव, तृप्ति, दंभ, दया, दुश्मनी, द्वेष, नफ़रत, नाज़, नाराज़गी, पछतावा, परवाह, परेशानी, पश्चात्ताप, प्यार, प्रीति, प्रेम, फ़िक्र, वहम, बेचैनी, बेताबी,

बेसब्री, भय, भरोसा, मलाल, मुहब्बत, मोह, यकीन, रंज, रश्क, रोष, विश्वास, बैर, शक, शर्म, शत्रुता, शिकवा, शिकायक, श्रद्धा, संकोच, संदेह, सहानुभूति, हमदर्दी, हैरत, हैरानी।

5.3.4 Liking/Habit

को-sentences are also often used in Hindi to express notions regarding the interest and habits of the animate noun These notions express the individual reaction of the animate noun and are related to the interest or the disinterest of the individual. Habits are also, in a way, the repetition of an interest and the liking of the individual. The को-notions of the liking and disliking of the individual are also expressed through को-verbs and को-complements, e.g.

(1) मेरी पत्नी को यह घर *पसंद है।* (को-verb)
(2) कांता को मेरी बात *चुभ गई।* (-do-)
(3) मुझे वह लड़का नहीं *जँचता।* (-do-)
(4) अशोक को पढ़ने का *शौक* है। (को- complement)
(5) शेखर को सुबह उठने की *आदत* है। (-do-)
(6) इन्हें इन चीज़ों में *दिलचस्पी* नहीं है। (-do-)

को-verbs expect an object in the sentence (घर, मेरी बात, लड़का) and the को-complement expects a phrasal object (पढ़ने का, सुबह उठने की, चीज़ों में). (see 5.3.2b)

(a) *Active Verb transformation* **:** Only a few को-notions of this category have the capacity to accept active verb transformation, e.g. मेरी पत्नी को यह घर पसंद है > मेरी पत्नी इस घर को *पसंद करती है*, उन्हें इन *चीज़ों* में *दिलचस्पी नहीं है* > ये इन चीज़ों में *दिलचस्पी नहीं रखते*।

(b) कि-clause (*that-clause*) **:** Only a very few को-notions of this category have the capacity to attach a that-clause, e.g. मुझे उनका यहाँ आना पसंद नहीं > मुझे पसंद नहीं कि वे यहाँ आएँ. Other को-notions like अफ़रना, जाँचना, माफ़िक आना, दिलचस्पी etc. are not capable of accepting that-clauses (*मोहन को दिलचस्पी है कि वह पढ़े-लिखे).

It may be noted that some nouns denoting the notion of liking, wish, ambition etc. demand the subject+की, e.g. मेरी लड़की की आगे पढ़ने की इच्छा है. > मेरी लड़की की इच्छा है कि वह आगे पढ़े.

A list of some major notions denoting liking/habit is being given below :

अखरना, अच्छा लगना, अनुभव, अभ्यास, आदत, खब्त सवार होना, चस्का, चाट (लगना), चाव, चाह, चुभना, झक सवार होना, जँचना, दिलचस्पी, पसंद होना, बुरा लगना, भाना, भूत सवार होना, मज़ा, माफ़िक आना, रास आना, रुचि, लत, व्यसन, शौक, हसरत, हवस।

5.3.5 Abstract Human Activities

The use of को-sentences in Hindi is not limited to only physical, mental and emotional experiences of the animate subject. It also at times extends to a number of abstract human activities and relationships. In such cases it is, however, not always easy to formulate the precise rules as to which abstract human activities require को- sentences and which do not.

One generalization can, however, be made in respect of the को-notions denoting abstract human actions: The को-subjects of these human actions or relations are experiencers, receivers, patients, inactive owners but never active agents. Moreover, most of them are related to human beings and not just the animate world. These को-notions can be broadly grouped into the following 6 semantic classes:

(a) Need class : आवश्यकता, इंतज़ार, खोज, चाहिए, ज़रूरत, तलाश, प्रतीक्षा।

(b) Availability class : उपलब्ध होना, टकराना, नसीब होना, प्राप्त होना, मयस्सर होना, मिलना, सुलभ होना, हासिल होना.

(a) Loss/Gain class class : अभाव, कमी, क्षति, घाटा, नुक्सान, परहेज़, फ़ायदा, बचत, मुनाफ़ा, हर्ज, हानि।

(d) Work class : अवकाश, काम, ख़तरा, गरज़, जल्दी, तमीज़, मतलब, देर, फुर्सत, लिहाज, समय, वक़्त, विलंब।

(e) Acceptance class : अमान्य, ग्राह्य, मान्य, सह्य, विलंब।

(d) Congrats class : अधिकार, अख्तियार, अनुमति, आदेश, आज्ञा, आज़ादी, कसम, धन्यवाद, धिक्कार, नमस्कार, प्रणाम, बधाई, लानत, शुक्रिया, स्वतंत्रता, हिदायत, रियायत, छूट।

(a) *Need-class* **:** A majority of को-notions of this class are expressed through complements and some through को-verbs. The complements demand a phrasal object and the को-verbs demand an object to complete its meaning:

(1) मनोहर को एक कार की **ज़रूरत** है। (को-complement)

(2) मुझे आप ही की **तलाश** थी।

(3) उसको मेरा **इंतज़ार** है।

(4) सीता को एक मकान **चाहिए**।

The को-sentences of this class do not have the capacity to accept a that-clause. For instance a sentence like *सीता को चाहिए कि एक मकान हो is not acceptable. It may be noted that an analogous sentence like सीता को चाहिए कि वह पढ़े is a sentence of obligation and not a need-based sentence. Secondly, they are structurally derived from a separate set of sentences (सीता को पढ़ना चाहिए).

Some को-notions like चाहिए are at times also used with reference to non-animate nouns. In such circumstances the inanimate nouns are supposed to have been personified and animate qualities are attributed to them, e.g. मोटर *को* पेट्रोल चाहिए.

(b) *Available-class*: The को-notions of this class are generally expressed through को-verbs and not को-complements, and, therefore, the को-notions generally require a regular object and not a phrasal object, e.g.

(1) राधा को सौ रुपए *मिले*। (को-verb)

(2) हमें सब चीज़ें *उपलब्ध हो गईं*। (को-verb)

The use of को-complements in this semantic category can be seen in some special contexts, e.g. in सब चीज़ों की उपलब्धि हो गई; उसे संतान की प्राप्ति हुई. को-verbs of this category can undergo active verb transformation, e.g. हमने सब चीज़ें प्राप्त कर ली हैं, though quite a few को-verbs are not compatible in this form, e.g. हमें सुख और आराम सभी चीज़ें नसीब हो गईं is an acceptable sentence but *हमने सुख और आराम की सब चीज़ें नसीब कर लीं is not an acceptable sentence. मिलना. The को-verb मिलाना is used in two senses-(a) to get or procure and (b) to meet. Their active verb transformation is possible in two ways: मिलना > पाना, मिलना < में मिलना See:

(1) राधा को सौ रुपए *मिले* > राधा ने सौ रुपए *पाए*।

(2) भाटिया को रास्ते में मेरी बहन *मिली* > भाटिया रास्ते में मेरी बहन से *मिला*।

(c) *Loss-gain class* **:** All the को-notions of this class are expressed through को-complements and require an object. See:

(1) सेठ जी को दस हजार रुपए का *नुक्सान* हुआ। (को-complement)

(2) आपको किस चीज़ का *अभाव* है? (को-complement)

(3) आपको मान जाने में क्या *हर्ज़* है? (को-complement)

Some को-notions of this class have the capacity to undergo active verb transformation, e.g. सेठ जी ने दस हजार रुपए का नुक्सान उठाया. The को-notions of this class are unable to *tag* a कि-clause.

(d) *Work-class:* The को-notions of this category are normally expressed through complements, out of which some complements anticipate a phrasal object while some others don't. In the following sentences the complements are self-contained and do not require any phrasal object, e.g.

(1) मुझे *काम* है। (2) पिताजी को *जल्दी* है।

(3) मुझे *फुर्सत* नहीं है। (4) आपकी जान को *खतरा* है।

(5) उनको *अभी* देर है। (6) आपको *तमीज़* नहीं है।

The को-complements in the following sentences require a phrasal object or a co-agent, though some of them can occur both along with the phrasal object as well as without it. See:

(7) मुझे *खाने तक की* फुर्सत नहीं। (phrasal object)

(8) आपको *बात करने की* तमीज़ नहीं है। (-do-)

(9) रमेश को *उन लोगों से* काम है। (co-agent)

(10) हमें आपके *पड़ोसियों से* कोई मतलब नहीं है। (-do-)

Only a few को-notions of this category have the capacity of active verb transformation, e.g. वे बड़ी जल्दी मचा रहे हैं./आप अपने से बड़ों का कोई लिहाज नहीं करते.

The को-notions of this class do not have the capacity to attach a कि-clause though we have a few exceptions, e.g आपको क्या गरज़ पड़ी है.

कि उसको बुलाएँ.

(e) *Acceptance class*: The को-notions of this class are expressed through को-verbs and not through compliments and, therefore, they require a regular object and not a phrasal object in the sentence. These को-verbs are normally formed through adjective + हो verbalizer. See:

(1) लड़के को हमारी सब शर्तें *स्वीकार्य* हैं।

(2) उन्हें मेरा रोज़ यहाँ आना *सह्य* नहीं।

(3) पिताजी को हमारी यह आज़ादी *गवारा* नहीं।

All the adjectives of this class are basically derived from active verbs. Hence their active verb transformation is easily possible, e.g. लड़का हमारी सब शर्तें स्वीकार करता है, वे मेरा रोज़ यहाँ आना स्वीकार नहीं कर सकते, पिता जी हमारी यह आज़ादी गवारा नहीं कर सकते.

Some verbs of this categry do have the capacity to attach a clause, but in a very limited number, e.g. उन्हें यह सह्य नहीं कि मैं रोज़ यहाँ आऊँ.

(f) *Congrats class:* The को-notions of the congrats-class have a separate entity of their own, because in its deep structure there is the entity of a recipient and a donor and the subject of the को-sentence is a recipient and not an experiencer. The को-sentences of this class can be said to have been derived from the same deep structure. Hence some grammarians do not include these sentences under general को-sentences. See:

(1) मैं आपको बधाई देता हूँ। > आपको बधाई है।

(2) किसी ने पुलिस को आदेश दिया है। > पुलिस को आदेश है।

(3) किसी ने हमें बोलने का आदेश दिया है। > हमें बोलने का अधिकार है।

Some को-notions of this class are self-contained and do not require any phrasal object for the completion of their meaning. See:

(4) आपको बधाई है।	(self-contained)
(5) आपको प्रणाम है।	(self-contained)
(6) पुलिस को गोली चलाने का आदेश है।	(phrasal subject)
(7) हमें बोलने का अधिकार है।	(phrasal subject)

Sub-pattern-21 (complement-based)

NP (subject) + को (subject) <+animate>	NP (complement) <+को-notion, +physical experience/काम-class, -कि, -कर>	हो-verb <-lexical>
क- Physical Experience		
(1) सुधीर को	बुख़ार	है।
(2) आपको	तक़लीफ़	होगी।
(3) ड्राइवर को	चोट	लगी है।
(4) यात्रियों को	भूख/प्यास	लगी है।
(5) बच्चों को	नींद	आई है।
(6) उसे	मज़ा	आ रहा है।
(7) रामदीन को	कँपकँपी	छूट रही है।
(8) पिता जी को	(दिन भर) हरारत	रहती है।
ख- काम-class		
(9) मुझे	काम	है।
(10) बड़े साहब को	फुर्सत	(नहीं) है।
(11) (क्या) आपको	जल्दी	है?

COMMENT: (SP-21)

(a) *Autonomy of the complement*: The complements in this sub-pattern require an animate subject, but no object, phrasal object or co-agent. This way the complements here are autonomous and do not require any object etc. for the completion of their meaning.

(b) *कि- clause and कर -activisation.* This sub-pattern can not attach a कि-clause nor can accept कर- activisation (*शीला को दर्द है कि--*शीला दर्द करती है). Some exceptions are तकलीफ़ करना, कष्ट करना etc.

(c) *Whole and part relationship*: The physical experience of the subject may generally relate to the total being or consciousness of the subject and not a part thereof. Subject +को is used only when it concerns the whole being. See:

ड्राइवर *को* चोट लगी है। (his total being)
ड्राइवर *के सिर में* चोट लगी है। (only a specific part of the body)

ड्राइवर के चोट लगी है। (= some part of the driver's body)

The two verbalizers most commonly used with the को-notions of this category are:

गर्मी, सर्दी, ठंड, जाड़ा (लगना)

प्यास, भूख, चोट (लगना)

पसीना, खांसी, छींक, नींद, पेशाब, जम्हाई, हिचकी (आना)

हँसी, रुलाई, शर्म, मज़ा (आना)

Sub-pattern-22 (Phrasal object)

NP +को (subject) <+animate>	Phrasal object <+का, ±कि>	NP (complement) <+को-notion, -physical, ±कर>	Verbalizer <-lexical>
(1) मुझे	आपका काम न कर पाने का	दुख	है।
(2) हमें	गाड़ी छूट जाने का	डर/भय	था।
(3) अशोक को	पढ़ने का	शौक	है।
(4) उन्हें	आप ही का	आसरा	है।
(5) आपको	किस बात का	घमंड	है?
(6) मुझे	इस बात का	पता	था/लग गया।
(7) पिता जी को	देर से सोने की	आदत	है।
(8) उसे	शराब की	लत	लग गई है।
(9) ठेकेदार को	पैसे की	ज़रूरत/कमी	है/पड़ी।
(10) इन लोगों को	डॉक्टर का	इंतज़ार	है।
(11) हमें	बोलने का	अधिकार	है।

COMMENT: (SP-22)

(a) *Phrasal object*: This sub-pattern requires a noun phrase complement together with a phrasal object. The phrasal object consists of a noun phrase (दुख) qualified by some marked modifier (काम न कर पाने का) as in sentence (1) above. The phrasal object is marked by some postposition (का) and its function is to complete the meaning of the sentence. This sub-pattern covers the expression of all such को-notions which require a marked object (i.e the object which is followed by some genitive postpotions like का, के लिए). This sub-pattern thus requires a co-agent which is marked by some phrasal object. A*phrasal object is thus an object which is followed by some postposition like से, पर, का etc.* e.g. अशोक **को** *पढ़ने का* शौक है. The को-notions that require this type of sentence patterns are those related to emotions, wish, habit, mental experience and certain types of abstract human behaviour, e.g. आपका काम न कर पाने का, गाड़ी छूट जाने का etc.

(b) *कर -activisation*: The transformation of कर-activisaton of many को-sentences of this sub-patterns is accomplished through verbalizers like कर, रख, or डाल, that is, these को-notions can be conveyed through verb-based sentences also, e.g.

इन लोगों को डॉक्टर का इंतज़ार है >

> ये लोग डॉक्टर *का इंतज़ार* कर रहे हैं।

आपको किस बात का घमंड है >

> आप किस बात *का घमंड* करते हैं।

हमें बोलने का अधिकार है >

> हम बोलने *का अधिकार* रखते हैं।

Similarly other कर-transformations are also possible, viz. आदत होना > आदत डालना, इच्छा होना > इच्छा रखना, जानकारी होना > जानकारी रखना etc. Many other को-notions of this category do not have the capacity to convert this type of transformation, e.g. उत्सुकता होना >*उत्सुकता करना, दुख होना >*दुख करना etc.

(c) *कि-clause*: Many sentences of this sub-pattern possess the capacity to affix a कि-clause, e.g. the sentence derived from the sentence: मुझे दुख है कि मैं आपका काम नहीं कर पाया, हमें डर था कहीं गाड़ी न छूट जाए. In some contexts the sentences of this sub-pattern necessarily ask for a कि-clause which can not be easily normalised, e.g मुझे यकीन है आप धोखा नहीं खाएँगे।

(d) *Animate को-subject*: The subjects of this sub-pattern are animate nouns. If the subject is replaced by an inanimate noun, the subject will attach a locative postposition को (*इस कार में* पेट्रोल की जरूरत है, and in some contexts where the subject +को is used, it should be treated as the extended or figurative use of the animate subject, e.g. *इस कार को* पेट्रोल की ज़रूरत है.

Sub-pattern-23 (Complement -based Co-agent)

NP +को (subject) <+animate>	**Co-agent** Supporting Participant <+से/पर,+(आलंबन),-कि>	**NP (complement)** <+को-notion -physical, ±कर>	**को-verbalizer** **(non-lexical)**
(1) रमेश को	उस लड़की से	नफ़रत	है।
(2) हमें	इन अदाओं से	प्यार	है।
(3) साहब को	ऐसी बातों से	चिढ़	है।
(4) शेखर को	तली चीज़ों से	परहेज़	है।
(5) आपको	इससे	(क्या) लेना-देना	है?
(6) शीला को	ड्राइवर पर	गुस्सा	आया।
(7) मुझे	भिखारी पर	दया	आई।
(8) डॉक्टर को	मुझ पर	यकीन	(नहीं) हुआ।
(9) मुझे	उनकी बातों पर	रोना/हँसी	आया/आई।
(10) उसे	इन बातों में	दिलचस्पी	(नहीं) है।

COMMENT: (SP-23)

This sub-pattern expresses को-sentences which are not related to physical experiences and which require a co-agent (उस लड़की से) which is marked by some postposition (से) and a noun phrase (नफ़रत) in order to complete the meaning of the sentence. All such को-notions which require a marked co-agent or participant are technically called आलंबन in literature. Some other exmples of this categry are प्यार, नफ़रत, सहानुभूति, हमदर्दी, शिकयत, चिढ़, परहेज, गुस्सा, दया, यकीन, शक, शर्म, दिलचस्पी, रुचि लेना-देना, मतलब, etc. All these को-notions expect one or the other आलंबन (supporting participant) as a consequence of which these notions or emotions arise. For instance, in the sentence रमेश को उस लड़की से नफ़रत है. रमेश is the abode of the feeling (or notion) and लड़की is the *आलंबन*, the one which triggers the feeling or को-notion. These co-participants or आलंबन are marked by some potpositions like से, पर and में. See:

उसे इन *बातों में* दिलचस्पी रहती है।

मुझे *आपसे/आपके प्रति* सहानुभूति है।

Sub-pattern-24 (object-based subject+को)

NP +को (subject) <+animate>	NP (object) <±concrete, ±कि>	को-verb <+को notion, +lexical>	
		Simple Verbs	
(1) सीता को	मकान	चाहिए।	
(2) स्मिथ को	हिंदी	आती है।	
(3) शेखर को	100 रुपए	मिले।	
(4) मुझे	आपकी बहन	मिली थी।	
(5) मुझे	लड़का	(नहीं) जँचा/भाया।	
(6) उन्हें	आपकी बात	खल/अखर रही है।	
(7) शीला को	तुम्हारा व्यंग्य	चुभ गया।	
(8) हमें	एक शैतानी	सूझी।	
		Complex Verbs	
(9) शर्मा जी को	यह गाड़ी	पसंद	: है/आई।
(10) मुझे	उनकी बातें	अच्छी/बुरी	: लगती हैं।
(11) बहू को	यहाँ का माहौल	रास/माफ़िक	: (नहीं) आया।
(12) रामदीन को	कुछ भी	दिखाई/सुनाई	: (नहीं) देता।
(13) मोहन को	यह बात	मालूम/पता	: है।
(14) मुझे	वे दिन	याद	: हैं।
(15) आपको	उनका नाम-पता	ज्ञात	: होगा।
(16) हमको	ये पुस्तकें	उपलब्ध	: हो सकती हैं।
(17) उसे	सारी कविता	कंठस्थ	: है।
(18) मुझे	आपकी शर्तें	स्वीकार्य	: हैं।

COMMENT: (Sub-pattern 24 (object-based sub+को)

(a) This sub-pattern requires a subject +को sentence with an animate subject. The object may be concrete (मकान, गाड़ी) or abstract (शैतानी, बात). The verbs used in these patterns are called subject+को verbs because it is these verbs which primarily anticipate or demand the *subjec+ को* construction (सीता को, आपको, मुझे).

(b) The verbs used here may be either a simple verb (like चाहिए, मिलना) or a complex verb (like पसंद होना, मालूम पड़ना).

(c) Some verbs used here may accept both the forms of verbalizers: कर as well as हो, e.g. पसंद होना : पसंद करना, but the form पसंद

करना does not attract the sub+को construction. See the difference:

-- रमेश *को* लाल वाली गाड़ी पसंद है।

-- रमेश *ने* लाल वाली गाड़ी पसंद की है।

(d) Some specific को-verbs like मालूम होना, आना, पता होना और जाना which belong to the same semantic fields have four syntactic forms in Hindi while English has a single word *to know* for all the three. See:

(1) स्मिथ को हिंदी *आती* है। (*मोहन को हिंदी मालूम है)

(2) मोहन को यह बात *मालूम* है। (*मोहन को यह बात आती है)

(3) मोहन को यह बात *पता* है। (*मोहन को हिंदी पता है)

(4) मोहन को इस बात का *पता* है। (*मोहन को हिंदी का पता है)

The verb आना in Hindi refers to the acquirement of *skill* which requires to be earned or practiced by a person. जानना, on the other hand, refers to the acquisition or collection of knowledge and not a *skill*.

Sub-pattern-25 object complement (noun)

NP +को (subject)	**NP (object)**	**NP (complement)**	**को-verb**
<+animate>	<±कि>	<+complement, +form similarity, +appearance>	<+को-notion, +lexical, +guess visual, +subjective
(1) मुझे	वह	धूर्त	लगता है।
(2) मुझे	वह	बिल्कुल अंग्रेज़	दिखाई देता है।
(3) मुझे	वह	पुलिस अफ़सर	लगता/दिखाई देता है।
(4) आपको तो	हर आदमी	ठग	नज़र आता है।

Sub-pattern-26 object complement (adjective)

NP +को (subject)	**NP (object)**	**NP (complement)**	**को-verb**
<+animate>	<±कि>	<+object complement >	<+को-notion, +lexical, +guess/ visual/taste, listening, touch, subjective>
(5) मुझे	नौकर	होशियार	लगता है।
(6) मुझे	लड़की	कुछ मोटी	दिखाई दे रही है।
(7) मुझे	सारी कहानी	गढ़ी हुई	जान पड़ती है।

(8) मुझे	यह सब दौड़-धूप	बेमानी	प्रतीत होती है।
(9) मुझे	दही	खट्टी	लगी।
(10) रमेश को	आपका गायन	बड़ा मधुर	लगा।
(11) मुझे	आपका हाथ	गरम	लग रहा है।

COMMENT: (for 25 and 26)

(a) *Structural Similarity*: Structurally both the sub-patterns (25) and (26) are primarily the same and share the same verbs e.g. (लगना, दिखाई देना, दीखना, नज़र आना, प्रतीत होना, जान पड़ना, etc. The को-verbs of both the sentences anticipate an object complement. The only difference is that in sentence (25) the complement is a noun while in sentence (26) it is adjective. In transformational grammar such sentences are supposed to contain an embedded sentence e.g.

मुझे (वह धूर्त है) लगता है।

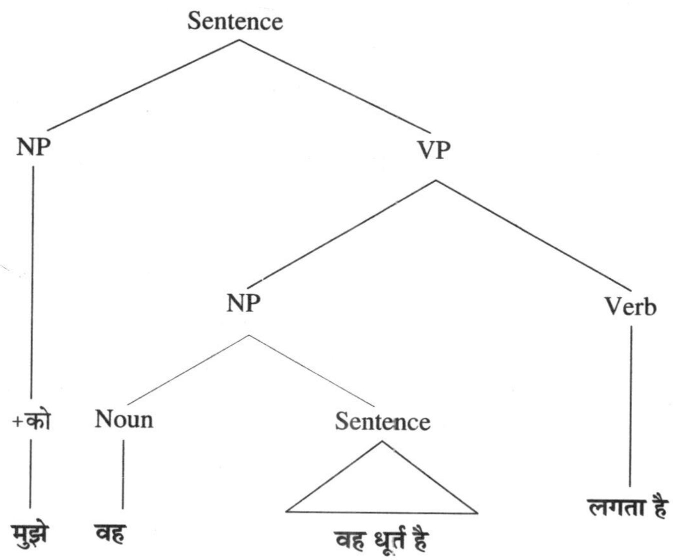

Sub-pattern-27 (possessor-possessed)

NP + postposition (subject) <+possessor >	**NP (complement)** <+possessed>	**हो-verb** <-lexical>
के पास : <+animate>	<+concrete, -body part >	
(1) मोहन के पास	तीस रुपये	हैं।
(2) शर्मा जी के पास	दो नौकर	हैं।
के : <+animate>	<+kith and kin/body part >	
(3) सुशीला के (की)	तीन बहनें	हैं।
(4) हाथी के (की)	एक सूँड	होती है।
के- : <±चेतन>	animate>	
(5) इस महल के	दस दरवाज़े	हैं। (Part and whole)
(6) रानी की	एक सहेली	थी।
(7) संस्थान का	अपना पुस्तकालय	है।
(8) इस किताब के	कई ग्राहक	हैं।
में : <+animate>	<-concrete, +permanent	
(9) शीला में	quality/feature>	है।
<-animate>	प्रतिभा	
	<-चेतन>	
(10) इस किताब में	सौ पृष्ठ	हैं।

□

Chapter-6

VERB-BASED SENTENCE PATTERNS

6.1 Verb-based Sentence Structure

There is normally a controlling constituent in every sentence which monitors or determines the formation and pattern of the of the sentence as to what type of sentence it will generate, how many participants it will contain, whether the sentence will require one object, two objects or no object, whether it needs a complement or an adverbial to complete the sentence. The constituent in the sentence that performs this function is a verb – a lexical verb). This is why it has been called a *verb-based* sentence. It is because of the requirement of a verb that the number and nature of the sentence is determined. See:

(1) राधा नाच रही है।	(subject)
(2) मैं आपकी बात नहीं समझा।	(subject x object)
(3) मोहन गाड़ी गैरेज में रखता है।	(subject x object x adverbial)
(4) मैं चंपा को नर्स समझता था।	(subject x object x object complement)

It is possible that a single verb may denote different meanings in different contexts as the verb समझना in sentences (2 and 4). Which verb can be used in how many sentence patterns depends on their semantic and functional features (3.5). Based on this it is possible to identify and categorize various categories of lexical verbs. The important relevant features of the verb-based sentences are being enumerated below: (Their explanation can be seen against the sub-pattern numbers given within brackets)

The relevant major features and sub-features for the verb-based sentences are being presented in the following chart (their explanation can be seen under the relevant numbers of the sub-patterns given within brackets):

I. INTRANSITIVE Sub-pattern No.

1. Existential (28)
2. General
   a. Agent (29)
   b. Patient (29)
   c. Natural Force (29)
   d. Natural Phenomenon (30)
3. Co-adverbial
   a. Locative (destinative, locative, ablative, spatial) (31)
   b. Temporal/manner/purpose (32)
4. Co-participant
   Coming together/separation (33)

II. TRANSITIVE

1. General
   a. Noun-transitive (object+0, object +को) (34)
   b. ना-transitive (+कि, -की) (35)
   c. -ने का transitive (36)
   d. object-prone complex verb- (37)
2. Co-adverbial
   a. Locative (38)
   b. Time, purpose etc. (38)
3. Co-participant
   a. Dative/ditransitive (non-mental, mental) (39)
   b. Ablative/source (non-mental, mental) (40)
   c. Comitative (emotional, verbal, imperative) (41)
   d. Instrument (intentional, voluntary) (42)
   e. Force (unintentional): natural, unintentional (42, 49)
4. Object Complement
   a. Nominal Object Complement (resultative, non-resultative) (43)
   b. Adjectival Object Complement (resultative, non-resultative) (44)
   c. Adverbial Object Complement (45)

6.2 Feature Analysis of Verb-based Sentence Patterns

Sub-pattern-28 (existential)

NP (subject)	**VP (existential हो)** (to be) <+existence, +beyond time/ space, +lexical, -या रह aspect>
(1) ईश्वर	है।
(2) प्रकृति नाम की कोई शक्ति	है।
(3) (शायद) ईश्वर	हो।
(4) क्या भूत	होते हैं?
(5) अगर ईश्वर	होता...

COMMENT: (SP-28)

(a) *Lexical verb*: On the face of it, this sub-pattern may appear like a copula sentence, but it is not. The verb है here functions as a main verb meaning *to exist* and secondly the sentence does not contain a complement which is the obligatory constituent of a copula sentence.

(b) *Beyond Time and Space*. This sub-pattern denotes the sense of existence beyond time and space, meaning that the subject either exists or does not exist, e.g. ईश्वर है, ईश्वर नहीं है. (God exists or does not exist). It does not make any reference to any time or place. The moment some time and space adverbial is attached to the sentence, the sentence becomes an adverbial copula sentence (*see* sub-pattern (18) e.g. मोहन *बाहर* है, यह *किला अठारहवीं शताब्दी में* था, मेरा नाम सूची में है, etc.

Sub-pattern-29 (intransitive)

NP (subject)	**VP (intransitive)**
a - <+animate, + active>	<+volition>
(1) राधा	नाच रही है।
(2) वे लोग	सो गए/लेट गए।
(3) चिड़िया	उड़ रही है।
b- <+animate +patient>	<-volition>
(4) मैं	ऊब गया/थक गया/चौंक गया।

(5) मेरा दिल	घबरा रहा है।
(6) बच्चा	डूब गया।
(7) मेरा सिर	चकरा रहा है।
(8) उसके हाथ-पाँव	थर्रा रहे हैं।
c- <-animate, +intention>	<-volition +denved informative>
(9) सभी किताबें	बिक गयीं।
(10) बिगुल	बजा।
(11) मंगलगान	शुरू हो गया।
(12) पतंग	उड़ रही है।
d- < -animate, +natural force, - intention>	<-volition>
(13) पृथ्वी	घूम रही है।
(14) बत्ती	बुझ गई। (हवा से)
(15) बादल	उमड़ रहे हैं।
(16) पत्ते	हिल रहे हैं।
(17) धूल	उड़ रही है। (आँधी से)

COMMENT (SP-29)

(a) *Semantic Classification of Hindi Intransitives*: Hindi intransitive sentences can be broadly classified into four semantic categories on the basis of their intrinsic semantic features:

(1) ***Intransitives with animate active subjects*** (राधा नाच रही है।): The active intransitive subject is the one which is free to perform or not to perform the action, e.g. राधा नाच रही है. In other words, to perform or not to perform the action depends upon the *volition* or discretion of the subject. Actions of this type are supposed to be in the control of the active subjects and are, therefore, called *controllable actions* and the subject is called an *active subject*. Verbs like नाचना, हँसना, लेटना, उड़ना etc. belong to this category of intransitive verbs having active subjects (sentence 1-3).

(2) ***Intransitives with inactive animate subjects*** (मैं थक गया।):

The subjects of the intransitive verbs belonging to this class are also animate but they are not *active* subjects because they do not have a full control on the action of the verb. They are merely *experiencers* or *patients* of the action with no volition of their own, e.g. मैं थक गया। The subjects of verbs of this class are, therefore, called *non-active* subjects, because they lack the feature of discretion or volition to influence the action. Verbs like थकना, डूबना, मरना, घबराना, चौंकना, ठहरना etc. belong to this category of non-active or patient verbs (sentence 4-8).

(3) ***Derived Intransitives*** (सभी किताबें बिक गईं।); The derived intransitives are the ones that are derived from the base transitive verbs. Their characteristic is that in the real world the performance of the action involves two participants - an active subject and the other an object but in the derived sentences they appear in the sentence in such a way as if they do not have any subject (doer) and the action is taking place on its own. Verbs like बिकना, धुलना, शुरू होना, बजना etc. belong to this category of intransitive verbs (sentences 9-12). In the real world, however, the actions of किताबें बिकने, बिगुल बजने, मंगलगान आरंभ होने etc. do not happen on their own. Behind them, there is always the hand of some animate and active subject, which remains unexpressed on the surface structure of the sentence. The objects of the real world (किताबें, बिगुल, मंगलगान) function as their grammatical subjects. These are intransitives which are the derived forms of their transitive counterparts like बेचना> बिकना, धोना > धुलना, बजाना > बजना.

(4) ***Natural Force*** (पृथ्वी घूम रही है) This action does not involve a human hand but the hand of Nature. It is part of the law of Nature, which can not be said to be an intentional or conscious action (see 2.8.5b, sub-pattern 42 b). These actions are not intentional actions, because the intended actions are, as a rule, related to the discretion or volition of the subject. On the contrary, the actions of derived intransitives are intentional, because in the real world it is performed at the discretions of the subject. [The unintentional actions are also possible to be expressed through derived intransitives in the subject + से construction, see 2.8.4, e.g. नौकर से गिलास टूट गया, मुझसे गलती हो गई. This is sometimes

called the *involuntary force*] See sub-pattern 42b and 2.8.5b. मुझसे गलती हो गई.

(b) *Volition-marked Sentences in Hindi*: The use of the following verb suffixes or constructs in Hindi makes the sentences subject-sensitive which means that the subject of the sentence can not be transformed or used in sentences in which the subject loses the capability or discretion to perform the action. In other words, in this the subject of the sentence is not active but is only passive or an experiencer. Such restrictions apply on (i) the verbs of obligation like (-ना है, -ना पड़), (ii) the incapabilitative subject + से construction and (iii) imperative verb-forms. These sentences represent actions which are performed with the volition or discretion of the subject. Consequently the active subject-based sentences can be transformed into the subject-volition based sentences whereas it is not possible in the case of the sentences belonging to class A, B, and C. See the difference:

Class A. (l) राधा नाच रही है। (Subject with Volition)
> राधा से नहीं नाचा जाता।
> राधा को नाचना है।
> राधा को नाचना पड़ा।
> नाचो।
> राधा जानबूझकर नाच रही है।

Class B. (4) मैं थक गया। (Subject without Volition)
*मुझसे नहीं थका गया, *मुझे थकना है। *मुझे थकना पड़ा। *थको, *मैं जानबूझकर थक गया।

Class C. सभी किताबें बिक गईं। (Subject without Volition)
> किताबों से नहीं बिका गया, *किताबों को बिकना है; *बिको; *किताबें जानबूझकर बिक गईं।

Class D. पृथ्वी घूम रही है। (Subject without Volition)
> *पृथ्वी से नहीं घूमा जाता; *पृथ्वी को घूमना है; *पृथ्वी को घूमना पड़ा।

(c) *Transitivisation*: The sentences of class C are semantically the passive forms of the base transitive verbs, (see 2.8.4). Hence it is possible to have their passive or transitive forms, for instance, सभी किताबें बिक गईं > दुकानदार ने सभी किताबें बेच दीं, मंगलगान शुरू हुआ > बच्चों ने मंगलगान शुरू किया. On the other hand, there is mainly the hand of the Natural Force (wind, sunshine and fire etc.) and not the human force. Hence their transitive forms are not possible, though in some stylistic constructions their transitive forms can be formed through personification, e.g. हवा धूल उड़ा रही है. It needs to be noted that some verbs can be used in more than one class depending upon the categories of the context and the category of the subjects , e.g. उड़ना, घूमना, हिलना etc. See:

(3) *चिड़िया* उड़ रही है। (active subject)
(12) *पतंग* उड़ रही है। (derived intransitive)
(17) *धूल* उड़ रही है। (as in storm)

(d) ***Animate Subject and its body Parts*:** In the place of the animate subjects, some parts of the body can also be used as symbolic, e.g. *मेरा दिल* घबरा रहा है. *मेरा सिर* चकरा रहा है।

Sub-pattern 30 (natural phenomenon)

NP (subject) <+ preverb, + natural phenomena>	**Verbalizer (हो)** <- active, -volition, - lexical>
बारिश	हो रही है।
गर्मी	हो रही है।
अकाल	पड़ रहा है।
बर्फ़	पड़ रही है।

COMMENT: (SP-30)

(a) *Natural Phenomena*: This sub-pattern accepts sentences which are formed by nouns denoting natural events/phenomena and inactive verbalizers (like हो, पड़, etc.). These events occur on their own for natural reasons and not because of the volition of an animate subject. That is why there is no entity of an agent or an active subject in this sub-pattern. There may be sentences like हवा से दरवाज़ा खुल गया but they are not intentional or intended actions and, therefore, they can not take the place of a logical subject.

(b) *Structure*: From the point of view of the structure, the internal format of the complex verb is almost similar to that of the complex sentence which is made up of two components: a noun and a verb, like बारिश होना, गर्मी होना, बर्फ़ पड़ना etc. The noun component of the complex verb is called a *preverb*. These preverbs also function as the grammatical subject of the sentence. It is important to note that in some languages where there is a *regular* provision of double and single unit verbs (like in English), an expletive '*it*', '*a*' or '*there* has to be used to complete the sentence, e.g. *It* is raining, *it* is snowing, *there* was famine in this part of the country last decade (2.4.1, sub-pattern 37).

(c) *कर - activisation*: बाहर बहुत गर्मी है is a stative sentence because it denotes the state of fact, but बाहर बहुत गर्मी पड़ रही है is a non-stative sentence because it denotes a process. In sentences having normal complex verbs there is the existence of a logical subject, hence it is possible to transform its activised form (e.g. गाड़ी की मरम्मत हो रही है > मिस्त्री गाड़ी की मरम्मत कर रहा है) but in the absence of the logical subject it is not possible to transform its activised form (बारिश हो रही है >* प्रकृति बारिश कर रही है). The mention of these causal forms is, however, possible in the sentence but only as a causal adverb and not as part of non-actvisation, e.g. बहुत गर्मी हो जाने से बारिश हो जाती है, कमरा बंद कर देने से और उमस हो जाएगी.

Sub-pattern-31 (locative intransitive)

NP (subject)	**NP (co-adverbial)** <place>	**Verb (intransitive)** <+location>
a-	<+ destination>	
(1) शेखर	घर	गया।
(2) वे लोग	यहाँ	आ चुके हैं।
(3) गाड़ी	स्टेशन	पहुँच गई है।
(4) यह बस	नई दिल्ली तक	जाएगी।

(5) पिता जी	गाँव	लौट आए हैं।
(6) नौबत	तू-तू मैं-मैं तक	आ गई। (figurative)
b-	<+locative>	
(7) प्रताप	गांधीनगर में	रहता है।
(8) सभी सदस्य	इसी होटल में	ठहरेंगे/टिकेंगे।
(9) आपका सामान	इस कमरे में	नहीं समाएगा।
(10) एक कंपन की लहर	सारे शरीर में	दौड़ गई।
(11) वह	कमरे में	घुसा।
(12) मैं	भीड़ में	धँस गया।
(13) शेर	बच्चे पर	झपटा।
(14) चोर	मेरी ओर	लपका/बढ़ा।
(15) मुस्कराहट	उसके होंठों पर	थिरक उठी।
c-	<+ablative>	
(16) वह	घर से	भाग गया।
(17) सभी पत्ते	पेड़ से	गिर गए।
(18) गंगा	हिमालय से	निकलती है।

COMMENT: (SP-31)

(a) *Locative Co-adverbial*. The verbs of this sub-pattern require a locative co-adverbial and, therefore, they are called locative verbs. The locative adverbial is the obligatory constituent of this sub-pattern and in its absence the sentence may remain rather incomplete at the level of communication, e.g. *प्रताप रहता है, *सुशीला गुज़रती है, *चोर लपका, *एक कंपन की लहर दौड़ गई, *वह घुसा.

(b) *Classification*: From the point of view of function and meaning, location verbs can be divided into three classes: destination, location and departure.

(c) *The Deletion of Postposition*: If the destinative verbs like जाना, आना, पहुँचना, लौटना etc. are used in the general sense, the tendency is to drop the postposition में., e.g. वह घर पहुँचा, मैं बाज़ार गया. But if the perception of the destination is in some specific part or place, the postposition में, पर etc. is generally retained.

Sub-pattern-32 (time, manner, purpose)

NP (Subject)	NP (co-adverbial)	Verb (intransitive)
a-	<+ time>	<+ temporal>
(1) यह कपड़ा	काफ़ी दिन	चलेगा।
(2) खेल	चार घंटे तक	चला।
(3) वह	ज़्यादा दिन	(नहीं) जिएगा।
(4) मैं	दिन भर	घूमा।
(5) हम	दो घंटे	चले।
b-	<+manner, + inherent function>	<+manner -based>
(6) यह कलम	अच्छा	लिखता है।
(7) यह मोटर	तेज़	चलती है।
(8) उषा मशीन	अच्छा	सिलती है।
c-	<+purpose>	<+purpose -based>
(9) हम	एक-एक पैसे के लिए	मोहताज हो रहे थे।
(10) पति-पत्नी दोनों	बच्चे के लिए	तरस रहे हैं।
(11) कुत्ता	पानी के लिए	तरस रहा है।
(12) उसका लड़का	विदेश जाने के लिए	मरा जा रहा है।

COMMENT: (SP-32)

(a) *Time Co-adverbial*: Just as some intransitive verbs require a locative adverbial (घर, यहाँ, कमरे में) to complete the intended meaning of the sentence, some intransitive verbs also anticipate some time adverbial as an obligatory component to complete the desired meaning of the sentence, e.g. *यह कपड़ा चलेगा and *खेल चला are incomplete without the durative co-adverbials like यह कपड़ा *काफ़ी* चलेगा and खेल *चार घंटे तक* चलेगा.

(b) *Co-adverbials of manner*: The adverbs of manner are normally supposed to be the optional or non-obligatory constituents of the sentence, but in certain usages they become obligatory constituents of the sentence and function as adjectives, e.g. यह पेन *अच्छा* लिखता है, यह गाड़ी *तेज* चलती है, यह सिलाई मशीन *अच्छा* सिलती है.

(c) *Purposive Co-adverbial*: A limited number of intransitive verbs anticipate a purposive co-adverbial के लिए, के वास्ते for the completion of their meaning, e.g. the sentences *कुत्ता तरस रहा है and *पति-पत्नी दोनों तरस रहे हैं are incomplete without the purposive co-adverbial पानी के लिए or बच्चे के लिए.

Sub-pattern-33 (Intransitive with से-agent)

NP (subject)	NP (agent) <+से>	Verb (intransitive) <+co-agentive>
a-	<association>	
(1) गोपाल	राधा से	लड़ता है/झगड़ता है।
(2) बच्चा	माँ से	लिपट गया।
(3) कार	स्कूटर से	टकरा गई।
(4) मैं	मोहन से	मिला।
(5) कुर्सियाँ	दीवार से	सट गई हैं।
(6) मैं	उनसे	(नहीं) जूझ सका।
b-	<+separation>	
(7) चोर	पुलिस से	डरता है।
(8) शीला	अपने पति से	रूठ गई।
(9) माया	उन लोगों से	कतराती/चिढ़ती है।
(10) वह	पुलिस से	(नहीं) बच सकता।

COMMENT: (SP-33)

(a) *Association and Separation*: Both the categories of verbs in their natural meanings require a co-agent because the actions like लड़ना, लिपटना and सटना etc. denoted by these verbs can not be accomplished without the existence of two persons or entities. Similary, the sentences (33a) give a perception of togetherness beteween the two entities (लड़ना, चिपकना) and the sub-pattern (33) gives the perception of separation e.g. डरना, रूठना.

(b) *Togetherness*: In the actions denoted by the sub-pattern 33a, the agent and the co-agent happen to be equal in status. In such sentences both of them may be linked together through some conjuncts like और and mutual adverbs like परस्पर, एक दूसरे से, आपस में etc. are suitably inserted. See:

(1) गोपाल राधा से लड़ता है > गोपाल *और* राधा लड़ते हैं।
> गोपाल और राधा *परस्पर* लड़ते हैं।

(3) कार स्कूटर से टकरा गई > कार *और* स्कूटर टकरा गए।
> कार और स्कूटर एक *दूसरे* से टकरा गए।

In the case of corresponding mutual actions where one party is active and the other is passive, the above transformation is not possible, e.g. *कुर्सी और दीवार परस्पर सट गए, *मैं और वह परस्पर नहीं जूझ सकते.

(c) *Mental Separation*: The verbs belonging to (33b) basically denote the perception of mental separation and consequently the subject and the co-agent can not be linked through the conjunct और. All the three sentences are structurally different. See:

(7) चोर पुलिस से डरता है।	(intransitive)
(11) शीला को शंकर से प्यार है।	(को- sentence)
(12) शीला शंकर से प्यार करती है।	(transitive)

Sub-pattern-34 (noun-based transitive)

NP (subject)	NP (object)	Verb (transitive)
a-	<-को,-definite>	
(1) हरी	पानी	पीता है।
(2) मैंने	बच्चों की पीठ	सहलाई।
(3) उसने	आग	बुझाई।
(4) रेखा ने	बनावटी मुस्कान	बिखेर दी।
(5) यह कार	बहुत पेट्रोल	खाती है। (figurative)
(6) पुलिस ने	कई चोर	पकड़े।
b-	<+को,+animate,+definite>	<+animate object+relatee>
(7) शेखर	अपनी पत्नी को	पीटता है।
(8) वह	आपको	बुला रहा है।
(9) मेरी याद	मम्मी-पापा को	सताती होगी।
(10) वे लोग	हमारे नौकर को	बहका रहे हैं।
(11) बड़े साहब ने	कई लोगों को	डाँटा।
	<+को,-animate,+definite>	
(12) उसकी आँखें	निर्जीव दीवारों को	देखती रहीं।
(13) उसने	लटकते चीथड़ों को	फेंक दिया।
(14) आप	उनकी बेकार बातों को	छोड़िए।
(15) भय ने	उसकी छाती को	संकुचित कर दिया।

COMMENT: (SP-34)

(a) *Marked and unmarked objects*: The verbs of this sub-pattern are transitive and require an object whether marked or unmarked. The *unmarked* objects are those that do not take any postposition after the object, e.g. हरी *पानी* पीता है. See also further sentences (1 to 6) above. The marked objects in this sub-pattern are followed by the postposition को etc, e.g. शेखर अपनी *पत्नी* को पीटता है. See further sentences (7 to 15) above. These object markers in Hindi are called *कारक or case markers*, because its presence or absence in the surface structure of the sentence depends on its intrinsic feaures (like animate-inanimate, definite-indefinite etc.).

(b) *Important rules for the use of object + को* are given below:

(i) Basically verbs which have the capacity to be used with reference to the animate objects require object + को, e.g. पीटना, डाँटना, सताना, गुड़गुड़ाना, चिढ़ाना, चौंकना, टाँगना, पुचकारना, फुसलाना, बहकाना, हराना, ललकारना, लुभाना etc. (7-11). Compare:

Object + को:

(11) बड़े साहब ने कई *लोगों को* डाँटा। (general)
*बड़े साहब ने *कई लोग* डाँटे। (general)
(9) मेरी याद *मम्मी को सताती* होगी। (definite)
*मेरी याद *कई लोग* सताती होगी। (general)

(ii) Inanimate nouns which have been expressed as specific objects may also accept the postposition को (see sentences 12 to 15)

Object + ϕ को:

In normal circumstances को is not used with the inanimate objects. On the contrary को is used with the definite or specific object as in (b) above. Compare:

(16) मैंने *रस्सी* पकड़ी। (general, inanimate)
(17) मैंने *रस्सी* को पकड़ा। (specific, animate)

(iii) In normal circumstances को is used along with the animate object, but if the animate object is indefinite and generalized, को may not be used with it (except in (i) above). See:

(18) पुलिस ने *रामू* को पकड़ा। (definite)

पुलिस ने *कई चोर* पकड़े। (generalised)

(19) मैंने स्टेशन में आपकी लड़की को देखा। (definite)

मैंने स्टेशन में *कई लड़कियाँ* देखीं। (generalized)

(b) There is a class of transitive verbs from which derived intransitives can be formed, as for instance, धुलना from धोना, छूटना from छोड़ना, बिकना from बेचना etc. Such transitive verbs are called*base transitive verbs*. The subjects of such base transitive verbs are animate and active and the objects are generally inanimate (In certain instances like पीटना-पिटना the object may be animate.)

Sub-pattern-35 (infinitive transitive with -ना)

NP (subject)	NP (object) <+ infinitive (-ना)>	Verb (transitive)
a- <+animate>	<+कि>	
(1) विजय	कार चलाना	जानता है।
(2) सुशीला	अंग्रेज़ी बोलना	सीख रही है।
(3) मैं	आपका चाय बनाना	देख रहा हूँ।
(4) मैं	इसे खोलना	भूल गया।
(5) सभी यात्री	नहाना	चाहते हैं।
(6) हम	उसका रोज़-रोज़ यहाँ आना	नहीं सह सकते।
(7) शकीला	चिट्ठी डालना	भूल गई।
(8) उन्होंने	गवाही देना	स्वीकार कर लिया।
b- <±animate>	<-कि>	
(9) इस मशीन ने	काम करना	बंद कर दिया है।
(10) रामलाल ने	सिगरेट पीना	छोड़ दिया है।
(11) मैंने	उसका गिड़गिड़ाना	ख़त्म कर दिया है।
(12) लोगों ने	गरम कोट पहनना	शुरू कर दिया है।

COMMENT: (SP-35)

(a) *Classification*: The transitive verbs of this sub-pattern have the capacity to accept infinitives as the object of the sentence, e.g. कार चलाना, नहाना etc. Such verbs are limited in inumber and can be grouped into two semantic classes:

(b) That-clause Complex Verb

Animate subject: The subjects of the sentences belonging to 1 to 8 are always are always animate.

(i) Verbs relating to mental activities, skills and wishes e.g. जानना, चाहना, सीखना, भूलना, देखना, सुनना, स्वीकार करना, मानना etc. The infinitive forms are also sometimes used in certain verbs like बताना, समझना etc. (e.g. मैं नियम का प्रयोग करना समझ गया हूँ, उन्होंने मुझे नियम का प्रयोग करना बता दिया है).

Sub-pattern-36 -ने का transitive

NP (subject) <+ animate>	**NP (object)** <verb + ने का, कि+ declinable>	**Verb <transitive>**
		<+ -ए, -एगा, +संकल्प>
(1) रंगनाथन	जाने की	सोच रहा है।
(2) उन्होंने	लौटने की	ठान ली है।
(3) शीला ने	शादी न करने का	इरादा किया है।
(4) हमने	सभी को बुलाने का	फ़ैसला किया है।
(5) मैंने	(इसी साल) परीक्षा देने का	विचार किया है।
(6) उसने	साड़ी लाने का	वादा किया था।
(7) हमने	देश की रक्षा करने का	संकल्प किया है।
		<±-ए, -एगा, +नाटक>
(8) बच्चों ने	सोने का	बहाना किया।
(9) नायिका ने	ज़हर खाकर मरने का	नाटक किया।

COMMENT: (SP- 36)

(a) *Structure*: This sub-pattern is also like the sub-pattern (35). The only difference is that the object in this sub-pattern is not a noun but an infinitive (आने की) followed by some postposition. According to the verb agreement pattern of Hindi, the -ना suffix in such situations becomes ए-ending, e.g. लौटने *की*, बुलाने *का* etc. (उन्होंने लौटने की ठान ली है).

(b) *कि clause*: Most of the verbs in this sub-pattern (sentence 1-7) express some type of resolution, pledge or decision like सोचना, ठानना, विचार करना, इरादा करना, संकल्प करना, प्रण करना, निश्चय करना, फैसला करना, निर्णय करना, ज़िद करना, हठ करना, आग्रह/दुराग्रह करना, वादा करना etc. Most of these verb forms have optative ए-ending. See:

(1a) रंगनाथन सोच रहा है कि वह चला *जाए*।

(2a) उन्होंने ठान लिया है कि वे लौट *जाएँ*।

The verbs (बहाना करना, नाटक करना, ढोंग रचना etc. used in sentences (8-9) are *factive* verbs, that is, they represent facts and not resolutions. Hence there are no such restrictons on their verb-forms e.g. बच्चों ने बहाना किया कि वे सो रहे हैं, नायिका ने यह नाटक किया कि वह ज़हर खाकर मर गई है.

(c) *Complex Verb*: In this sub-pattern the finite verbs used are mostly complex verbs because the use of a noun word after the postposition का is obligatory in such a sentence construction. Like most of the Hindi complex verbs formed by noun + verbalizer, these verbs also expect an object + का before them, e.g. का इरादा करना, का संकल्प करना, का वादा करना, का बहाना करना. One class of complex verbs which does not require the postposition का after the object is: याद करना (मैंने पाठ याद किया), प्रारंभ/शुरू करना, व्यय/खर्च करना, बर्दाश्त करना, पसंद करना, इंकार करना, बलिदान करना, दान करना, भेंट करना, (को) क्षमा करना, रवाना करना etc.

(d) *Animate subject*: The subject in this sub-pattern is always animate because the notions of pledge, wish or resolution are essentially related to an animate subject (human being) and not an inanimate subject.

SUB-PATTERN-37 (object-based complex verbs)

Transitive with Complex Verbs

A- Object-based

NP (subject)	**Object-plus**	**Verbalizer** <+active, +कर>
(1) मज़दूर	हड़ताल	कर रहे हैं।
(2) वह	सत्याग्रह	कर रहा है।
(3) रामू ने	आत्महत्या	कर ली है।
(4) लोग	काम	कर रहे हैं।
(5) उसकी पत्नी	एक जघन्य कृत्य	कर बैठी।
(6) मैंने	एक गलती	की।

B- Phrasal NP based

NP (subject) <±ने>	Phrasal NP (object) <+ का>	Noun with verbalizer <+pre-verb> Noun-based	<+कर> verbaliser
(7) मिस्त्री	कार की	मरम्मत	: कर रहा है।
(8) उन्होंने	इसी दवा का	सेवन	: किया।
(9) उसने	अपने जिस्म का	सौदा	: किया।
(10) मैंने	आपकी	चर्चा	: नहीं की।
(11) मैं	उनकी बातों का	विश्वास	: (नहीं) करता।
(12) वे	मंदिर के	दर्शन	: करेंगे।
(13) शिक्षामंत्री ने	इस भवन का	उद्घाटन	: किया।

COMMENT: (SP-37)

(a) *Noun pre-verb as object*: The verbs of both the categories of sentences A and B above are transitive complex verbs which are formed with noun+कर, e.g. हड़ताल करना, मरम्मत करना etc. Their noun portion is called a preverb (see 2.4.2) which carries the lexical meaning of the verb phrase. कर is a verbalizer which provides a verbal meaning to the preverb but in itself does not carry any lexical meaning.

All the complex verbs of this sub-pattern are functional (see 2.4.3), i.e. they perform a grammatical function in the sentence, for instance in the perfective environment the first component (i.e. the noun component) controls the verb agreement of the sentence in the same way the unmarked object of the simple verb does it. See:

(1) मज़दूरों ने *हड़ताल की*। (complex verb agreement)

(14) चंपा ने *चाय पी*। (simple verb agreement)

Despite this, the noun element can not be said to be the objects because it is basically a constituent of the verb phrase, carries the lexical meaning of the verb phrase and forms an independent semantic unit. It also lacks many structural featues of an object like the use of object + को (*लोगों ने हड़ताल को किया). Hence the first component of the complex verb performs only a partial function of an object in the sentence and has, therefore, been called a *proxy* object. Semantically, the proxy object (or the the object-based noun) is a part of the adverb phrase whereas the entity of a regular object is always outside the adverb phrase.

(b) *Object+का*: The complex verbs belonging to class (a) of this sub-pattern are semantically self-contained in themselves but the complex verbs belonging to the class (b) require the use of regular objects for the completion of their meaning. e.g. *मिस्त्री मरम्मत कर रहा है and उन्होंने सेवन किया are respectively incomplete without the mention of the objects कार की and दवा का. The use of the postposition का after the object is the structural characteristic of the functional complex verbs (see 2.4.3).

(c) *Intrasitivisation*: The transitive sentences of this sub-pattern can be transformed into intransitive sentences through the process of subject deletion and से-passivisation, e.g.

(i) (deletion of subject) हड़ताल हो रही है/कार की मरम्मत हो रही है।
(subject + से) मुझसे गलती हुई। (unintended action)
(ii) उनसे इस दवा का सेवन नहीं होगा। (incapability)
(iii) इस भवन का उद्‌घाटन शिक्षामंत्री द्वारा हुआ।
(iv) मुझे उनकी बातों का विश्वास नहीं है/होता।

Sub-pattern-38 (locational transitive)

NP (Subject)	**NP (Object)** <±को>	**Co-adverbial** <+locative>	**Verb <transitive>** <+place -relative>
(1) मोहन	गाड़ी	गैरेज में	रखता है।
(2) मैंने	नौकर को	बाज़ार में	भेजा।
(3) डॉक्टर ने	दवा	ज़ख्म पर	लगा दी।
(4) हीरो ने	तलवार	राजा के पेट में	भोंक दी।
(5) मैनेजर ने	हम सभी को	हॉल में	घुसाया।
(6) छात्रों ने	सभी किताबें	बक्से में	डाल दीं।
(7) उन्होंने	सारी ज़िम्मेदारी	मेरे ऊपर	थोप दी।
(8) सरकार ने	भिखारियों को	नई कॉलोनी में	बसा दिया।
(9) वैज्ञानिकों ने	तेल	ज़मीन से	निकाला।

COMMENT: (SP- 38)

(a) *Locative Adverbial*: This sub-pattern is the transitive counterpart of the locative intransitive sentence pattern (प्रताप गांधीनगर में रहता है). Hence the transitive or first causative forms of many locative adverbials are possible in this sub-pattern, e.g. घुसाना, लटकाना, टाँगना, गाड़ना,

पहुँचाना, बसाना, निकालना etc. Locative transitive verbs expect locative co-adverbials. These co-adverbials are the obligatory constituents of this sub-pattern without which the sentences are incomplete at communication level. For instance the sentences *मोहन गाड़ी रखता है and *उन्होंने किताबें डालीं are incomplete without the co-adverbials गैरेज में and बक्से में respectively unless, of course, the meaning is derived from the context.

(b) *False Locative Sentences*: At a surface level some sentences may outwardly look like locative sentences, but they are infact not. They are false locatives. The locative adverbials are obligatory constituents of the sentence and can not be removed without the loss of meaning. See the following:

(1) a. मोहन गाड़ी *गैरेज में* रखता है। (obligatory)
b. मोहन गाड़ी *गैरेज में* धोता है। (optional/false
(5) a. मैनेजर ने हम सबको *हॉल में* घुसाया। (obligatory)
b. मैनेजर ने हम सभी को *हॉल में* बुलाय। (optional/false)

(c) *Intrasitive Transformation*: Some transitive locative sentences can be transformed into intransitive forms through the process of subject deleton and copula है. See:

(10) मैंने नौकर को बाज़ार *भेजा* > नौकर बाज़ार *गया*।
(11) मैनेजर ने हम सभी को हॉल में *घुसा दिया* > हम सभी हॉल में *घुस गए*।
(12) उन्होंने सारी जिम्मेदारी मेरे ऊपर *थोप दी* > सारी जिम्मेदारी मेरे ऊपर *पड़ गई*।
(13) मोहन गाड़ी गैरेज में *रखता है* > गाड़ी गैरेज में *है/रहती* है।

Sub-pattern-39 (dative bi-transitive)

NP (subject)	NP (dative)	NP (object)	Verb (ditrinsitive)
<+donor>	<+indirect object>	<+direct object>	<+दे-class>
A -		<+recipient>	<-mental>
(1) सेठ जी ने	नौकर को	पैसे	दिए।
(2) उसने	मुझे	यह मकान	बेचा।
(3) उन्होंने	मंत्री को	एक टी-सेट	भेंट/प्रदान किया।
(4) मैंने	पिता जी को	चिट्ठी	लिखी।
(5) मोहन ने	राधा को	सामान	भेजा।
(6) अशोक	मुझे	सभी कागज़ात	लौटा/सौंप देगा।
(7) माँ ने	सभी को	खाना	परोस दिया।

B-	<+receiver>	<+mental>	<+bilateral>
(8) अध्यापक	छात्रों को	गणित	पढ़ाते हैं।
(9) माता जी ने	नई बहू को	सभी बातें	समझा दी हैं।
(10) मैं	सिल्वी को	हिंदी	सिखा रहा हूँ।
(11) गायिका ने	श्रोताओं को	एक नया गाना	सुनाया।

COMMENT: (SP-39)

(a) *Bilateral Verbs*: Most of the verbs of this sub-pattern are bi-directional or bilateral and represent both the sides of the same action, e.g. देना-लेना, भेजना-पाना etc.

The objects so transferred from one place to the other may be something concrete like money, house, letter, food etc. (sentences 1 to 7 above) or it may be something abstract like mathematics, song, language etc. (sentences 8 to 11 above (गणित पढ़ाना, गाना सुनना-सुनाना). This category of bilateral or bi-directional actions of giving or taking is expressed through different lexical words like लेना-देना, खरीदना-बेचना etc. The bilateral actions in category A above are denoted through different lexical words (like लेना-देना) whereas in group B it is expressed through bi-lateral causative pairs like पढ़ना-पढ़ाना, समझना-समझाना etc.

(b) *Direct and Indirect Object*: The verbs of this sub-pattern are called *di-transitive* verbs because they contain two objects – direct object and indirect object. The direct object is also called a *dative*. The direct object answers the question *what* and the indirect object answes the question to *whom*. So if we consider a sentence, सेठ जी ने नौकर को एक हज़ार रुपए दिए, the question asked will be: *what* was given and *to whom* was it given? एक हज़ार रुपए will be a direct object and नौकर will be an indirect object.

(c) *Donor and Receiver Relationship*: At the root of the semantic structures of all the words denoting di-transitive verbs we find that there is an inherent sense of *giving* or *donating* in these actions. This is a bilateral action which requires two parties – the donor (subject) and the receiver (dative case). Amongst the bilateral verbs *to give* is a central theme devoid of any specific type or manner of giving. In this sense they are supposed to contain an added mixture of two semantic elements, e.g. बेचना = to give away by accepting money, भेंट करना = to give with respect, परोसना = to lay food and serve, भेजना = to send through some medium, लिखना, लिखाना = to write and send (in the sense of sentence (4).

(d) *Dative and Benificiary*: There is a very fine distinction between the dative and the beneficiary. See:

(1) सेठ जी ने *नौकर को* पैसे दिए। (dative *to*)

(15) मैंने *अपनी पत्नी को* एक गाड़ी खरीदी। (benificiary *for*)

If you delete नौकर को from the sentence (1) the sentences will remain incompletee, but if you delete अपनी पत्नी को from sentence (15), the sentence मैंने एक गाड़ी खरीदी is complete in itself. Here अपनी पत्नी को is beneficiary and not dative. It is possible to substitute के लिए in place of *को* (e.g. मैंने अपनी पत्नी के लिए एक गाड़ी खरीदी). This is not possible in the case of dative.

(e) *Similar but False Sentences*: Some sentences may look alike on the surface structure but may in part belong to different sentence patterns. See the following:

(1) मैंने बच्चों को कपड़े *दिए*। (ditransitive)
मैंने बच्चों को कपड़े *पहनाए*। (causative)

(2) मोहन ने राधा को सामान *भेजा*। (ditransitive)
मोहन ने राधा को बाज़ार *भेजा*। (locative tansitive)

Sub-pattern-40 (Ablative/Source)

A - Ablative

NP (subject) <+receiver>	**NP (ablative)** <+से, + animate>	**NP (object)** <- mental>	**Verb (transitive)** <+ले-class>
(1) नौकर ने	सेठ जी से	पैसे	लिए।
(2) शीला ने	पति से	तीस रुपये	माँगे।
(3) चोर ने	रामू से	बटुआ	छीन लिया।
(4) मैंने	उनसे	यह मकान	खरीद लिया।
(5) दुकानदार ने	मुझसे	दस रुपये	ठग लिए।

B- Source

NP (subject) <+recipient, - active>	NP (ablative) <+से, + active>	NP (Object) <- concrete>	Verb (Transitive) <+पढ़-class>
(6) ये छात्र	अध्यापक से	गणित	पढ़ते हैं।
(7) नई बहू ने	माता जी से	सभी बातें	समझ ली हैं।
(8) सिल्वी	मुझसे	हिंदी	सीख रही है।
(9) श्रोताओं ने	गायिका से	एक नया गाना	सुना।

COMMENT: (SP-40)

(a) *Bi-directional Actions*: Both the ablative and the source (1-5) denote a perception of separation in the same way as the ditransitive verbs like देना and लेना give a perception of taking and giving. The subjects of both (the ablative and the *source*) are marked by the postposition से and denote a sense of separation in the same way the ditransitive verbs like लेना-देना denote the sense of taking and giving. In sentences where both the subject and the ablative are animate, the action of mutual exchange is normally bilateral. लेना and देना are the two ends of the same action, e.g. नौकर ने सेठ जी से पैसे लिए > सेठ जी ने नौकर को पैसे दिए. In sentences where the ablative is inanimate, functions as it locative adverbial and the verb is not bilateral. The locative adverbial can be either optional or obligatoy depending upon the context and the verb-class. If they are obligatory they will be included under locative transitive. See:

(10) मैंने दही *बाज़ार से* ख़रीदी। (optional)

(11) वैज्ञानिकों ने *ज़मीन से* तेल निकाला। (obligatory) (sub-pattern 38)

(b) *Ablative and Source*: In the sentences of both the groups there is the connotation of giving and taking. In Group A this exchange is concrete and non-mental while in group B it is abstract and mental. See:

(6) ये छात्र *अध्यापक से* गणित पढ़ते हैं। (source)
> *अध्यापक* इन छात्रों को गणित पढ़ाते हैं। (subject)

(1) नौकर ने *सेठ जी से* पैसे लिये। (ablative)
*सेठ जी नौकर को पैसे लिवाते हैं।

Remember that there are some misleading similarities between the ablative verbs and the second causative verbs, e.g.

(12) मैंने डॉ. बोस *से* यह तरीका सीखा। (source)

(13) मैंने डॉ. बोस *से* यह बात मनवाई। (second causative)

(c) *Encapsulated Verbs*. The association or collocative use of some specific objects is so strong and exclusive with certain verbs that the verb assimilates the direct object in its meaning. These are called the *encapsulated verbs*, i.e. the verb itself encapsules the object, for instance, (दूध) दुहना, पैसे ठगना, धूल झाड़ना, पानी (निचोड़ना) (खून/द्रव) चूसना etc. In the sentence ग्वाला गाय दुह रहा है and दुकानदार ने मुझे ठग लिया, the words दूध and पैसे remain omitted because here these notions are encapsulated or assimilated in the verbs themselves.

Sub-pattern-41 (mutual transitive)

A - complex verb based

NP (subject)	**NP (co-agent)**	**Verb (transitive)** <+ mixed>	
<+ animate>	<+ से, + co-agent>	object-based <+preverb, - noun, - कि>	verbalizer
		<+event>	
(1) प्रताप ने	शीला से	शादी	की।
(2) उन्होंने	मंत्री से	भेंट	की।
(3) उसने	सभी लोगों से	परिचय/मेल	कर लिया है।
(4) सुशीला	अपनी पड़ोसन से	बहस/झगड़ा/लड़ाई	कर रही है।
(5) मैं	आपसे	परामर्श	करूँगा।
(6) उन्होंने	किससे	बात	की ?
(7) हम	आपके दल से	कोई संबंध/सरोकार	(नहीं) रखेंगे।
		<+feeling>	
(8) मैं	तुमसे	प्यार	करता हूँ।
(9) सभी लोग	आपसे	सहानुभूति	रखते हैं।
(10) नई लड़कियाँ	हमसे	ईर्ष्या	करती हैं।

B- Verbal (statement)

NP (subject) <+ speaker>	NP (co-agent) <+ party, + co-agent>	NP (object) <+ statement, - कि>	Verb (transitive) <+ से - based>
(11) सुधीर ने	भाभी से	एक बात	कही।
(12) छात्र	अध्यापक से	प्रश्न	पूछ रहे हैं।
(13) पुलिस ने	चोर से	वही सवाल	दोहराया।
(14) वह	(मुझसे)	कुछ नहीं	बोला।
		<+ ना object, +को/के लिए>	<+order>
(15) डॉक्टर ने	मरीज़ से	कल आने को	कहा है।
(16) मैंने	पिताजी से	आपको साथ लाने के लिए	कहा था।

COMMENT: (SP 41)

(a) *Co-agent*: The sentences of this sub-pattern are basically transitive. Secondly, both the subject and the co-agent are animate and occur together sharing the same function in the sentence. For instance, the transitive verbs of this sub-pattern (1) require an animate subject (प्रताप) as well as a co-agent (शीला से). The subject (प्रताप) and the co-agent (शीला) are mutually linked to each other performing the same function or action.The only thing worth noting here is that the verb here is a *complex verb* (शादी करना). What is important here is that the transitive verb physically splits into two segments -- शादी and करना, but semantically they form a single unit. The relationship between the subject and the co-agent is that of togetherness or separation. The postposition that links them together is से, and sometimes, के साथ. They are called *transitive complex verbs* (शादी करना). This is the transitive counterpart of the sub-pattern 33a (गोपाल राधा से लड़ता है). See:

गोपाल राधा से *लड़ता है vs*.: गोपाल राधा से *लड़ाई करता* है।

(b) *Notion, event, verbalization*: Semantically, the objects in this category of sentences may appear as a notion, an event or a verbalization. See the following sentences:

(1) प्रताप ने *शीला से* शादी की। (co-agent)

(2) सुधीर ने भाभी से *एक बात* कही। (statement)

(3) डॉक्टर ने मरीज़ से कहा कि *आप कल आएँ।* (verbalisation)

(4) डॉक्टर ने मरीज़ को कल आने को कहा। (nominalisation)

(c) *Intransitivisation* : The transitive forms of complex verbs can be achieved through two processes – by substituting the active verbalizer -कर with the passive verbalizer हो and secondly by devaluating the subject. The devaluation of the subject can be achieved in two ways in this sub-pattern by i) transformation of transitive forms (कर) into हो forms into intransitive one can be achieved through two ways: by using subject + का or using subject + को, e.g.

(1) प्रताप ने शीला से **शादी** की > **प्रताप की** शादी शीला से हुई।

(2) मैं तुमसे प्यार करता हूँ > **मुझे** तुमसे प्यार **है/हो गया।**

(d) *Nominalisation* : Verbs like: कहना etc. which freely use कि -clauses in Hindi have the capacity to be expressed in the normalised from also as verb + ना + को/के लिए. is:

(15) डॉक्टर ने मरीज़ से कहा कि *आप कल आएँ।*

(15a) <डॉक्टर ने मरीज़ से कहा कि *आप कल आइए*>।

Sub-pattern-42 (Instrument/Force)

A- Instrument

NP (subject) <+ volition + intentional>	NP (instrument) <- animate>	NP (object) <±animate, ±को>	Verb (transitive) <+instrument-based>
	<+से>		
(1) बढ़ई ने	आरी से	लकड़ी	चीर दी।
(2) पुलिस ने	डंडे से	चोर को	पीटा।
(3) नौकर	(चाकू से)	फल	काट रहा है।
(4) नौकरानी	(झाड़ू से)	कमरा	बुहार रही है।
(5) पिता जी ने	<-से>		
(6) बड़े बाबू ने	अपने कानों	यह बात	सुनी।
	अपनी आँखों	सब कुछ	देखा।

B- Force

NP (force) <+ unintentional>	NP gram. subject) <- animate>	Verb (derived intransitive) Derived intransitive
Natural force>		
(7) हवा से	दरवाज़ा	खुल गया।
(8) गर्मी से	घी	पिघल गया।
(9) पानी से	कागज़	फूल गया।
(10) धूप से	कपड़े	सूख गए।
<Unintentional force>		
(11) हाथ लगने से	बटन	बंद हो गया।
(12) चाकू से	मेरी उँगली	कट गई।
(13) नौकर से	गिलास	टूट गया।

COMMENT: (SP-42)

(a) *Instrument and Force*: Instrument* (case) is an inanimate medium of accomplishing an action which is executed by an animate subject having the power of discretion or volition, e.g. बढ़ई ने आरी से लकड़ी चीर दी. Here the action accomplished by the instrument is intentional, performed in the full knowedge of the subject. There is, however, always the hand of some human being behind every such action (2.7.2) which is executed by the the instrument, e.g. चीरना, काटना and बुहारना. Verbs of this category are shown under the class A of this sub-pattern.

Some actions which are normally supposed to be accomplished through instruments may sometimes occur on their own without any other support. e.g. हवा से दरवाज़ा खुल गया. There is normally a hand of nature behind these actions which is called the Natural Force (2.8.5). This action is not intended or intentional. The sentences (7-10) in the above sub-pattern B belong to this category. The actions under Natural Force in relation to intransitive sentences falls under a separate category (see sub-pattern 29 d)

Some actions may, however, take place on their own without the knowledge or intention of the subject, or by mistake, e.g. नौकर से गिलास टूट गया. This is also an unintended action but without the knowledge of the subject. Hence नौकर is an ignorant force or instrument. Behind the ignorant force there is no conscious hand of the subject as happens in the case of the *instrument*. The sentences of this category are given under category B (11-13).

One characteristic of the sentences of the B category (see 2.7.4d) is that they are the derived intransitives of the base transitive verbs. The main marker of both the instrument and the force is the postposition से. In the case of instrument, however, the use of some other particles is also possible, e.g. के ज़रिए (रमेश ने बड़े भाई *के ज़रिए* दाखिला ले लिया), के द्वारा) वह *अपने एजेंटों द्वारा* सब खबर प्राप्त कर लेता है), के हाथ, (उसने *नौकर के हाथ* सामान भिजवाया), plural suffix (बड़े बाबू ने *आँखों से* सब कुछ देखा), zero suffix (लड़कों ने कुत्ते को *पत्थर* मारा).

(b) *Instrument-based Verbs*: Some instruments करण कारक and verbs have exclusive relationships between them so much so that the verb itself encapsulates (i.e. contains inside it) the meaning of the instrument. Halliday calls them *encapsulated* verbs. The verb बुहारना itself, for instance, covers or envelops the meaning of the instrument झाड़ू, the verb कुतरना contains inside it the meaning of tooth, etc. The semantic structure of these words themselves captures the meaning of the instrument in the verb. Halliday says that for certain specific actions accomplished through certain instruments or instrument classes, every language develops, by tradition, certain conventional specific words like झाड़ू से बुहारना, दाँतों से कुतरना, डंक से डसना), आरी से चीरना etc*. Where the mention of the medium is specifically necessary or

---

*Here the notion of instrument is a little different from that of Fillmore. According to Fillmore all the the underlined words in italics in the following sentences are instrument in case:

मैंने *चाबी से* दरवाज़ा खोला। *आँधी ने* कई पेड़ उखाड़ दिए। *बारूद ने* कई मकान उड़ा दिए। *इस फ़ोटो ने* मुझे मेरा बचपन याद दिला दिया। *आपका सम्मान होना* हम सभी के लिए खुशी की बात है।

*Some important instrument-based nouns are as follows:

(कैंची से) कतरना	(मूसल से) कूटना	
(पेंचकस से) कसना	(पानी से) खंगालना	(डंक से) डँसना
(चाकू से) काटना	(नुकीली चीज से) खरोचना	(तराजू से) तौलना
(सुई से) काढ़ना	(करछी से) खुरचना	(लाठी से) पीटना
(तकली से) कातना	(आरी से) चीरना	(झाड़ू से) बुहारना
(दाँतों से) कुतरना	(चाकू से) छीलना	(बेलन से) बेलना

desirable, or where there is no intrinsic relationship between the verb and the instrument, the mention of the instrument in the surface structure is necessary, e.g. मैं *कोलगेट* से दाँत साफ करता हूँ, उसने दोनों हाथों से मूर्ति उठाई और नीचे पटक दी. From this angle, the instrument is not the obligatory constituent of the the sentence. It is only an optional constituent. In this sentence pattern the instrument has been shown within brackets. From the point of view of basic sub-patterns, these sub-patterns do not come under the present instrument-based sub-pattern but under instrumentless transitive sub-patterns.

(c) *Subject and Instrument*: The instrument is basically inanimate and without a volition of its own while the active subject (or agent) is animate with discretion of its own. The agent in such cases executes its action rhrough the instrument but in cases where there is no animate subject or doer mentioned in the sentence, the instrument may assume the designate role of the subject, even though metaphorically, and execute the action, e.g.

(14) इस *उस्तरे ने* बड़े-बड़ों की हजामत बनाई है।

(15) यह *पॉलिश* जूता अच्छा चमकाता है।

(16) *सर्फ़* कपड़े साफ़ धोता है।

(17) अनजाने में *चाकू से* मेरी उँगली कट गई। (unintentional)

(d) *Object and Instrument*

The instrument does not only perform the function of a subject in a sentence, but can sometimes also perform the function of an object. In certain usages, the postposition से is deleted after the the instrument and the instrument adopts many characteristics of the object, e.g.

(18) लड़कों ने कुत्ते को *पत्थर से* मारा।

(19) लड़कों ने कुत्ते को *पत्थर* मारा।

In both these sentences the structure of the events is the same, in which the पत्थर has been used as an instrument, but according to the grammatical structure, पत्थर in sentence (18) is an instrument and in sentence (19) it is object, because in sentence (18) it answers the question लड़कों ने कुत्ते को क्या मारा? (पत्थर) and controls the verb agreement in the ने-environment (पत्थर मारा, लाठी मारी).

The number of verbs which can perform the inherent function of the object is, however, limited, e.g. पत्थर मारना, लात मारना/जमाना, थप्पड़ मारना, घूँसा मारना, डंडा/बेंत मारना, छुरा मारना, etc. The verbs of this class are mostly related to physical assault and their objects are animate and subject+को marked. The perception of *manner* in these instruments is important here. For instance, the verb मारना denotes an *action*. पत्थर and लात etc. denote the manner of killing. The verb and the manner put together constitute a single action or a semantic unit and in many languages they constitute a single word, e.g. to pelt, to kick, to slap, to knock, to cane, to shoot, to stab etc. In Hindi also the words like थप्पड़, लात, घूँसा have such an exclusive relationship with the verbs that a construction like थप्पड़ से मारना and घूँसे से मारना would appear artificial. Hence it will be more appropriate to consider them as complex perbs.

Sub-pattern-43 (Object Complement Noun)

NP (subject)	**NP (object)** <+ को>	**NP (complement)**	**VP (transitive)** <object comple-ment-based>
a- Non-resultative			<-resultative>, +कि>
(1) मैं	चंपा को	नर्स	समझता था।
(2) वह	मुझे	अपना भाई	मानता/समझता है।
(3) लोग	उसे	विद्वान	मानते हैं।
(4) मैं	आपको	शरीफ़ आदमी	समझता/मानता हूँ।
b- Resultative			**<+resultative>**
			<-कि,>
(5) लोगों ने	रामलाल को	अपना नेता	चुना।
(6) वे	अपनी लड़की को	डॉक्टर	बनाना चाहते हैं।
(7) मैनेजर ने	रीता को	अपना सचिव	नियुक्त किया।
(8) कंपनी वालों ने	मुझे	अपना वकील	मुकर्रर किया है।
(9) बच्चे	पंडित नेहरू को	चाचा	कहते हैं।
			<+कि, +कथ्य>
(10) वकील ने	जग्गू को	चोर	सिद्ध कर दिया।
(11) डॉक्टर ने	गुप्ता जी को	तपेदिक का मरीज़	बताया।
(12) सभी घर वाले	उसे	कामचोर	कहते हैं।

Sub-pattern-44 (Adjective Complement)

NP (subject)	NP (object)		VP (transitive) <object complement-based>
a- Non-resultative	<+ को>		<+कि -in transitive>
(13) मैं	आपको	ईमानदार	समझता था।
(14) हम	इसे	फायदेमंद	समझते हैं।
(15) मोहन	लता को	शरीफ़	समझता/मानता है।
(16) लोग	जग्गू को	बेकसूर	मानते हैं।
(17) किशन ने	अपनी पत्नी को	दुखी	पाया।
(18) मैंने	बिटिया को	खुश	देखा
b- Resultative		<-optional>	<+intransitive sation> <- कि>
(19) आपने	लड़के को	निकम्मा	बना दिया है।
(20) किशन ने	अपनी पत्नी को	दुखी	रखा।
(21) निदेशक ने	अधीक्षक को ही	दोषी	ठहराया।
			<+कि>
(22) डॉक्टर ने	रोगी को	मरा	घोषित किया।
(23) वकील ने	श्यामू को	निर्दोष	सिद्ध कर दिया।
(24) डॉक्टर	इस रोग को	लाइलाज	बताते हैं।
	<±को>	<+optional >	
(25) उसने	कपड़े	साफ़	धोए हैं।
(26) शीला ने	गोश्त	कच्चा	पकाया है।
(27) उसने	अपनी साड़ी	लाल	रंग ली है।
(28) वह	चीज़ें	सस्ती	बेचता है।

Sub-pattern-45 (Adverb Complement)

NP (Subject)	NP (Object)	ADV (Complement)	Verb (Transitive)
(1) रामलाल ने	लड़की को	यहाँ से गुज़रते	देखा।
(2) मैंने	कइयों को	पैसे के लिए जान देते	देखा है।
(3) मैंने	शोभा को	कभी शिकायत करते	(नहीं) सुना।
(4) उन्होंने	जग्गू को	शराब पीते हुए	पाया।
(5) अधीक्षक ने	लड़के को	नकल करते हुए	पकड़ा।
(6) वह	मरीज़ को	तड़पते हुए	लाया था।

COMMENT: (SP- 44 & 45)

(a) *Structure* : The sub-patterns 43, 44 and 45 are a little different from others in the sense that they contain an additional slot for complements i.e. noun complement, adjective complement and adverb complement. See

मैं चंपा को *नर्स* समझता था. (noun complement)
मैं जग्गू को *शरीफ़* समझता था। (adjective)
रामलाल ने लड़की को *यहाँ से गुज़रते* देखा। (adverb)

The verbs of sub-patterns 44 and 45 require a noun phrase in the place of the noun complement, e.g. मैं चंपा को **नर्स** समझता था whereas the sub-pattern 45 requires an adjective phrase in the place of the adjective complement e.g. मैं चंपा को **शरीफ़** समझता था. Some verbs, however, can accept both-the noun phrase as well as the adjective phrase as in the above sentence. Some verbs, however, accept only noun phrases in the place of the complement like छूना, बनाना/नियुक्त करना, मुक़र्रर करना, स्वीकार करना etc. (sub-pattern 43). Some verbs, can accept only adjectives as a complement, like पाना, देखना, झाँकना, बदलना, रंगना, धोना, पकाना etc. (sub-pattern 44). Some verbs can, however, accept both -- noun as well as adjective as complemets, e.g. समझना, मानना, सिद्ध करना, घोषित करना etc.

Remember that many verbs out of these can also be used as normal transitive verbs which is a different construction all together, e.g. मैंने एक लड़की चुनी है, मैं आपकी बात मानता हूँ etc. As normal transitive verbs, some actions related to mental activity like मानना, समझना, स्वीकार करना etc. can accept only abstract nouns as objects, but there is no such restriction in the case of noun complement constructions, e.g मैं चंपा को (आपकी बहन) समझता था, मैं चंपा को शरीफ़ समझता था.

(b) *Resultative and non-resultative Verbs*. On the basis of the inherent features the verbs, the object complements of the sentence can be divided into two types – resultative verbs and non-resultative verbs. The non-resultative complements denote its pre-existing state or quality of the object which is not the result of the efforts of the subject. For instance, in the sentence the main verbs denote the change of state or quality of the object which is mainly because of the object.

For instance in the sentences मैनेजर ने रीता को अपना सचिव नियुक्त किया and आपने लड़के को निकम्मा बना दिया, the objects (रीता or लड़का) was not already in the position of the secretary or the boy had been made निकम्मा. The change happened as a result of the efforts of the subject. This will become more evident in the following sentences:

(17) किशन ने अपनी पत्नी को दुखी *पाया*। (non-resultative)

(20) किशन ने अपनी पत्नी को दुखी *रखा*। (resultative)

The resultative verbs (like sentence 20) are controlled by the subject and hence their subjects are active subjects (i.e. doer).Hence these sentences can be detransitivised when necessary, e.g.

(दुखी) रखना > दुखी रहना,

निकम्मा बनाना > निकम्मा बनाना/होना, साफ धोना > साफ धुलना, रंगना > रंगना (उसने साड़ी रंग ली),

सिद्ध करना, सिद्ध > होना,

वकील ने रामू को निर्दोष सिद्ध किया > रामू निर्दोष सिद्ध हुआ।

The detransitivisation of this type is, however, not possible in the case of resultative verbs like समझना, मानना etc. It is also not possible in the case of verbs denoting mental perception like समझना, मानना etc. because these verbs are mainly mental experiences in which the subject is experiencer or recipient which can not be the active subject or doer.

(a) *That-clause*: Certain sentences having noun phrase as complements are capable of formimg a कि-*clause*, e.g.

(10) वकील ने जग्गू को चोर सिद्ध कर दिया। (object complement)

(11) वकील ने सिद्ध कर दिया *कि जग्गू चोर है*।

Though the statement stated in a sigle sentence without a that-clause and the one stated through a that-clause should give the same meaning, but at the level of discourse one finds subtle differences in their meanings or their nuances. See the differences:

(29) a- अमीन आपकी बात *समझ गया*। (understand)

(29) b- मैं *समझ गया* आप देर से क्यों आए।

(30) मैं *समझता हूँ* कि अब वह नहीं आएगा। (guess)

Appendix - 1

CONSOLIDATED LIST OF HINDI SENTENCE PATTERNS

I. Copula Sentence Pattern

S Pt	Sub-Pattern		Page No
(1) Nominal Copula Sentence Pattern: NP X NP X LV			
1	है[1] (identification)	रफ़ी मेरा ड्राइवर है।	161
2	है[2] (class-member)	मेरे पिता जी अध्यापक हैं।	161
3	हो[1] (class inclusion)	ऊँट एक जानवर होता है।	162
4 a	है[1] (demonstrative)	यह कलम है।	163
4 b	रह[1] (demonstrative)	ये आपके रुपए रहे।	163
5 a	हो[2] (relation)	रामलाल मेरा बड़ा भाई होता है।	164
5 b	लग[1] (relation)	साधना मेरी बहन लगती है।	164
6 a	हो[3] (change of state)	चंपा युवती हो गई।	165
6 b	बन[1] (change of state)	चंपा नर्स बन गई है।	166
7	रह[2] (duration)	मैं (कुछ दिनों) इस समिति का अध्यक्ष रहा।	166
8	सिद्ध हो (confirmation)	वह कुशल अध्यापक सिद्ध हुआ।	167
9	दिखाई दे - class	वह पुलिस अफ़सर दिखाई देता/लगता है।	168
10 a	*निकल* (unexpected)	जग्गू चोर निकला।	169
10 b	*बन*[2]	वह बड़ा तीसमारखाँ बनता था।	169
10 c	*आ*	आप कहाँ के नवाब आए !	170
10 d	*ठहर* (prior notion)	आप तो साहब ठहरे।	170
(2) Adjectival Copula Sentence Pattern: NP X ADJP X LV			
11	है (as member)	राधा सुंदर है।	171
12	हो (class)	कौवा काला होता है।	172
13 a	हो (change of state)	लड़का बीमार हो गया (=हुआ)।	173

(5) Object Complement (Noun): NP + को x NP (Object) x Complement x को-Verb

24 Object-based   सीता को मकान चाहिए।   207

(6) Object-Based को-Sentence Pattern: NP + को x NP (Object) x Complement x को-Verb

25 Object complement (noun)   राधा को नौकर चोर लगता है।   208

26 Object Complement (adj)   राधा को नौकर होशियार लगता है।   208

(7) Possessor-Possessed Sentence Pattern: NP+ के पास x Noun x हो-Verb

27 कर्ता+के पास/के/में   मोहन के पास तीस रुपए हैं।   210

सुशीला के/की तीन बहनें हैं।   210

शीला में प्रतिभा है।   210

III. Verb-based Sentence Patterns

(8) Simple Intransitive Sentence Pattern: Subject x Verb

28 Existential

ईश्वर है।   213

29 Intransitive

(a) राधा नाच रही है।   (active subject)   213

(b) मैं ऊब गया।   (patient)   213

(c) सभी किताबें बिक गयीं।   (derived intransitive)   214

(d) पृथ्वी घूम रही है।   (Natural Force)   214

30 Natural Phenomenon   बारिश हो रही है।   217

(9) Co-Adverbial x Adverbial

31 Locative intransitive

(a) शेखर घर गया।   (destination)   218

(b) प्रताप गांधीनगर में रहता है।   (locative)   219

(c) वह घर से भाग गया।   (ablative)   219

32 Time/manner/purpose

(a) यह कपड़ा काफ़ी दिन चलेगा।   (time)   220

□

Appendix - 2

BIBLIOGRAPHY

Allen, Austin (2007) J.P.B. & Buren, P.V. (1971) *Chomsky : Selected Readings*, New York : Oxford OUP

Bahl, Kalicharan (1967) *A Reference Grammar of Hindi*, Chicago : The University Of Chicago. (1974) *Studies in the Semantic Structure of Hindi*, Vol. I. Delhi : Motilal Banarsi Das.

Bahri, U.S. (1981) ed., *Topics in Hindi Linguistics*, Vol. I. New Delhi : Bahri Publications

Barker, Russel H. (1939) *The Sentence.*

Bloch, Bernerd & Trager, G.L. (1942) *Outline of Linguistic Analysis.* Baltimore : Linguistic Society of America.

Bloomfield, Leonard (1933) *Language*, New York : Holt.

Burton-Page, J. (1957) Compound and conjunct verb in Hindi in *Bulletin of the School of Oriental and African Studies* 19(3), p.468-479

Chafe, Wallace L. (1970) *Meaning and the Structure of Language* Chicago : University of Chicago Press.

Chomsky, Noam (1957) *Symantic Structures*. The Hague : Mouton.- (1965) *Aspects of the Theory of Syntax*. Cambridge, Mass. : MIT Press.- (1972) *Studies on Semantics in Generative Grammar*, the Hague : Mouton.

Comrie, B. (1976) *Aspect*. Cambridge : Cambridge University Press.

Crowell, *Dictionary of English Grammar.*

Crystal, David (1971) *Linguistics*. England, Middlesex : Penguin.

Fairbanks, G.H. & Bal Govind Mishra (1966) *Spoken and Written Hindi*. New York : Cornell University.

Fillmore, C.J. (1967) *The case for case* in E. Bach & R.J. Harms. Eds., *University in Linguistic Theory*. New York : Holt, Reinhart & Winston.

Fillmore, C.J. & D. Terence Langendoen eds. (1971) *Studies in Linguistic Semantics*. New York : Holt, Reinhart & Winston.

Firth, J.R. (1957) *A Synopsis of Linguistic Theory* in Blackwell, *Studies in Linguistic Analysis.*

Fries, C.C. (1952) *The Structure of English*, New York : Harcourt Brace.

Gardiner, A.H. (1926, 1932) *Speech and Language*, Oxford : Clarendon.

Goodenough, Ward H. (1956) *Componential analysis and the study of meaning*; in *Language 32,*

Halliday, M.A.K. (1961) Categories of the theory of grammar, in *Word* 17.p.- (1967a) Notes on transitivity and theme in English, Part 1 in *Journal of Linguistics 3,* p.- (1967b) Notes on transitivity and theme in English, Part 2 in *Journal of Linguistics 3,* p -(1970) *Language structure and language function* in John Lyons, ed., (1970) *New Horizons in Linguistics*, Middlesex, p.- (1973) *Explorations in the Functions of Language*, London : Arnold.

Halliday, M.A.K., McIntosh, A & Strevens, P. (1964) *the Linguistic Science and Language Teaching*, London : Longman.

Hill, A.R. (1957) *Introduction to Linguistic Structures*. New York : Harcourt, Brace and World.

Holisky, D.A. (1981) *Aspect theory and Georgian aspect* in Tedese-chi, P. and Zaenen, A. (eds.) *Syntax and Semantics* Vol. 14. New york : Academic Press.

Hook, Peter Edwin (1974) *The Compound Verb in Hindi*. University of Michigan.- (1978) 'The Hindi Compound Verb : What it is and what it does' in K.S. Singh, ed., *Readings in Hindi-Urdu Linguistics*. New

Delhi : National Publishing House,

Hornby, A.S. (1948) *The Advanced Learners Dictionary of Current English*. London : Oxford University Press. (1954) *A Guide to Patterns and Usage in English*. London : OUP.

Jacobs, R.A. & Rosenbaum, P.S. (1968) *English Transformational Grammar*. London : Blaisdell.

Jagannathan, V.R. (1973) State verbs is Hindi' in *Proceedings of the Fourth All India Conference of Linguists*. Agra : LSI and CIH.

Jain, Jagdish (1977) The Hindi Passive in Universal Grammar (unpublished paper). San Francisco State University.

Jesperson, Otto (1924) *the Philosophy of Grammar*. London : Allen & Ulwin.

Johnson, Marion R. (1981) *A unified temporal theory of tense and aspet* in Tedeschi, P. and Zaenen, A. (eds.) *Syntax and Semantics* Vol. 14, New York : Academic Press.

Kachru, Yamuna (1966) *An Introduction to Hindi Syntax*. Urbana : University of Illinois.- (1968) The copula in Hindi' in J.W.M. Verhaar, ed. *The Verb be and its* - (1970) Note on possessive constructions in Hindi-Urdu in *Journal of Linguistics* 6(1), p.- (1970) The syntax of *ko*-sentences in Hindi-Urdu in *Papers in Linguistics* 20 p.- (1973) Causative sentences in Hindi revisited' in Braj Kachru & others, eds., - (1978) On relative clause formation in Hindi-Urdu in *Linguistics* 277, p.- (1979) Pragmatics and verb serialization in Hindi-Urdu' in *Studies in Linguistics Sciences* (2) Urbana : University of Illinois, p.- (1980) *Aspects of Hindi Grammar*, Delhi : Manohar.

Katz, J.J. & J.A. Foder (1963) 'The structure of a semantic theory' in *Linguistics* 3, p.

Keenan, E.L. (1975) Some universals of passive in relational grammar in *Papers from the eleventh Regional Meeting of the Chicago Linguistic Society*.

Kelkar, Ashok (1978) *Tense and aspect in French* in *Indian*

Linguistics Vol 39, p.

Kiparsky, P. & Kiparsky, C. (1968) 'Fact' in Steinberg, D.D. & Jacobovits, L.A., eds., (1971) *Semantics*, London : C.U. Press, p.

Koul, Omkar Nath (1974) Co-coordinating conjunctions in Hindi' in *Indian Linguistics* 35, p. - ed., (1981) *topics in Hindi Linguistics* Vol.II, New Delhi : Bahri Publishers

Kress, Gunther, ed., (1976), ed., (1976) *Halliday : System and Function in Language*, London : Oxford University Press.

Kucera, Henry (1981) Aspect, markedness and to' in Tedeschi P. and Zaenan A. (eds.) *Syntax and Semantics* Vol. 14, New York : Academic Press.

Lakoff, George (1966) *Stative Adjectives and verbs in English*, Harvard University.

Lakshmibai, Balanchandran (1973) *A Case Grammar of Hindi*, Agra : C.I.H.- (1978) Modal auxilaries in Hindi' in *Proceedings of the Fourth All India Conference of Linguists*. Agra : L.S.I. & C.I.H.

Lamb, S.M. (1964) ;The semantic approach to structural semantics' in A.K. Romey & others, eds., *Transcultural Studies in Cognition* 66 (3), Part 2, p.

Leech, Geoffrey N. (1969) *Towards a Semantic Description of English*, London and Harlow : Longman, Green.

Lefevre, Carl A. (1964) *Linguistics and the Teaching of Reading*. New York : McGraw Hill.

Lyons, John (1968) *Introduction to Theoretical Linguistics*. C.U. Press.- ed., (1970) *New Horizons in Linguistics,* Middlesex : Penguin.- (1977) *Semantics* Vol. I & II Cambridge : C.U. Press.

McGregor, R.S. (1972) *Outline of Hindi Grammar*, Oxford : Claredon Press.

Morgan J, (1969) On the treatment of presupposition in TG in *Papers from the Fifth Regional Meeting of the Chicago Linguistic Society*, p.

Mourelatos, A.P.D. (1981) 'Events, processes and states, in

Tedeschi, P. and Zaenen, A. (eds.) *Syntax and Semantics* Vol. 14. New York : Academic Press.

Nichois, A.E. (1965) *English Syntax*.

Nida, Eugene A. (1958) 'Analysis of meaning and dictionary making' in *IJAL* 24, p.

Nilsen, D.L.F. & Nilsen, A.P. (1975) *Semantic Theory : A Linguistic Perspective*, Massachusetts : Newbury House Publishers

Olphen, H. Van (1970) *The Structure of the Hindi Verb Phrase*. Austin : University of Texas.

Palmer, Frank (1971) *Grammar*, England : Penguin.

Perlmutter, David M. & Postal, Paul M. (1977) 'Towards a universal characterization of passivisation' in *Papers from the Third Annual Meeting of the Barkerly Linguistic Society*, p. - (1974) Lectures on relational grammar at *Summer Linguistic Institute of the Linguistic Society of America*, Amherst.

Pike, K.L. (1963) A syntactic paradigm' in *Language 39.* - (1966) *Language in Relation to a Unified Theory of the Structure of Human Behaviour.* The Hague: Mouton.

Porizka, Vincenc (1954) Notes on R.L. Vale s theory of verbal composition in Hindi, Bengali, Gujrati and Marathi' in *Archiv Orientalni* 22, p- (1967, 1968, 1969) On the perfective verbal aspect in Hindi in *Archiv Orientalni* 35, 36, 37.- (1981) On the aspectual contrast in Hindi in O.N. Koul, ed., *Topics in Hindi Linguistics* Vol. II. New Delhi: Bahri Publishers.

Roberts, Paul (1964) *English Syntax*. New York: Harcourt, Brace & World.

Satyanarayan P. (1981) *The syntax of hona* in Hindi' in O.N. Koul, ed., *Topics in Hindi Linguistics.* New Delhi: Bahri Publishers.

Schwab, William (1967) *Guide to Modern Grammar and Exposition*. London: Harper & Row.

Sharma, Aryendra (1958) *A Basic Grammar of Modern Hindi.* New Delhi: Central Hindi Directorate.

Singh, Amar Bahadur (1978) Auxiliary in Hindi in *Proceedings of the All India Conference of Linguists.* Agra : LSI & C.I H.

Singh, Kripa Shankar. Ed., (1978) *Readings in Hindi-Urdu Linguistics.* New Delhi: National Publishing House.

Singh, Suraj Bhan (1979) A feature analysis of equational sentences in Hindi in *Indian Linguistics* 40 (1) p.- (1980) Theoretical and applicational implications of Functional grammar' in *Revue Roumaine de Linguistique* (French) XVII No. (2) Bucharest, Romania.- (1980) Concepts of semantic field and collocation in Hindi-Urdu lexicography' in *Stvdia et Acta Orientalia* (French) X, Bucharest, Romania. (3) Hindi ka vakyatmak vyakaran (1980).

Sledd, James & Scott (1959) *A Short Introduction to English Grammar.* Chicago: Scott, Foresman.

Srivastava, Ravindra Nath (1971) How empty is the abstrart verb (+cause)? A Case grammar of Hindi causal verb morphology in *Proceedings of the First All India Conference of Linguists*. Poona, p.

Subbarao, K.V. (1976) Complementizers in Hindi' in *Indian Linguistics* 37 (2), p.- (1981) Syntactic criteria for some semantic class of predicate in Hindi' in O.N. Koul, ed., *Topics in Hindi Linguistics* Vol. II. New Delhi: Bahri Publishers.

Sweet Henry (1891) *A New English Grammar*. Oxford: Clarendon Press.

Tedeschi, Philip and Zaenen, A. (1981) (eds.) *Syntax and Semantics* Vol. 14. New York : Academic Press,

Varmeer, H.J. and Aryendra Sharma (1966) *Hindi Lautlehre mit Einfuhrung in die Devnagri Schrift.* Heidelberg: Julius Gross Verlag.

Vendler, Z. (1967) *Linguistics in Philosophy.* Ithaca: Cornell University Press.

Verma, M.K. (1971) *The Structure of the Noun Phrase in English and Hindi.* Delhi: Motilal Banarsi Das.

Verma, Shivendra Kishore (1970) Word order in Hindi' in *Archiv Orienralni* 38 (1), p.- (1974) The semantics of

Hindi *caahiye*' in *Foundations of Language* 12, p.- (1981) Reflections on thematisation in Hindi' O.N. Koul, ed., *Topics in Hindi Linguistics* Vol. II. Delhi: Bahri Pub..

Verhaar, J.W.M. (1968) etc.) *The Verb be and its Synonyms* Vol. I, II. Holland: Reidel.

Wallace, Anthony F.C. & John Atkins (1960) 'The meaning of kinship terms' in *American Anthropologist* 62, p.

Weinreich Uriel (1963) On the semantic structure of language' in J.H. Greenberg, ed., *Universals of Language*. Cambridge, p.- (1966) 'Explorations in semantic theory' in T.A. Sebeok, ed., *Current Trends in Linguistics*-3. The Hague : Mouton.

- काचरू , यमुना (1973) **हिंदी व्याकरण के कुछ प्रकरण।** आगरा, केंद्रीय हिंदी संस्थान।
- (1980) **हिंदी का समसामयिक व्याकरण।** दिल्ली : मैक्मिलन कम्पनी ऑव इंडिया।
- कालरा, सुधा (1971) हिंदी की प्रेर्णार्थक क्रियाएँ , भाषा - हिंदी भाषा विज्ञान अंक, पृ. 211-213
- गुरु, कामता प्रसाद (1920) हिंदी व्याकरण। काशी मागरी प्रचारिणी सभा।
- जगन्नाथन, वी. रा. (1973) 'हिंदी ज-प्रकार के सम्मिश्रण वाक्यों में विशेषीकरण' भाषा-हिंदी भाषाविज्ञान अंक, पृ. 303-309।
- तिवारी, भोलानाथ ((1973) 'हिंदी यौगिक क्रिया' भाषा-हिंदी भाषाविज्ञान अंक, पृ. 224-232।
- (1979) हिंदी भाषा की संरचना। दिल्ली : वाणी प्रकाशन ।
- बहल, कालीचरण (1973) 'हिंदी समापिका क्रियारूपों का अर्थतात्विक विवेचन', भाषा-हिंदी भाषाविज्ञान अंक, पृ. 341-366।
- रस्तोगी, कृष्णगोपाल (1973) हिंदी क्रियाओं का अर्थपरक अध्ययन। दिल्ली : अर्चना प्रकाशन।
- वाजपेयी, किशोरी दास (1959) **हिंदी शब्दानुशासन।** वाराणसी : नागरी प्रचारिणी सभा।
- श्रीवास्तव, रवींद्रनाथ (1973) काल और पक्ष, **भाषा-हिंदी भाषाविज्ञान अंक**, पृ. 199-210
- श्रीवास्तव, रवींद्रनाथ तथा शारदा भसीन (1983) **प्रयोजनमूलक हिंदी व्याकरण।** आगरा : केंद्रीय हिंदी संस्थान।
- (1975) हिंदी में विशेषण उपवाक्य : गवेषणा 26, पृ. 28-34।
- (1975) हिंदी में कर्मवाच्य', गवेषणा 27, पृ. 48-53।
- सहाय, रमानाथ (1959) 'अन्य भाषा शिक्षण में टेग्मेमिक्स की उपयोगिता', **भाषा शिक्षण तथा भाषा विज्ञान** (सं.)। आगरा : केंद्रीय हिंदी संस्थान।
- (1978) हिंदी में काल, वृत्ति और पक्ष, **गवेषणा** 31, पृ. 20-33।
- सिंह, सूरजभान (2003) English Hindi Translation Grammar, Prabhat Prakashan, New Delhi
- (1978) सिस्टेमेटिक व्याकरण-हिंदी के संदर्भ में, **गवेषणा** 28, पृ. 36-40। ☐

WORD INDEX